The Study of Greek and Roman Religions

Scientific Studies of Religion: Inquiry and Explanation

Series editors: Luther H. Martin, Donald Wiebe, Radek Kundt, and Dimitris Xygalatas

Scientific Studies of Religion: Inquiry and Explanation publishes cutting-edge research in the new and growing field of scientific studies in religion. Its aim is to publish empirical, experimental, historical, and ethnographic research on religious thought, behaviour, and institutional structures. The series works with a broad notion of scientific that includes innovative work on understanding religion(s), both past and present. With an emphasis on the cognitive science of religion, the series includes complementary approaches to the study of religion, such as psychology and computer modelling of religious data. Titles seek to provide explanatory accounts for the religious behaviors under review, both past and present.

The Attraction of Religion
Edited by D. Jason Slone and James A. Van Slyke

The Cognitive Science of Religion
Edited by D. Jason Slone and William W. McCorkle Jr.

The Construction of the Supernatural in Euro-American Cultures
Benson Saler

Contemporary Evolutionary Theories of Culture and the Study of Religion
Radek Kundt

Death Anxiety and Religious Belief
Jonathan Jong and Jamin Halberstadt

Gnosticism and the History of Religions
David G. Robertson

The Impact of Ritual on Child Cognition
Veronika Rybanska

Language, Cognition, and Biblical Exegesis
Edited by Ronit Nikolsky, Istvan Czachesz, Frederick S. Tappenden, and Tamas Biro

The Learned Practice of Religion in the Modern University
Donald Wiebe

The Mind of Mithraists
Luther H. Martin

Naturalism and Protectionism in the Study of Religion
Juraj Franek

New Patterns for Comparative Religion
William E. Paden

Philosophical Foundations of the Cognitive Science of Religion
Robert N. McCauley and E. Thomas Lawson

Religion, Disease, and Immunology
Thomas B. Ellis

Religion Explained?
Edited by Luther H. Martin and Donald Wiebe

Religion in Science Fiction
Steven Hrotic

Religious Evolution and the Axial Age
Stephen K. Sanderson

The Roman Mithras Cult
Olympia Panagiotidou with Roger Beck

Solving the Evolutionary Puzzle of Human Cooperation
Glenn Barenthin

Understanding Religion Through Artificial Intelligence
Justin E. Lane

The Study of Greek and Roman Religions

Insularity and Assimilation

Nickolas P. Roubekas

BLOOMSBURY ACADEMIC
LONDON • NEW YORK • OXFORD • NEW DELHI • SYDNEY

BLOOMSBURY ACADEMIC
Bloomsbury Publishing Plc
50 Bedford Square, London, WC1B 3DP, UK
1385 Broadway, New York, NY 10018, USA
29 Earlsfort Terrace, Dublin 2, Ireland

BLOOMSBURY, BLOOMSBURY ACADEMIC and the Diana logo are trademarks of
Bloomsbury Publishing Plc

First published in Great Britain 2022
This paperback edition published 2024

Copyright © Nickolas P. Roubekas, 2022, 2024

Nickolas P. Roubekas has asserted his right under the Copyright, Designs and
Patents Act, 1988, to be identified as Author of this work.

For legal purposes the Acknowledgments on pp. x–xiii constitute an
extension of this copyright page.

All rights reserved. No part of this publication may be reproduced or transmitted in any
form or by any means, electronic or mechanical, including photocopying,
recording, or any information storage or retrieval system, without prior
permission in writing from the publishers.

Bloomsbury Publishing Plc does not have any control over, or responsibility for, any
third-party websites referred to or in this book. All internet addresses given in this
book were correct at the time of going to press. The author and publisher regret any
inconvenience caused if addresses have changed or sites have ceased to exist, but
can accept no responsibility for any such changes.

A catalogue record for this book is available from the British Library.

Library of Congress Control Number: 2022932189

ISBN: HB: 978-1-3501-0261-3
PB: 978-1-3503-3624-7
ePDF: 978-1-3501-0263-7
eBook: 978-1-3501-0262-0

Series: Scientific Studies of Religion: Inquiry and Explanation

Typeset by Newgen KnowledgeWorks Pvt. Ltd., Chennai, India

To find out more about our authors and books visit www.bloomsbury.com
and sign up for our newsletters

When these books were first admitted into the public libraries, I remember to have said, upon occasion, to several persons concerned, how I was sure they would create broils wherever they came, unless a world of care were taken; and therefore I advised that the champions of each side should be coupled together, or otherwise mixed ... And it seems I was neither an ill prophet nor an ill counsellor; for it was nothing else but the neglect of this caution which gave occasion to the terrible fight that happened on Friday last between the Ancient and Modern Books in the King's library.

Jonathan Swift, The Battle of the Books (1704)

Contents

Acknowledgments   x

1   "Closing a Book None the Wiser"; Or Should a Scholar of Religion
    Happen to Meet a Classicist   1
2   Burning Bridges?   19
3   (No) Greek and Roman "Religion"   37
4   Comparative Nausea   53
5   The Departing Gods   69
6   Re(ap)proaching the Study of Greek and Roman Religions   89

Appendix I—Re: Hesiod   109
Appendix II—On Belief   114
Appendix III—A Typology of Religions   119

Notes   123
References   143
Index   171

Acknowledgments

The idea for writing this short volume was born in October 2017 in Toronto. After the kind invitation by Donald Wiebe, I spent a week as a visiting scholar at Trinity College of the University of Toronto, where I gave two presentations kindly sponsored by the Institute for the Advanced Study of Religion (IASR). One of the two talks was titled "Neglecting the Ancients: The Insularity of Ancient Religion," which was eventually published as "The Insularity of the Study of Ancient Religions and 'Religion'" in the *Bulletin for the Study of Religion* in 2018 (vol. 47, no. 2, pp. 2–7). Among the people attending my (then still work-in-progress) presentation was also Luther H. Martin of the University of Vermont. Both Don and Luther made my visit at Toronto a memorable one, while during my week-long stay we had the opportunity to further discuss the idea of turning the broad (and, frankly, unsystematic then) arguments I made there into something more substantive than merely a journal article. It was undoubtedly their insights, advice, and passionate support for such a project that eventually convinced me to go for it. In addition, their suggestion to include the volume into their series kind of obliged me to agree and work on the project. I thank them both for their support, always informative and interesting discussions, and their friendship.

I had the pleasure to discuss some of the ideas found in the next pages with a number of friends and colleagues, whose comments, arguments, and criticisms helped me refine my initial positions, and I thank them for their time and insights: Lukas Pokorny, Panayotis Pachis, Leonardo Ambasciano, and Robert Segal. Moreover, and sometimes going unnoticed, many of the points made in this volume owe their existence to my students at the University of Vienna, who were always curious, posed the most interesting questions, and offered some unexpected but valuable comments when I presented them with the ideas, theories, and arguments of the ancients in the course *Religions of Greek and Roman Antiquity*. Finally, I would like to thank the four anonymous reviewers who offered very valuable remarks and thoughts that helped me restructure the volume and address some topics that I had not initially thought of or had overlooked.

My appreciation also goes to my editor Lalle Pursglove and the amazing editorial assistant Lily McMahon, who were always willing to allow me "a little more time" so I could finalize the manuscript and helped me immensely through the review, production, and publication process. I would also like to thank Megan Jones and Metilda Nancy for spotting various mistakes and making the book so much better and clearer. It goes without saying that any remaining mistakes are my own.

Some of the ideas presented in the following chapters were initially published elsewhere. A portion of Chapter 2 was previously published as "Review of *The Oxford Handbook of Ancient Greek Religion*, edited by Esther Eidinow and Julia Kindt," *Revista Classica* 29.2 (2016): 221–4, used with permission according to Creative Commons Attribution License (CC By 3.0). Chapter 3 is partly based on "*Thrēskeia*: From Etymology to Ideology and the Academic Study of Ancient Greek Religion," *Journal of Hellenic Religion* 12 (2019): 39–59, used with permission by Éditions Méduse d'Or SARL, France. Part of Chapter 6 is based on "Whose Theology? The Promise of Cognitive Theories and the Future of a Disputed Field," *Religion & Theology* 20.3–4 (2013): 384–402, used with permission by Brill, The Netherlands. I would like to thank these publishers for allowing me to use portions of those previously published materials.

Finally, I would like to extend my appreciation to a number of people who were involved, unknowingly, with their choices and decisions to further forcing me to write this short volume. First, the translators and publishers who evidently struggled with how to translate and thus advertise one of Martin P. Nilsson's (1874–1967) books—which indicates how problematic the terminology related to ancient Greek and Roman religion(s) was and still remains among scholars working within this subfield. Originally published in Swedish with the title *Grekisk Religiositet* (Hugo Gebers Förlag, 1946), the book drew great attention given the prominence of its author, which led to two translations, one in English and one in German. The former appeared with the title *Greek Piety* (Clarendon Press, 1948; translated by H. J. Rose), the latter as *Griechischer Glaube* (A. Francke Verlag, 1950; translated in German by Benedict Christ). For anyone acquainted with the basics of the languages involved, the linguistic and terminological choices made are superb indications of how the study of Greek and Roman religion(s) has been saturated by linguistic, methodological, and theoretical backgrounds and choices that have not allowed the field to proceed beyond them, although, as I will discuss in the following pages, there are some admirable attempts and projects that seek to overcome such persisting obstacles.

Second, I need to wholeheartedly thank the anonymous reviewer of Chapter 2 (this volume), which I deliberately submitted to a journal of the "Classics bend" after writing it so as to see whether I was on the right path (and the reactions I received convinced me that I was). Due to an elementary mistake made by the reviewer, her comments on the text came with her full name above them, alloying me therefore to be absolutely sure whether she was a classicist or not. (She is one of the most renowned classicists working in the French world, whose anonymity I will here maintain out of collegiality.) Her final assessment was the following:

> I felt very uncomfortable with the paper. On the one hand, the claim for more interdisciplinarity and a more precise theoretical framework is right, and I share it. On the other hand, the analysis is based on different assumptions that I disagree with. First, the "quintessential" role assigned to religious studies. Secondly, the method for identifying who does and does not make "religious studies," with very subjective criteria (and not explicit criteria). Third, the tendency to consider one specific cartography of fields as universal, whereas it is not pertinent at all for many countries. I think there is a deep misunderstanding of the historical approach to ancient religions, which is interdisciplinary even if "religionists" are not involved.

Although my exposition in the next pages will eventually address what is condensed in this assessment, it suffices here to point out an initial diagnosis: scholars working in the subfield of Greek and Roman religion(s) are apparently content with their interdisciplinary work which excludes specialists on the very term and category that determines the subfield, namely "religion(s)," which in turn makes me and a number of others equally uncomfortable.

—//—

The bulk of the book was completed in 2020 and 2021, perhaps the most difficult period humanity has faced in the last fifty years due to the Covid-19 pandemic. Millions lost their lives during this awful period, and when these lines are penned, the pandemic seems to persist, and the loss of human lives remains regrettably high. Like myself, millions of people around the world suffered greatly, both professionally, personally, and mentally. From an academic perspective, in person teaching was ceased, academic libraries were closed for prolonged periods, research became even more burdensome, conferences went online, and personal interactions were restricted to a minimum, making scholarly work a real challenge to say the least. Within such insecurity, difficulties, and uncertainty, I am indebted to my family and my closest friends who kept me going, listened to my musings about this project (often not knowing at all what I was talking about), and were there to save the day. Sometimes, the smallest things matter so much—something we often take for granted.

1

"Closing a Book None the Wiser"; Or Should a Scholar of Religion Happen to Meet a Classicist

What? Am I to be a listener only all my days? Am I never to get my word in—I that have been so often bored by the Theseid of the ranting Cordus?

Juvenal (c. 60–c. 127 CE)[1]

For the versed reader, the latter part of this introductory chapter's perhaps odd title is a slightly modified version of the title of chapter 1 in Marcel Detienne's *Comparer l'incoparable* (2000). Contrary to Detienne's aim, who sought to contextualize and foster a large-scale comparativism by inviting historians and anthropologists to work closely together, in the following chapters I am proposing a more fundamental project: instead of focusing on the strengths and weaknesses of a particular methodological approach, such as that of the comparative method,[2] I am advocating for a deeper interdisciplinary collaboration that I (and hopefully others) deem necessary. The thesis expounded throughout the volume is straightforward albeit startling in some respects: between classics (more so) and ancient history (less so) on the one hand, and the study of religion on the other, joint work in researching what has been traditionally labeled "Greek and Roman religion(s)" seems to be meager—for the most part superficial, often one-sided, occasionally ill-informed, or by and large nonexistent. Be that as it may, one would expect the contrary, given the continuing calls for interdisciplinary work within the modern university. Although interdisciplinarity has become an oft-invoked scholarly jargon—which, nevertheless, frequently receives whispered criticisms since conforming and expressing loyalty to disciplinary fields remains the preferred attitude ultimately—it is rarely put into practice in respect to the study of ancient Greek and Roman religion(s) by scholars working in the two respective fields. The present study aims at presenting such a lack of cooperation, tracing the possible causes, and offering some (hopefully) helpful suggestions, while concurrently addressing some critical issues that seem to have been tantalizing the two disciplines, thus acting as barriers for a more wide-ranging and productive joint effort.

In some respects, my project resembles similar ones attempted by scholars working in adjacent subdisciplines, such as the work by scholar of religion Thomas A. Lewis, who recently pointed out the following concerning the lack of collaboration between scholars of religion and philosophers of religion:

> In probing what philosophy of religion should be learning from as well as contributing to religious studies as a whole, I hope to speak not only to philosophers of religion but to a broader audience of students and scholars interested in philosophy's role in the study of religion. Although the book is centrally concerned with articulating a conception of philosophy of religion adequate to religious studies, i.e., the academic study of religion, it also addresses what philosophy of religion as a whole—including as practiced in departments of philosophy—should learn from recent developments in religious studies. (Lewis 2015: 6; for a similar project, see Schilbrack 2014)

Before proceeding with my exposition, however, I need to justify my admittedly disheartening diagnosis which will be most likely received with skepticism—if not outright pugnacity. When push comes to shove, it is understandably unpleasant for scholars to read that their respective fields might eventually be theoretically and methodologically insufficient or biased to study a topic that is diachronically deemed their "own." And this is the point where protectionism often becomes the approach par excellence, with stringent disciplinary boundaries and histories—let alone praised "divinized" scholars of the past—functioning as invisible shields of a type of "unique" scholarly work that outsiders cannot fathom nor advance in any constructive manner. In order to justify such a grim portrayal, I am returning to the title of this chapter, but now to its former part. The quoted phrase is partly based on the concluding words of Greta Hawes in her review of my book *An Ancient Theory of Religion: Euhemerism from Antiquity to the Present* (2017) in the *Bryan Mawr Classical Review*, the flagship periodical publishing reviews of new works from predominantly the fields of classics and ancient history (Hawes 2017).

I am not of course planning to cunningly use these pages with the intention of countering a negative review. Numerous scholars have had the experience of an unfavorable criticism, and I take no personal offense whatsoever. Being fully aware from the outset that my work balances between disciplines, I had no doubt that some scholars from classics (and, perhaps, ancient history) would react as guardians of their disciplinary cherished principles and theories after the publication of that said volume—as I strongly anticipate to be the case with the current volume as well. In her review, Hawes chose a recognizable counterargumentation strategy, namely *responding to tone*. By apparently taking offense for criticizing her colleagues and their approaches pertaining to the enigmatic figure of Euhemerus of Messene (c. third century BCE) and his theory, Hawes made the following observation:

> Roubekas ... lavishes praise on scholars quoted in support of his argument, while undermining the contributions of others. Patrick O'Sullivan is dismissed as "lack[ing] a deeper understanding of how theorizing about religion functions" on account of "neglect[ing] discussions in the field of religious studies in the last 300 years or so" (39). Scott Scullion and Hugh Bowden are mistaken when they describe Herodotus and Xenophon respectively as "theorists," in contradiction of Roubekas' definition (43, nn. 68, 72). Such comments cast a pall of mean-spiritedness, suggesting little of worth in scholarship which did not ascribe to Roubekas's argument in advance of his having formulated it. They gratuitously highlight Roubekas' tendency to argue semantics with the secondary tradition rather than arguing from the primary evidence.

There is a lot to be discussed in this excerpt. Instead, however, of replying in defense of my thesis in *An Ancient Theory of Religion*—which would be of little (if any) interest to the reader of the present volume—I seize here the opportunity to make a more substantial criticism in view of what I am arguing in the book at hand. It is, I reckon, far more appealing to examine Hawes's points as an indication of scholarly protectionism and a point of contention within an academic debate that exceeds the strict limits of a book under review. In my reading, Hawes's polemical tone—to the point of *ad hominem*—does not seem to be about euhemerism; rather, it appears to be about disciplinary methods and theories, and ultimately about who *can* or *should* study the religious ideas of the ancient Greeks and Romans. In her attempt to defend her field (O'Sullian, Scullion, and Bowden mentioned in the quoted excerpt are all prominent classicists), Hawes makes elementary mistakes with regard to how scholarly research is conducted and the manner with which theories are formulated. First, claiming that when one agrees with some scholars while undermining others constitutes an indication of wobbly scholarship, one could readily respond that the foundational principle of any academic research is to debate or even eventually dissolve cherished ideas irrespective of who formulated them. As Karl Popper put it in his magisterial *The World of Parmenides* (1998), theories are guesswork. Functioning as such, they are neither stable nor steadfast principles: "If you ask me, 'How do you know?' my reply would be, 'I don't; I only propose a guess. If you are interested in my problem, I shall be most happy if you criticize my guess, and if you offer counter-proposals, I in turn will try to criticize them'" (Popper 1998: 24). Second, when Hawes argues that one does a disservice to scholarship when criticizing other scholars' classifications or definitions "in contradiction of his/hers," she again fails to acknowledge how definitions and other theoretical formulations come about or are being applied. Any classification (of anything) is liable to scrutiny if the one who renders it invalid formulates an alternative. For example, the debate on defining religion has been central and yet unresolved in the field of the academic study of religion for more than a hundred and fifty years, whereas it has remained largely (if not entirely) mute among classicists and historians—a pivotal issue to which I will return in various places throughout this volume. Moreover, as Mary Douglas (1921–2007) taught us many years ago, classifications are not fixed but culture-specific (see Douglas 1984 [1966])—and, in view of Hawes's protectionism, discipline-specific as well, I would add. Third, by functioning primarily as a custodian of her field and secondarily as a reviewer of a given work and its thesis, Hawes dismisses the book under review with the following closing remark:

> A colleague once patiently explained to me that scholars should begin all papers by punching (figuratively) their intellectual rivals, as if incivility were a hallmark of impressive scholarship. Roubekas' rhetoric brought this back to mind. … I closed Roubekas' book none the wiser.

Any reader has the right to claim or suggest that a book is to be dismissed or celebrated. However, "incivility" or "mean-spiritedness" could be rather unfortunate descriptions of an author's motivations or style—as if such features could be precisely measured in any adequate manner (hence Hawes's formulation: "*cast a pall of* mean-spiritedness" [my emphasis])—that have, I think, little value in scholarly debates. However, what one could take from Hawes's criticism is the broader picture she painted, and which has little to do with my thesis on euhemerism in the said volume. The issue, if my reading and hunch are correct, touches upon more important problems pertaining to the way scholars of the study of religion approach the religions of antiquity, as well as the clash between their methods and theories and the ones formulated and argued about by their colleagues in Departments of Classics and/or Ancient History.

Hawes's tacit protectionism, however, is neither peculiar nor shocking. Lately the field of classics (and, often, ancient history) has received fierce criticisms and not merely for its academic methods and theories. Rather, like many (if not all) other fields under the broader umbrella of the humanities, the current (largely postmodern) critique related to identity politics and power balances has increasingly dealt with the humanities as a cluster of academic fields that, anchored to previously hegemonic ideas, support, tolerate, or even propagate ideologies that conceal strong racial, misogynistic, anti-LGBTQ+, and other sentiments and ideas of inequality and oppression. The ensuing result of such criticisms has recently led the humanities in general into a period of introspection and possible restructuring from the bottom-up. Classics (and ancient history) as well as the study of religion have not evaded such a critique—although the former has lately received harsher attacks. For example, the controversy over Martin Bernal's *Black Athena: The Afroasiatic Roots of Classical Civilization* (1987) still in many respects haunts the discipline as Denise Eileen McCoskey recently opined (2018). The issue of systemic racism within classics, as was reported, tormented the 2019 Society of Classical Studies at its annual meeting in San Diego (Bond 2019). The result was a series of online posts presumably unveiling not merely the alleged embedded racist ideology surrounding classics as a discipline, but also an inherent exceptionalism that classicists feel and perhaps occasionally maintain about their field. As Donna Zuckerberg puts it, "I believe that classicists are particularly in thrall to the notion that our discipline is objectively *more* important—and, relatedly, more difficult—than other humanities disciplines" (Zuckerberg 2018; emphasis in original). Moreover, the field has been severely criticized for espousing and nurturing an ideal of "Western triumphalism," with new generation scholars aiming at not only acknowledging such a problem, but, more importantly as it is put, "further exposing … the damage done by the old hardline on Classics and 'Western civilization'" (Hanink 2017; cf. Appiah 2016; Dhindsa 2020).

Concurrently, there are many alarming messages coming from voices within the discipline of classics regarding low student enrollments, threats of defunding, or occasionally dismantling whole departments, as well as the "uselessness" of classical education to persons of the twenty-first century—all leading to but also feeding from a popular catchphrase: the humanities are in crisis.[3] It is by no accident thus that a heated discussion recently erupted online following a proposal by the Faculty of Classics of Oxford University to remove Homer and Virgil from the compulsory first-year classics syllabus in response to a diversity gap (Turner and Kavanagh 2020; Badhe 2020)[4]—or another debate at the other side of the Atlantic after Princeton University's decision to alter the structure of its classics undergraduate program in connection with the teaching of Greek and Latin, as well as similar decisions elsewhere in the country (including the shrinking or even closure of departments of Classical Studies).[5]

I must here, however, turn my attention to my own field as well, that is, the study of religion, since the volume at hand is not an attack on classicists—although it will be most likely be seen as such; rather, it is an investigation of the reasons the two disciplines, classics and the study of religion, have failed or avoided to productively collaborate (and, as it seems, continue to do so) when studying the religion(s) of the Greeks and the Romans. A feeling of exceptionalism is likewise apparent among scholars of religion when it comes to their field; but the "invisible enemy" is not the nonspecialist or outsider in general but rather a specific cognate field: theology.[6] Ever since the launching of non-confessional chairs and departments in Europe in the late nineteenth century, the study of religion (also encountered, for example, as comparative religion, history of religions, *Religionswissenschaft*, religious studies, or science of religion among others—although each nomenclature has its own serious pitfalls)[7] has struggled and occasionally still does so to justify its position in the modern university vis-à-vis primarily theology, and secondarily other social sciences (such as anthropology, sociology, psychology, etc.).[8] The common argument put forward is typically conveyed based on the following general basis: the academic study of religion cannot and should not be confessional. It must be scientific, although many scholars working within the field of the study of religion tend to be crypto-theologians or, to recall Russell McCutcheon's (2001) classification, "caretakers rather than critics." Although McCutcheon is a strong player in the field and has ever since turned toward other methodological and theoretical venues as well—to which I will return in Chapters 3 and 6—his argument remains as vivid today as it was twenty years ago (e.g., see Ambasciano [2019] as well as Franek [2020]).[9]

Apart from the ongoing disciplinary struggles, however, a new approach to the study of religion has slowly emerged since the mid-1980s, primarily due to perhaps the most quoted phrase in the field ever since, to wit, the late Jonathan Z. Smith's (1938–2017) popular aphorism:

> While there is a staggering amount of data, of phenomena, of human experiences and expressions that might be characterized in one culture or another, by one criterion or another, as religious—*there is no data for religion*. Religion is solely the creation of the scholar's study. It is created for the scholar's analytic purposes by his imaginative acts of comparison and generalization. Religion has no independent existence apart from the academy. (Smith 1982: xi; emphasis in original)

It is hardly an exaggeration to say that this statement has initiated a new movement within the study of religion, with a number of scholars adopting Smith's words ever since and presenting them as the theoretical starting point of any type of research conducted within the field. This, in effect, has exerted great influence on scholars working in the field of ancient Mediterranean religions broadly speaking, and, more particularly, in the study of Greek and Roman religion(s). For example, Brent Nongbri's *Before Religion: A History of a Modern Concept* (2013) and Carlin A. Barton and Daniel Boyarin's *Imagine No Religion: How Modern Abstractions Hide Ancient Realities* (2016), both highly influential and two works I will be returning to in Chapter 3, take their cues largely from Smith's famous words. What is more, Barton and Boyarin open their introduction with the words of historian Edwin Judge that Nongbri cites as personal communication. It is important to remember Judge's controversial opinion, since along with Smith's position (whose name regularly appears in both aforementioned works), essentially constitute today the "proper way" to approach the "religions" of premodern societies (including, of course, Greek and Roman antiquity) for many scholars:[10]

> When one encounters the word "religion" in a translation of an ancient text: First, cross out the word whenever it occurs. Next, find a copy of the text in question in its original language and see what word (if any) is being translated by "religion." Third, come up with a different translation: It almost doesn't matter what. Anything besides "religion." (Nongbri 2013: 156; Barton and Boyarin 2016: 1)

In other words, "religion" as a descriptor apparently cannot and does not work when studying cultural phenomena before the advent of Christianity. However, such a categorical approach eventually causes severe tribulations to the study of Greek and Roman religion(s) as I will discuss in Chapter 3—and instead of our modern abstractions hiding ancient "realities" (to use Barton and Boyarin's subtitle, but placing the term *realities* within quotation marks to indicate that having your cake and eating it too leads to further complications; e.g., what is exactly meant here by "realities?"), the counter proposal is essentially to reject the abstraction altogether. Yet, such a dismissal, as I will argue, largely unveils the failure—as well as conscious evasion—of scholars of religion to actually define their terminologies.

This is further evident in some recent online short publications in which scholars who passionately argue in favor of a "critical study of religion" have practically transformed into scholars who study not what could be classified as "religion"—therefore avoiding to deal with any data—but with those who do the classification (such as scholars, political and social actors, etc.). For example, Malory Nye, author of the very widely used textbook *Religion: The Basics* (2008)—currently in its second edition while the third one is being prepared—nicely illustrates what the study of religion has in some respects become today when he argues that

> I am a student of religion who does not study religion. … I don't think religion is a "thing" to be studied. "It" is not an entity in itself. … I study the *idea* of religion. … And behind such ideas of religion, race, and gender

are relations of power. They are means by which power and influence are exerted—rich over poor, men over women, white over black, and so on. (Nye 2017a; emphasis in original)

Nye is correct. Like other descriptors used by people (with the list, when championing such an approach, containing everything, from "culture" to "politics" and from "race" to "economy" to name a few examples), "religion" is undeniably a human construction. The very classification of phenomena as "religions" is indeed a human activity (to return to Smith's influential words). However, not everything is about "power"—and, if it is, then Nye (along with similar-minded scholars) needs to explain what is meant by the term. Because, clearly, the term is not only applicable in the Nietzschean or Foucauldian manner. But Nye et al. take "religion" to solely mean ideology-exerting-power that leads to societal disparities—the classification can also function as such, of course, and religion has been, currently is, and will be used as a means for exerting power by those who wish so according to their own agendas. Nonetheless, in order to come to such a conclusion, scholars need to honestly unveil their own ideological outlook and point of departure as well as their sought outcome. Similarly to my call for working definitions of religion (see Chapter 4), one also has to demand clear explications of these scholars' ideological motivations and goals. Otherwise, a scientific study of religion simply becomes an ideological study of religion and only that. And although scholars have of course the choice to focus on the latter, this does not instinctively imply that their focus is the best or the only proper way to study religion; nor does it mean that they can severely criticize other scholars as nonscientific, biased, or even accuse them of bigotry without serious and substantial argumentation (e.g., see Driscoll and Miller 2019, as well as my criticism to their positions in Roubekas 2019c).

By extension, if scholars cannot come into grips with the necessity of demarcating what they mean by "religion" whenever they use the term, then one may readily argue that the discipline itself has no actual subject, and thereby no reason to exist. Take, for instance, Russell McCutcheon's response to Christopher Kavanagh's essay on the value of the said term—which Kavanagh does not consider it to be "semantically incoherent," as he puts it. McCutcheon, among other points he makes, also stresses the following: "While I agree that such variability does not make the term religion 'semantically incoherent' but, as just suggested, *it makes the field studying it scientifically incoherent* and, more than likely, *institutionally nonviable*; for there apparently there is no 'it' to study but, rather, all sorts of potentially different its that many have nothing to do with one another" (McCutcheon 2016; my emphasis—mind the similarities in McCutcheon's position here with Nye's words cited earlier). These are serious arguments made from within the field. But, in my view, it is McCutcheon's own rhetoric here that makes the field *look* scientifically incoherent rather than the other way around. According to McCutcheon's line of thought, one should then also argue that a number of fields should be similarly deemed "scientifically incoherent and institutionally nonviable." There is little (if any) agreement on what consciousness or unconsciousness is among psychologists; hardly any sociologist is in a position to offer a definition of the term "society" without being immediately criticized by her peers; anthropologists and other social scientists have struggled with what is the nature of "culture" without any viable result to date; and mathematicians—another field dedicated to "no 'it' "—have been working on a purely "human-made" domain. This means nothing *in essence*—another term, incidentally, that has had philosophers debating for centuries. But when rhetorical tools and sophistic means are being utilized, then apparently anything goes.

— // —

As has hopefully become apparent, my interest in this book is not what constitutes "Greek and Roman religion(s)," but the study of such cultural phenomena classified as religion(s) by the two aforementioned distinct academic fields.[11] In proceeding, however, I must briefly deal with the very descriptor of those phenomena, that is, *religion*—a rather difficult pursuit, as it seems, which I virtually discuss throughout the volume. I will be repeatedly returning to the issue of definition, since, in my view, most contemporary scholars of the study of religion have deliberately avoided to provide an adequate way to approach this classificatory descriptor, whereas classicists and ancient historians have largely dismissed the need for a definition altogether. The latter typically restrict their discussions by constantly invoking a dichotomy that seems to have been transformed into and functions as a quasi-definition by and of itself: Greek and Roman religions are not like Christianity (or, more broadly, the Abrahamic monotheistic religions). This strategy, however, does not actually offer a definition; on the contrary, I deem it a rhetorical device that primarily aims at separating Greek and Roman antiquity (and its religions—and, therefore, their "special nature") from whatever it is that religion means from a Christian perspective. In other words, I maintain that such a classification primarily aims at demarcating academic fields rather than actually offering an adoptable or even useful tool for those studying the religions of the Greeks and the Romans.

This strategy has found additional fertile ground at what has now become the most common and elementary form of dismissing valuable theoretical work being done in the field of Greek and Roman religions: the principle that the term "religion" is an anachronism. This axiom, however, is the equivalent of bringing sand to the beach from a scientific perspective. Whereas all scholars agree—and have done so for centuries—that all our language is anachronistic, in the last roughly twenty years the problem of anachronism has become *the* cardinal sin in historical scholarship. One could imagine the reasons—say, to mention a few: a lack of competent linguistic training, a way out of dealing with the actual sources while appearing to be scientific with jargon-laden language and thus speak about everything irrespective of specialization and/or knowledge, an exclusive interest in deconstructionist routes that feed from linguistic theory games—but such assumptions would only be grounded on mere speculation at this point. Nevertheless, despite the triggers behind the reemergence of frivolous anachronism as a serious problem—one that, presumably, was put into rest already in the nineteenth century by Friedrich Max Müller (1823–1900), the founding figure of the field of the study of religion[12]—the call for attention when dealing with source languages and renderings is neither new nor is it something that scholars keep overlooking, as critics want us to believe. Hence,

> two fundamental questions were therefore kept in mind: how to express ancient concepts that are in some way similar to, but at the same time profoundly different from modern concepts in our language? How to explain these differences to a modern reader? (Imhausen and Pommerening 2010: 4)

> Thus, historians are faced with two alternatives: either to echo the terminology used in their evidence, or to use a terminology which is foreign to it. (Ginzburg 2013: 98)

> But there is another problem here, again one of language. When the historian comes to write his or her true story, how does he or she translate a past *mentalité* for a modern audience? Whose words do you use to explain the source (and therefore the past): those of the dead or those of the living? (Arnold 2000: 104)

> We do not have the option of a neutral, transparent, "normal" language; we simply have to choose from a range of possible vocabularies, some more precise and technical than others but all equally time-bound and laden with anachronistic baggage. (Morley 2004: 26)

> ... [S]ensitivity to anachronism is a later phenomenon more closely coinciding with the formation of the disciplinary divisions under whose aegis we still mainly work. To speak of anachronism *avant la lettre*, then, would itself be an anachronism. But that should not be taken to mean that we have not been sufficiently historical: when our propositions go so self-reflexively circular, it is a sure sign that we are banging our heads against our disciplinary walls. (De Grazia 2010: 32)

Margreta De Grazia's words here are closer to what I deem the essential problem of distancing between classics (and ancient history) and the study of religion pertaining to the study of Greek and Roman religion(s). Although, as it has been recently argued, and in part convincingly so, the ancients themselves also had an advanced sense of anachronism (Rood, Atack, and Phillips 2020), the issue is not whether anachronism is a modern or an ancient concept but whether, when encountered in the works of contemporary authors, the drawn conclusion that the author has gravely failed is a valid one and on what basis.

Firstly, no ancient term or concept is an island. Take, for example, the case of "superstition." The Greek term usually translated into English as superstition is *deisidaimonia*. The English term has no positive meaning, typically interpreted as an excessive but irrational belief in supernatural powers and/or influences. The Greek word, however, as Dale Martin has cogently demonstrated, had a range of meanings among the ancient authors. The term

> could be a positive or neutral [one] ... referring to piety or the respect of sacred things that most people would have considered quite appropriate. But it could also be taken to be a term of reproach, referring to irrational or exaggerated fear of benign or nonexistent beings and forces. Hence the term, even in its basic definitional sense, spanned the range of meanings

from "respect for the gods" or "awe appropriate to sacred things" to "craven and irrational fear of divinities or demons." (Martin 2004: 19)

What one should take from Martin's assessment thus is apparently not that by translating *deisidaimonia* as superstition one commits the sin of anachronism. On the contrary, one needs to double check whether the excerpt in which the term appears utilizes it as we would nowadays—that is, negatively instead of positively, the latter typically meaning as an expression of "deep and pious" religiosity. As I will discuss in Chapter 3, the same process is applicable to the term *thrēskeia*, for which (primarily) Barton and Boyarin and (less so) Nongbri argue against translating it as "religion."

Secondly, if some scholars are willing to utilize postmodern critical theory onto ancient texts in order to demonstrate social injustices in the ancient world, then anachronism becomes an empty concept that we should do away with it at a stroke. Take for example, the position of Joel P. Christensen, currently Professor of Classical Studies at Brandeis University, who argued on his website/blog *Sententiae Antiquae*:

> Saying the Homeric epics are misogynistic or using Marxist theory to show how they (re-)produce structural oppression does not erase their beauty or their impact. Instead, it shows that their beauty may also have a harmful impact. It helps us understand how they work and how *we work* as human communities. (Christensen 2018; emphasis in original)

It is impossible to be given an easy ride when arguing both. Either our conceptual anachronisms are problematic and thereby prohibited, given that *we* assign—for instance, when arguing that the Greeks and the Romans had "religion"—*our own* conceptual tools to a historical period that lacked them, or one can apply modern concepts to antiquity as heuristic tools to further elaborate on how those ancient societies structured their worlds and what we can make of them. The latter point will also become apparent when I will be discussing the question whether "theology" is an appropriate category/term before the Christian era (see Chapter 5).

The bewildering and pressuring problem of anachronism as a result of historization and wordsmithing in the two fields within the last two decades or so has its own merit but commonly misses another important and far more crucial issue in my view regarding concepts, terms, and categories. As the positivist Claude Bernard argued almost two centuries ago in his *Introduction à la médecine expérimentale* (1865):

> When we create a word to characterize a phenomenon, we then agree in general on the idea we wish it to express and the precise meaning we are giving to it; but with the later progress of science the meaning of the word changes for some people, while for others the word remains in the language with its original meaning. The result is often such discord that men using the same word express very different ideas. Our language, in fact, is only approximate, and even in science it is so indefinite that if we lose sight of phenomena and cling to words, we are speedily outside of reality. (Translated by and cited in Ginzburg 2013: 99)

Although one may disagree with Bernard, I am intrigued by and in full agreement with his opening sentence. If Jonathan Z. Smith's "religion is solely the creation of the scholar's study" is correct, then Bernard's presupposition that conceptual creations are based on mutual agreement in respect to both the idea expressed by and the precise meaning of the term should make us seriously think twice. Given the lack of agreement regarding the idea expressed by and the exact meaning of "religion" among scholars, it seems somehow paradoxical to argue that, say, the Greeks and the Romans had no religion. And as Anders Klostergaard Petersen (2017a) recently put it, "To be able to identify a culture as being without a concept of religion you need—whether acknowledged or not—to subscribe to such a concept, albeit a vague one, that enables you to recognize the absence of the element you are searching for." Failing to do so renders anachronism as well as any debate over such concepts simply repetitive and pointless.

— // —

Instead of merely summarizing the argument of each chapter that follows, I find it more alluring to turn to two of the most prominent and revered scholars of Greek and Roman religion(s), respectively: Jean-Pierre Vernant (1914–2007) and John Scheid (b. 1946). Although both prolific authors, I have chosen here their inaugural lectures at the Collège de France on the occasion of their appointment to professorial chairs—Vernant in the "Comparative Studies of Ancient Religions" (Étude comparée des religions antiques) from 1975 until 1984 and Scheid in "Religion, Institutions, and Society of Ancient

Rome" (Religion, institutions et société de la Rome antique) from 2001 to 2016. Given that inauguration speeches act as events of publicly formulating the past, present, and future research agenda of a newly appointed holder, it is of interest to see how Vernant and Scheid articulated their approach to ancient religion—in some respects wonderfully demonstrating what I will be arguing about throughout this book. (This, however, does not mean that I unreservedly agree with their overall take, as it will also become evident.)

Vernant's inaugural speech entitled "Greek Religion, Ancient Religions" ("Religion grecque, religions antiques"), presented on December 5, 1975, is a masterfully crafted call for interdisciplinary work as the *sine qua non* for a productive, meaningful, and truly scientific study of ancient religions. Vernant naturally does not dismiss the grassroots work of classicists, but clearly indicates that in order to interpret our sources one needs to be receptive and adopt the theoretical concepts, tools, and methods from other social scientific domains as well—he himself was a passionate structuralist influenced by the work of the French anthropologist Claude Lévi-Strauss (1908–2009). As he put it:

> As for those scholars who … decided to keep strictly to Greek facts, they have carried out as philologists and historians the indispensable task of collecting, restoring, and carefully arranging various kinds of documents of religious significance. Nothing can be achieved without their help. Interpretation, however, seems to need other methods of approach. (Vernant 1991: 271)

Although throughout his lecture Vernant constantly returns to his cherished structuralism—for example, Greek gods should only be understood "by virtue of [their] relative position" and by "the structure of relations" (ibid.: 273)—it is only through cooperation with other disciplines that he deemed it possible to actually reach meaningful conclusions about the religious ideas and practices of the ancient Greeks: "research would be meaningless if specialists in religions other than Greek did not take part and did not feel equally involved" (ibid.: 275). Despite the occasional pitfalls in Vernant's structuralist approach to ancient Greek religion, his 1975 call for collaboration and exchange of methods and theories with other disciplines has not yet been actualized to its full potential. As I will be arguing in the chapters that follow, disciplines have become more insular rather than the opposite.

Scheid's lecture, entitled "Religion, Institutions and Society in Ancient Rome" ("Religion, institutions et société de la Rome antique") and delivered on February 7, 2002, is more hooked on the conventional view of classics and ancient history, with his main call being for a return to the sources as essentially the primary and most important step one needs to take to study the religion of the Romans. And although Scheid does not refute the utilization of concepts and categories from the modern world in the study of antiquity, his cautionary language is indicative of his more traditional (which, by the way, means neither problematic nor conservative) approach to Roman antiquity. In his words:

> Thirty years ago, historians of Rome could draw on their reading and classical culture to reconstruct the appropriate context for asking the right questions. Once they have lost the ability to use ancient languages, the history of Rome is very likely to resemble medicine in Molière's day. … [W]ithout concepts there is no history, even with sources. But where are these concepts to be found? … Things get out of hand however when concepts, often forged by researchers studying civilizations and societies very different from those of the Ancients, are transposed without any precaution onto Roman data. (Scheid 2002: §13; §§26–7)

Scheid's *ad fontes* recommendation has never, of course, lost its significance. On the contrary, it is (or must be, I should add) the fundamental condition for studying the Roman (and Greek) world altogether—and not merely its religious institutions, beliefs, and practices. (Scheid, however, is among the most ardent exponents of the dismissal of the notion of belief from the study of Roman religion—a position I find not only problematic but also damaging for the study of the religious world of the Romans. The "lack of any orthodoxy" principle [ibid.: §§31–2] features prominently in his inaugural lecture. For more on belief, see Chapter 6 and Appendix II.)

Notwithstanding the problems one encounters in Vernant's and Scheid's inaugural lectures, when considered in tandem they constitute a "how-to" map for the study of Greek and Roman religion(s) from which classicists, on the one hand, and scholars of religion, on the other, have a lot to gain. As such, although theory is unquestionably required, Scheid reminds modern scholars of religion of antiquity that any theoretical or meta-theoretical endeavor becomes untenable and even harmful when lacking knowledge of the original languages and sources. (And, in my view, his position should be seen as the most important criticism to scholars of religion who [over-]theorize about the ancient world while often not being able to read one line of source materials.) Concurrently, Vernant's 1975 interdisciplinary outlook indicates that no field needs custodians, and its existence is not predicated on some idea of exceptional and unique work conducted only within its disciplinary limits. (And, in my view, such a position should be embraced by classicists without necessarily meaning that it should be restricted to a "critical study" that today merely means a deconstructionist one. Foucault, Bourdieu, or Derrida are undoubtedly important, and in many respects undeniably indispensable, but not a panacea.)

— // —

It might often be the case that one may close a book none the wiser, and if this will be the case with this slim volume for some or many, so be it. Authors who write with an agenda in mind of solely making the majority of their peers positively nod rarely offer any valuable insights in my humble opinion. Being fully aware that what follows might make some (or most) readers from both aforementioned fields raise their eyebrows and dismiss the argumentation altogether, I will merely repeat Friedrich Max Müller's words in his letter to A. P. Stanley, the Dean of Westminster, on December 7, 1878: "Of course I know that many people will be angry with my *Lectures*. If it were not so, I should not have written them" (cited in Chaudhuri 1974: 358).

2

Burning Bridges?

Now, the majority of people do this either at random or with a familiarity arising from habit. But since both these ways are possible, it is clear that matters can be reduced to a system, for it is possible to examine the reason why some attain their end by familiarity and others by chance; and such an examination all would at once admit to be the function of an art.

Aristotle (384–322 BCE)[1]

In 2019, Peter Thonemann published an important and eye-opening article in the *Council of University Classical Departments Bulletin* (*CUCD*) dealing with the representation of female and male scholars in two hundred "Companion" volumes published in the period between 2001 and 2019. The aim was to investigate how and if female scholars are underrepresented in such publications primarily due to editorial choices as Thonemann demonstrates.[2] Such scholarship is undeniably necessary and essential—and it is neither restricted within classics nor solely deals with gender representation but has righteously so expanded, inter alia, into race, disabilities, and sexual orientation (e.g., see Rowe 2020).

"Companions" and "Handbooks" are in general presented as publications that are received as the current state-of-the-art of each field, used extensively by undergraduates, graduates, and scholars alike, while written by the most influential contemporary academics. Even the advertisement of such typically rather hefty volumes by the publishers promote them as exhaustive introductions to the most important topics, debates, innovations, future research, and so on, of the corresponding research fields. For example, the celebrated Oxford Handbooks series is marketed as follows:

> Oxford Handbooks offer *authoritative* and up-to-date surveys of original research in a particular subject area. Specially commissioned essays from

leading figures in the discipline give critical examinations of the progress and direction of debates, as well as a foundation for future research. Oxford Handbooks provide scholars and graduate students with compelling new perspectives upon a wide range of subjects in the humanities, social sciences, and sciences.[3]

Similarly, the Cambridge Companions series advertises its more than five hundred volumes in the following manner:

Cambridge Companions are a series of *authoritative* guides, written by leading experts, offering lively, accessible surveys to major writers, artists, philosophers, topics, and periods.[4]

Admittedly, these publications on the whole function as superb introductory surveys for the interested reader, and I have also been benefitted from such works numerous times when preparing lectures, course syllabi and materials, or writing articles and book reviews. (As a matter of fact, some chapters from such volumes have informed or even shaped some of my ideas in this book as it will become evident to the attentive reader.) However, the presentation of these works as "authoritative" and written by "leading" experts in each discipline begs some questions since, in my reading, such language—even if it is merely used for the sake of marketing, as one may readily object—creates some problems. By no means do I here imply that the authors of those surveys are not good scholars, knowledgeable, erudite, or that they fail to offer comprehensive, informed, and more often than not splendid short essays that can many a time help their audience move into new directions or reevaluate previously held positions. What I do wish to point out, however, is that such characterizations (i.e., "authoritative") also seemingly attempt to demarcate that whatever lies outside the scope of what the "leading experts" maintain could potentially be non-authoritative, uninformed, or possibly dismissible altogether.

One of the questions that naturally follows[5] is whether within the humanities "leading experts" are to be solely found within specific fields—especially so when the topic under consideration refers to broader concepts, categories, and classifications rather than narrower or specialized areas of research. For example, the concept and classification of phenomena as "religion(s)," or similarly objects, texts, and people as "religious," are not specific to one culture, historical period, or geographical area. There is hardly any field that does not also address the topic of religion in one form or another—ranging from geography and political science to sociology and economics. Therefore, one would expect that specialists in such fields would also resort to the work of scholars working in the study of religion to inform their own research given that the latter are deemed the quintessential specialists on matters related to "religion" as a category and as a phenomenon across time and space—at the very least from a theoretical and methodological point of view. (Examining whether this is the case in all these various disciplines would require independent studies as one might imagine, whereas whether the study of religion is indeed a distinctive "field" is in some ways disputable among some scholars.)[6] Whether classicists (and/or ancient historians) do also base their own "authoritative" studies about the religion(s) of the Greeks and the Romans on the theoretical and methodological work conducted by specialists in the study of religion is the main topic of this chapter. In doing so, I am examining such standardized works found within the genre of "Companions" in order to trace how and if scholars working in the field of the study of religion are either directly represented in such multi-authored volumes or are their works being considered—or, at least, suggested in the "Further Readings" section often encountered at the end of individual chapters in works of this kind. That is, by loosely imitating Thonemann's work, I am paying attention not on gender, race, sexuality, or otherwise, but on interdisciplinarity, which I consider essential in further examining and advancing the study of Greek and Roman religion(s).[7]

–1–

I have chosen four popular volumes that belong to the "Companion" genre that are specifically dedicated to the study of Greek and/or Roman religion, while I also discuss an additional one that expands into the Mediterranean world more broadly.[8] I could have also added in my discussion similar works related to myth and/or mythology in Greek and Roman antiquity. But given that "myth" is not restricted to religion but had more functions within Greek and Roman societies (from legitimation of kingship to foundation of cities, and from genealogical narratives to identity formation processes), I will not be touching upon that category here.⁹

Daniel Ogden (ed.), *A Companion to Greek Religion*. Malden, MA and Oxford: Blackwell, 2007

The volume is comprised of twenty-seven chapters written by twenty-eight scholars. The latter are classified as follows: twenty-five scholars are classicists or historians of Greek antiquity, whereas three are hailing from different disciplines. More specifically: Jan N. Bremmer (religious studies), Françoise Dunand (history of religions), and Scott B. Noegel (biblical and ancient near eastern studies). Despite one's objections whether Bremmer and Dunand are scholars indeed working in the broader field of the study of religion,[10] the ratio is still astounding: 89.3 percent classicists and historians of Greek antiquity and 10.7 percent "other," with the ratio shrinking further down if the classification of "other" is restricted to the "Study of Religion" alone (7.14 percent).

In terms of works cited, the contributors have used the works of just a handful of scholars outside the fields of classics and ancient history (who are related directly or indirectly with the field of the study of religion), with the following names appearing: Mary Douglas (two works, pp. 182, 189), Émile Durkheim (one work, pp. 283, 285, 295), Mircea Eliade (two works, p. 23), E. E. Evans-Pritchard (three works, pp. 376, 381–3), J. G. Frazer (two works, pp. 24, 194 as "Further Reading"), Sigmund Freud (one work, p. 35), Victor Turner (one work, p. 295 as "Further Reading"), René Girard (one work, p. 22), Marcel Mauss and Henri Hubert (one work, p. 22), Bronisław Malinowski (one work, p. 25), Edward Said (one work, p. 23), Jonathan Z. Smith (four works, pp. 22, 32, 144 as "Further Reading"), and Roy Rappaport (one work, p. 22). For the observant reader, it turns out that with the exception of Douglas (cited by Andreas Bendlin in his chapter "Purity and Pollution," pp. 178–89), Durkheim and Turner (cited by Charles W. Hedrick Jr. in his chapter "Religion and Society in Classical Greece," pp. 283–96), and Evans-Pritchard (cited by Thomas Harrison in his chapter "Greek Religion and Literature," pp. 373–84), all the rest (!) are cited by Scott B. Noegel in his chapter "Greek Religion and the Ancient Near East" (pp. 21–37). In other words, in a tome of xxi + 497 pages, of which thirty-seven pages provide an extensive bibliography comprising 1,147 entries, the almost absolute majority of works cited, used, and suggested to the student of ancient Greek religion comes from within the fields of classics, archaeology, and ancient history, with other disciplines being barely represented.

One could readily object to such a "superficial" presentation, given that individual contributors do indeed tackle issues in their essays that go beyond the strict boundaries of their field—that is, classics and ancient history. For example, in her essay on "'Something to do with Aphrodite': *Ta Aphrodisia* and the Sacred" (pp. 311–23), Vincianne Pirenne-Delforge opens with the following statement: "The validity of some concepts and interpretative categories for the study of ancient societies, such as those of 'myth', 'rite', and 'religion', has recently been called into question" (311), but does not offer any citation nor suggestion to lead the reader to further discussions. The same in encountered in Matthew W. Dickie's "Magic in Classical and Hellenistic Greece" (pp. 357–70), where, without bibliographical suggestions, it is stated that

> religion is a more problematic notion than magic. It is notoriously difficult to give an adequate rendering of the English word "religion" in either Greek or Latin; there is no single word in either ancient language that fits the bill. That is not to say that it is impossible to put into Greek or Latin *whatever is meant by the use of the English word "religion" in any given context*. That it is always possible to render what is meant by "religion" in Greek or Latin gives the lie to those who assert that the Greeks and the Romans had no concept of religion. A more accurate, though less dramatic, statement of the true state of affairs would be that the Greeks and the Romans have no one word that covers everything comprehended in the English word "religion." (357; my emphasis)[11]

The overall approach to Greek religion without theoretical inputs from fields outside classics and ancient history is apparent in the editor's introductory chapter, in which Ogden prefers to merely delineate the volume's structure rather than focus on the actual category "ancient Greek religion" and the theoretical and methodological issues arising by the very claim that the ancient Greeks "had religion"—let alone attempting to actually define what is meant by "religion" in this Companion. The only two contributors who offer such discussions are Thomas Harrison and Charles W. Hedrick Jr., with the latter also offering a definition of religion that he then applies to his essay: "By 'religion' I mean beliefs, manifested in word and deed (or myth and ritual), in the transcendental, the deathless, unchanging, true or natural: what is other than the world of contingent, practical experience, and thus can serve as a model for it" (285). It is surprising that, apart from Hedrick Jr., no other contributor attempts to clearly define their object of study. But this is not a problem restricted to this Companion alone.

Jörg Rüpke (ed.), *A Companion to Roman Religion*. Malden, MA and Oxford: Blackwell, 2007

Edited by perhaps the most influential contemporary scholar in the field of Roman religion, this Companion is consisted of thirty-one essays. However, only two of the respective authors work in fields other than classics, ancient history, and archaeology, namely Jack L. Lightstone (biblical studies/ Judaism) and Stefan Heid (theology). This makes for an astounding 93.5 percent of authors from classics and adjacent disciplines and a mere 6.5 percent from "other," whereas the study of religion as a discipline is not represented at all.

Contrary, however, to Ogden's introductory chapter, Rüpke touches upon more theoretical issues in his own introduction. Although he does not risk offering a clear definition of "religion" (or "Roman religion" specifically), he nonetheless gives the overall view of what is classified as "Roman religion" within the Companion: "'religion' is *conceptualized by the authors of this book* as human actions and communication. These were performed *on the presupposition that gods existed* who were part of one's own social or political group, existed in the same space and time" (6–7; my emphasis). One, however, should pay attention to the care with which this statement is phrased by Rüpke, especially the highlighted parts. The former one could be seen more as an observation rather than what the editor himself maintains, whereas the latter one indicates a reluctance to use the term "belief."[12] Rüpke does not eventually offer a definition of "religion" or "Roman religion" other than a circular presentation in the following manner: "'Roman religion' as used here is an abbreviation for 'religious signs, practices, and traditions in the city of Rome'" (5), which, of course, leaves the term "religious" undefined in turn.

Similarly to *A Companion to Greek Religion*, the works used and suggested to the reader in the thirty-eight pages of bibliography are overwhelmingly related to or stem from the fields of classics, ancient history, and archaeology. Hence, from the 983 works cited, only a couple of dozen are written by scholars not working in the aforementioned fields: twenty-two works written by thirteen scholars directly or indirectly related to the field of the study of religion are used or referred to, bringing the latter's percentage to roughly 2.3 percent. It is worth noting that ten works written by six scholars—namely, Russell T. McCutcheon, Catherine Bell, George Stocking, Donald Wiebe, Robert Segal, and E. J. Sharpe—are only mentioned by one contributor: C. Robert Phillips, III, in his essay "Approaching Roman Religion: The Case for *Wissenschaftsgeschichte*" (pp. 10–28). Likewise, five works written by three scholars—that is, Mary Douglas, Peter Berger, and Clifford Geertz—are only cited by Jack L. Lightstone in his essay "Roman Diaspora Judaism" (pp. 345–77). The remaining eight works are found scattered in the rest of the volume—penned by Robert Bellah (one work appearing once), Ugo Bianchi (two works appearing in two papers), Burkhardt Gladigow (one work appearing once), and Jonathan Z. Smith (four works appearing in three different papers, with two of them only to be found in C. Robert Phillips's paper again).

Phillips's paper, along with parts of Rüpke's introduction, are the only ones that actually address some theoretical issues that are of interest to the non-classicist—with the former being much more profound and appealing than the latter, in my view. Phillips not only offers an interesting outline of how classical studies functions in relation to methodological and theoretical issues, but also effectively summarizes the main problem the field faces when it comes to the study of Roman religion—which can be certainly extended to Greek religion as well, thus encompassing the whole historical period of Greek and Roman antiquity that the field has historically claimed to have mastered. In his words:

> Thus, while deplorable, it is understandable why there is no *Wissenschaftsgeschichte* of Roman religion. It seems highly specialized to do *Wissenschaftsgeschichte*, but for Roman religion one must attend not only to the *Wissenschaftsgeschichte* of classical studies, but also to the *Wissenschaftsgeschichte* of anthropology, sociology, the history of universities, religious studies; thus the study becomes a specialty inside a specialty. (12)

Although crucial, Phillips's call for interdisciplinary work, which he correctly observes as absent due to a dictum that has historically guided the classics methodologically—"the empirico-positivist context 'the facts speak for themselves'" (11) that has led to the downplaying of theory in general—does not seem to have great influence on the rest of the contributors of this Companion (or on classicists by and large as I am arguing throughout this book). This is not the first time Phillips gets his hands dirty, as it were, since he has offered similar criticisms in regard to the study of Greek and Roman mythology (Phillips 2000 [1991])—a topic which would naturally require an independent study.

Rubina Raja and Jörg Rüpke (eds.), *A Companion to the Archaeology of Religion in the Ancient World*. Malden, MA and Oxford: Wiley Blackwell, 2015

This is a more peculiar Companion given that it focuses on the materiality of religion[13] in the ancient world through the lens of archaeology—restricted as the editors inform the reader to the Greco-Roman world (6). The thirty-seven authors of the thirty-six essays, again, hail from classics, ancient history, and archaeology (thirty-four in particular, which translates into 91.9 percent of the contributors), with only three exceptions that work in theology (one), Hebrew culture (one), and Jewish history (one)—the latter two combined amounting to 8.2 percent. Similarly to the previous publication (also edited by Rüpke), no individual author has studied religion at the undergraduate or graduate level, or holds a PhD in the study of religion (or of any of its other nomenclatures). Of interest, perhaps, as Raja and Rüpke indicate in their introduction, is the fact that five of the contributors (including the editors themselves) were supported by the European Research Council (ERC) funded project run by Rüpke at the University of Erfurt entitled "Lived Ancient Religion" (p. 24). What they do not disclose, however, is that other contributors were also involved in the project as visitors at Erfurt, by participating in conferences organized as part of the project, or publishing under the auspices of the project: for example, Richard Gordon, Gregory Woolf, and Eric Rebillard.[14] In many respects, thus, the Companion directly or indirectly follows a very specific methodological and theoretical path informed by Rüpke's project and conceptualization in regard to what is "religion" (and "Roman religion" specifically).[15] This becomes even more apparent when Raja and Rüpke explicitly reject one of the most recent and perhaps promising approaches to ancient religion, that is, the cognitive study of religion (see, e.g., Larson [2016] and my discussion in Chapter 6). In their words:

> It is above all the local, situational, and individual dimension of religion which has been neglected. ... The primacy given to the systematic and the dogmatic is a normative decision. It is a decision to describe religion, as it should be rather than as it is. There are two ways out of the problem. One group of researchers opts for a scientific approach. They base their claims on cognitive studies and attempt to reach firm ground by starting from "conceptual metaphors" of self and superhuman powers supposedly grounded in universal ways of perception and an evolutionary theory of religion. ... This way will not be followed in this Companion. Instead, we opt for a cultural and historical approach, lived religion. (3)

In and of itself, there is nothing wrong with adhering to a particular methodological and theoretical principle. This has been and still remains the most common way of approaching one's subject. However, this becomes quite complicated when a whole Companion—presumably presenting an inclusive and rather broad overview of current research—is conceived of and formulated in this manner. In one sentence: whoever disagrees with or has reservations in relation to the "lived religion" project might find very little of interest in this particular Companion—and will definitely not consider it a state-of-the-field publication as such works are typically advertised and dealt with.[16]

Given the specific topic of the Companion, that is, archaeology/religion/Greek and Roman world, it would be anticipated that, methodologically and theoretically speaking, the field of archaeology would be the most represented one. Equally, the fields of classics and ancient history would be the ones informing the volume. But there is an astonishing gap in works related to the field of the study of religion: out of the 1,411 sources used in the Companion by the contributors, only roughly ninety are directly related to the study of religion, with the former three disciplines representing 93.9 percent of the bibliographical entries and the latter a mere 6.1 percent. It is indeed startling that the third main element of the Companion's focus, that is, "religion," can be adequately covered theoretically by classicists, ancient historians, and archaeologists alone, thus making the discussions by scholars of religion simply nonessential—despite the fact that none of the contributors offer any definition of "religion." It is equally alarming that the vast majority of the works related to the study of religion are cited by Rüpke (in his co-authored introduction to the volume as well as in his chapter on "Individual Choices and Individuality in the Archaeology of Ancient Religion," pp. 437–50), with the rest of the contributors only scarcely utilizing the works of scholars working in the study of religion. To put it in perspective: Jonathan Z. Smith appears only once (p. 214), Clifford Geertz twice (pp. 2, 349), Victor Turner once (p. 446), Catherine Bell, five times (pp. 4, 41, 57, 127, 468), Mary Douglas twice (pp. 5, 170), Peter Berger once (p. 438), whereas scholars such as Robert Segal, Bruce Lincoln, Russell McCutcheon, Donald Wiebe, Luther H. Martin, Hans Penner, and numerous others do not feature, nor one learns anything about, say, the comparative method—the very foundation of the field of the study of religion. It is merely Rüpke who incorporates into his contributions here various theoretical and methodological aspects that expand into different disciplines and, specifically, into the study of religion. And it is Rüpke again, along with Rubina Raja, that attempts a definition of religion, without nonetheless being clear whether the contributors accept, are critical of, or simply reject such a definition given that no hints are found into the individual chapters: "Such 'religion' is understood as a spectrum of experiences, actions, and beliefs and communications hinging on human communication with super-human or even transcendent agent(s), for many, but not all societies conceptualized as 'gods'" (4).

Esther Eidinow and Julia Kindt (eds.), *The Oxford Handbook of Ancient Greek Religion*. New York: Oxford University Press, 2015

Edited by two of the most learned and influential contemporary scholars in the field of Greek religion, this Handbook constitutes the most recent addition for the interested student and scholar working on the religious beliefs and practices of the Greeks. A little over seven hundred pages long, it is admittedly a very broad and informed textbook. Eidinow and Kindt's aim is clear: to "highlight crucial developments in the study of ancient Greek religion, with a special focus on problems and debates" thus offering "a comprehensive overview of the current state of the field" (1). Yet again, based on the choice of contributors and their respective specializations, the "field" here is conceptualized rather narrowly.

The volume contains forty-three chapters in addition to the introductory essay penned by forty-seven contributors in total. Of those, forty-one are historians of antiquity and classicists; one is a comparative literature/philosophy scholar (Lisa Raphals); one is a historian of art (Maya Muratov); and four are identified as scholars of religion, namely, Jan Bremmer, Sarah Iles Johnston, Gabriella Pironti, and Giulia Sfameni Gasparro. From the latter subgroup, however, only Pironti and Sfameni Gasparro can be considered scholars of religion, and only the latter by training (having also published an introduction to the study of religion; Sfameni Gasparro 2011), whereas Bremmer and Johnston are trained classicists and should be counted among the first subgroup. This translates into 91.5 percent trained and working in classics and ancient history and 8.5 percent in other fields, with the study of religion represented by two scholars (meaning 4.2 percent—or, if Pironti will be classified as a historian of Mediterranean religions specifically, then 2.1 percent).

This has some implications. For example, in the first part entitled "What is Ancient Greek Religion?" (pp. 11–47)—perhaps the most important question from a theoretical perspective—and comprised of four chapters, normally one would expect either a rudimentary or a fully fledged definition as an answer to this fundamental question which, however, is not to be found in this or in any of the other parts of the volume. For example, Robin Osborne's chapter, "Unity vs. Diversity," dedicates a mere few lines to the issue in the beginning of his contribution, where it is argued that "the term 'religion' cannot be translated into Greek. The Greeks knew that different people worshipped different gods and did so in different ways. … But no Greek writer known to us classifies either the gods or the cult practices into separate 'religions'" (11). Although most scholars today would agree with such a statement, it does not answer the main question of this first part of the book. The claim that Osborne's chapter is "challenging the very term 'religion' itself," as the editors put it in their introduction (2) is hardly justified from a study of religion perspective.[17]

This leads us to the sources consulted and found in the Handbook. Compared to the previously discussed works, the Handbook contains the largest number of chapters as well as works mentioned. In total (although many are repeated in the different chapters), we encounter 1,952 bibliographical entries, of which only fifty-three are from outside classics, ancient history, or archaeology and related to the study of religion and adjacent disciplines. This is broken down as follows: 97.3 percent and 2.7 percent, respectively. From those works, the vast majority is encountered in specific papers, such as: Thomas Harrison's "Belief vs. Practice" (pp. 21–8), Caitlín E. Barrett's "Material Evidence" (pp. 113–30), Robert Fowler's "History" (pp. 195–209), Verity Platt's "Epiphany" (pp. 491–504), and Sarah Hitch's "From Birth to Death: Life-Changing Rituals" (pp. 521–36). These five chapters refer to thirty-nine of the fifty-three aforementioned works that are not penned by classicists, ancient historians, or archaeologists, amounting to 73.5 percent of all "other" works used. It becomes therefore evident that for the interested student and scholar of ancient Greek religion, the Handbook's suggested academic path leads predominantly (if not exclusively) to the fields of classics, ancient history, and archaeology, whereas the questions what constitutes "religion" as well as how and why "religion" came about as a phenomenon within the ancient Greek world is (seemingly) silently agreed upon without further insights from the study of religion or the social sciences more broadly.

–2–

What informs such a shortage in volumes of this kind can be first and foremost traced in the history of disciplinary divisions and the ensuing training dictated by a rhetoric of "specialness" and "uniqueness" typically permeating curricula and—above all—mindsets. Thankfully, some classicists and scholars of religion alike are becoming rampantly conscious of such a trend and seek collaborations (cf. the different approaches in Roubekas [2019b]), despite the disheartening landscape sketched by many volumes belonging to the "Companion" genre. One such attempt is exemplified in a volume that is part of the Cambridge Companions series. Although not belonging to the field of Greek and Roman religion(s) *strictu sensu*, it is nevertheless a very good example of disciplinary inclusivity and may function as a paradigm worth examining and, perhaps, imitating.

Barbette Stanley Spaeth (ed.), *The Cambridge Companion to Ancient Mediterranean Religions*. New York: Cambridge University Press, 2013

Edited by a classicist with a specialization in Greek and Roman religion(s), the Companion comprises merely fourteen single-authored chapters along with the editor's introduction. In terms of disciplinary representation, this is by far the most inclusive volume of its kind, but with a caveat. Given that the Companion deals with more geographical areas and peoples than a typical multi-authored volume dedicated to Greek and/or Roman religion(s) alone, some of the contributors feature in its pages precisely due to the need for input on religions of diverse peoples and places such as: Egypt (Emily Teeter, an egyptologist), Mesopotamia (Beate Pongratz-Leisten, a near eastern studies specialist), Syria-Canaan (Shawna Dolansky, a specialist in biblical studies), Israel (Mayer I. Gruber, a biblical archaeologist and near eastern studies specialist), Anatolia (Billie Jean Collins, a specialist on the Hittites and the near east), Iran (W. W. Malandra, a specialist on Iranian religion), and (the usual suspect) Early Christianity (H. Gregory Snyder, a New Testament specialist).

Of interest here, however, is that the editor also invited a group of scholars of religion who engage in a discussion of more general categories often either neglected or underrepresented in similar volumes. Hence, Bruce Lincoln, Kimberly B. Stratton, Elizabeth A. Castelli, and Ross Shepard Kraemer discuss umbrella terms such as violence, identity, body, and gender. Overall, the volume is penned by classicists (20 percent), scholars of religion (26.5 percent), theologians and biblical studies scholars (20 percent), and specialists of the near east and Egypt (33.5 percent). It is due to such diversity in terms of disciplinary voices that this particular volume stands out in both the treatment of the religions of Mediterranean antiquity and the works informing the individual chapters. It would be futile to go over the whole bibliographical list, since merely by looking at the chapters authored by the non-classicists, one encounters a plethora of sources from a wide variety of disciplines. But to put it in perspective, even Spaeth's nine-page introductory chapter cites the works of theoreticians such as Talal Asad, Timothy Fitzgerald, John R. Hinnells, Bruce Lincoln, and Russell T. McCutcheon. Containing eighteen bibliographical entries, one realizes that more than one quarter of the cited works stem from outside Spaeth's own discipline.

Expanding on her introduction, it is refreshing to see Spaeth's take on religion in conjunction with antiquity as a subfield. She does not deny the possibility to categorize things as "religious," offering at the same time an implicit definition: "Nevertheless, it seems clear that phenomena that we would categorize as 'religious' did exist in the ancient Mediterranean, including such things as beliefs about divine beings, rituals devoted to these beings, and institutions connected with the performance of those rituals" (1). One can point out some apparent problems with such an indirect definition of religion: from essentializing religion in the likes of E. B. Tylor's minimal definition of religion to (more commonly) Christianizing other cultures' religions by connecting the phenomenon to belief, practices, and formal institutions—one perhaps may add here that Spaeth's take also implies a Durkheimian functionalist approach to religion.[18]

However, Spaeth's articulation here functions as a definition of the subject matter (i.e., "religion") positioning therefore the volume within a specific theoretical framework. Nevertheless, Spaeth's introductory chapter shines when she explains and justifies the rationale of choosing scholars from a variety of disciplines to contribute to her Companion. In many respects, her position here anticipates my own in regard to the study of ancient religions—in my case, Greek and Roman; in her Companion, the broader Mediterranean basin. Her words are worth citing since they encapsulate the broader problem as exemplified in this chapter and in the rest of book at hand:

> The academic discipline of the study of ancient Mediterranean religions, however, is still in its nascent stages. The relatively recent development of this field may be attributed to a variety of factors. First, the trend toward academic specialization in the twentieth century has meant that *until recently most scholars have been traditionally trained in fields that have had relatively rigid boundaries.* ... Second, the problem of academic specialization is compounded when one considers the large number of scholarly fields that comprise the study of ancient Mediterranean religions, among them classical studies, Near Eastern studies, biblical studies, Egyptology, art and art history, history, archaeology, and religious studies. *Scholars are often uncomfortable stepping outside of their own fields and into comparative or*

interdisciplinary work, and hence often do not attempt research that requires such work. Finally, communication among scholars who work on different aspects of ancient Mediterranean religions has been limited. *Scholars tend to associate with others in their field, and so do not come into dialogue with those in other areas.*[19] (2; my emphases)

I will be discussing such issues throughout the book, but suffice it here to say that, although invaluable, Spaeth's diagnosis partly overlooks the inwardly outlook of scholars when it comes to interdisciplinary work: it is in many respects the rhetoric of "exceptionality" and "distinctiveness" that drives such absence of different voices within the type of works that belong to the "Companion and Handbook" genre. And things become even more "rigid," to use her term, when turning our attention to monographs or journal articles.[20]

–3–

Scholars working within the field of classics and ancient history have recently attempted to identify why the field seems more reticent than unreserved. The common thread observed in such works is a continuous tendency of the field to cling onto the basic foundational principles that distinguished, shielded, and cultivated its reputation. This is aptly presented by Joshua Billings in his study of ancient Greek tragedy and German philosophy since 1800. As he observes:

> A conception of *Wissenschaft* is at the heart of the modern understanding of research in the humanities (though it is worth remembering that this conception is only two hundred years old). ... *Wissenschaft* and slow reading are distinct practices, with incompatible relations to history: "scientific" research tends to the goal of perspective-free knowledge of the past, while "literary" study tends towards an experience of meaningfulness in the present. Their coexistence in classical studies is rooted in a founding antinomy of the discipline, which defines its method historically and its object ahistorically (through the concept of the "classical," which draws arbitrary boundaries around cultures thought to be uniquely educative).[21]

Billings's thesis here encapsulates, at least partly, the argument presented in this chapter. A quick examination of the manner departments of classics advertise themselves seems to corroborate Billings's assessment that classicists seem more hooked on Ulrich von Wilamowitz-Moellendorff's (1848–1931) legacy than that of Friedrich Nietzsche's (1844–1900).[22] Wilamowitz's understanding of how to study antiquity holistically has largely led the discipline to its present standing, which is not restricted to philology *tout court* but encompasses art, archaeology, history, geography, and philosophy into one entity—what became known as *Altertumswissenschaft* with its *Totalitätsideal*.[23] So, indicatively:

> "Classics" refers to the study of the languages, literatures, material culture, and history of the societies of the ancient world, together with their influence on later periods and cultures right up to the present day. It is one of the most varied and interdisciplinary of all subjects and can include literature, history, philosophy, art and archaeology.[24]

> Classics in this broad sense includes the study of language and creative literature, of political and social history, of economics and law, of philosophy, religion, and art, and of the material remains of the ancient world. The organizing idea of the field is not a method or a discipline, but the culture of Greco-Roman antiquity in all its richness and diversity (often its strangeness). Classics in this sense is the original and most wide ranging of interdisciplinary fields.[25]

> Classics is the integrated study of ancient Greek and Roman civilization through its languages, literature, and artistic and material remains. ... Topics include Greek and Roman archaeology and art history, ancient theater, mythology, women's history, humor, cultural exchange across the Mediterranean, the translation of Greek and Latin poetry, the history of slavery, sexuality, and ethnicity in ancient society, film studies, and the reception of classical antiquity in the modern era.[26]

> Classics is an intensely interdisciplinary field of study comprising the culture, history, languages and material remains of ancient Greek and Roman civilizations.[27]

Nevertheless, Wilamowitz's take was not interdisciplinary per se but saw antiquity beholding its "own" interdisciplinarity restricted within the confines of the aforementioned fields but always limited within the chronological boundaries of antiquity—whatever those are, given their constant reshaping in scholarly works.[28] Hence, it comes as no surprise that in the volumes examined in this chapter, certain disciplines are readily represented whereas others are overlooked or deliberately not being considered.

Wilamowitz's discipline-centric outlook was evident, for example, in his reaction to James G. Frazer's (1854–1941) comparativism in regard to magic and religion as cross-cultural phenomena.[29] Moreover, Wilamowitz was not an admirer of Ellen Harrison's (1850–1928) work either—one of the most renowned female scholars belonging to the so-called Cambridge Ritualists group[30]—and in a letter to, perhaps the most influential British classicist of the first half of the twentieth century, Gilbert Murray (1866–1957)[31] he expressed his disdain for Harrison's work, which is of interest here: "In matters of religion I remain old-fashioned … I can't get along with historians of religion; not with those who really dispose of everything with magic and superstition and in the end have a more intimate relation with old women of both sexes than to Plato, Spinoza and Goethe."[32] This neatly summarizes a more "aristocratic" approach to antiquity, so to speak, which was engrained in Wilamowitz's view of the ancient world, as did the Greek gods whom he considered of possessing the two quintessential aristocratic features, that of unaccountableness and that of only interested in the select few than in the many as Arnaldo Momigliano put it almost three decades ago.[33]

One might object that nowadays no modern classicist or student of antiquity remains hooked on Wilamowitz's peculiar or even one-sided view of Greek antiquity. However, there are still many persons voicing their concerns when Wilamowitz's name (and the tradition he represents) is lacking from or does not receive the proper attention in new publications. Such an episode is recorded in a heated exchange in the *Times Literary Supplement* (TLS) following Johanna Hanink's review of *Postclassicisms*.[34] What triggered the debate is Hanink's following statement: "Classics as an academic discipline might have developed in nineteenth-century Germany, but that does not mean that the field must hold Nietzsche and Wilamowitz ever in view. … Wilamowitz's name occurs fifty times, just as often as Plato's. The notion that nineteenth-century Germany is as important to today's classicist as ancient Greece and Rome is troubling."[35] In a letter to the editor of *TLS*, Edward N. Luttwak strenuously criticized Hanink's review by stating that many parts of Wilamowitz's work "remain unsurpassed," lamenting that a faculty member of Brown University would maintain such ideas.[36] A week later, Helen Morales of the University of California, Santa Barbara, wrote to the editor pointing out that Luttwak "manages to work himself into a lather about Wilamowitz not being adored enough,"[37] which in turn led to the arrival of yet another letter to the editor penned by Josef Kessler, in which both Hanink and Morales are vigorously attacked: "When a classicist brags in the TLS of her ignorance of Wilamowitz and Nietzsche, one can only feel sympathy for her unfortunate students. That a letter condoning such ignorance and illiteracy is couched in terms of pop culture rather than engaging in intellectual dialectic should come as no surprise: *abyssus abyssum invocat*, as Auden would have sadly observed."[38] Hence the question persists: what type of *Wissenschaft* should scholars of ancient religions embrace and promote? Wilamowitz's conception of *Altertumswissenschaft* (still partly hegemonic as observed in departmental descriptions as well as in some major publications as this chapter has attempted to show) or otherwise? The aforementioned debate indicates that the question has neither been settled yet nor may do so within the disciplinary borders of one or two fields. And despite the various attempts to bridge disciplines from scholars working in the field of classics,[39] this is rarely (at the very least) the case in the "Companions and Handbooks" genre despite their importance as sources for the discipline-outsiders, undergraduates, postgraduates, and other general readers.[40]

3

(No) Greek and Roman "Religion"

Nothing could be more ridiculous than to reject an author's judgement because he is following the received customs of his age and his people.

Jacob Perizonius (1651–1715)[1]

It was the year 1962 when Wilfred Cantwell Smith (1916–2000), one of the most influential North American scholars of comparative religion, published what eventually became—for North American scholars above all—the point of departure of a series of attempts to "historicize religion" as a category. *The Meaning and End of Religion: A New Approach to the Religious Traditions of Mankind* has had a surprising albeit puzzling reception history: it immediately became a big hit among scholars of religion for different and rather divergent reasons. On the one hand, readers that had a Christian background (like Smith himself who was an ordained Presbyterian minister) and thus a Christian-centric view of what religion is rejoiced in Smith's call for putting stress on the term "faith" rather than "religion." On the other hand, and since the other influential Smith (Jonathan Z.; 1938–2017) explicated his approach to "religion" as a category, contemporary scholars have initiated a series of discussions and publications that seek to deconstruct the descriptor "religion" in several ways, from explicitly advocating its abandonment to drawing attention to the evident anachronism of the category when utilized outwith monotheistic milieus, given, as the argument goes, the Christian-centric birth and history of the category.[2] The latter group, however, often invokes or starts from Cantwell Smith considering his seminal work as the quintessential piece of scholarship on the matter, thereby seemingly overlooking (consciously or not) Smith's Christian-centric and phenomenological approach while cherry-picking from his theory to support their position—that is, to demonstrate the supposed inadequacy of "religion" as an analytical category.[3]

Smith held a very particular and Christian-derived understanding of the term "religion," which he deemed one that misleads rather than helps us. As he argued:

> My own suggestion is that the word, and the concepts, should be dropped—in all but the ... personalist sense. ... I suggest that the term "religion" is confusing, unnecessary, and distorting. ... I have become strongly convinced that the vitality of personal faith, on the one hand, and, on the other hand (quite separately), progress in understanding—even at the academic level—of the traditions of other people throughout history and throughout the world, are both seriously blocked by our attempt to conceptualize what is involved in each case in terms of (a) religion. (Smith 1962: 48–9)

For Smith, the preferred term and focus is "faith" rather than religion, and the "personalist sense" is that of "religion as faith." Smith's suggested shift is one that eventually incapacitates the study of religion as a human by-product and practice, given that it deflects scholars from the study of texts and practices and pleads for a study of adherents and insiders, undoubtedly favoring the latter's input over and beyond the scholar's observations, evaluations, and explanations. As he famously put it, "no statement about a religion is valid unless it can be acknowledged by that religion's believers" (Smith 1959: 42).[4]

Naturally, one wonders how a scholar of, say, Greek and Roman religion(s) may proceed from here given the impossibility of verification since Greek and Roman "believers" are long dead. Smith did not shy away from such a question, maintaining that

> personalization can be achieved also, however, in the case of the religion of an historical community that has ceased to exist ... as a study of people over against a study of data. ... Perhaps one should say, with more precision, the study of a people's religious life over against a study of their gods, their doctrines, their institutions, and the like. (Smith 1959: 35)

Therefore, for Smith, ancient religion(s) can be studied by reconstructing ancient peoples' "religious life"-qua-faith instead of studying those peoples' gods, ideas, institutions, and so on. Such a faith-based approach differs little (if at all) from a theological one, thereby transforming the study of ancient religions into a study of Christian-like and theologically informed discussion, as if the religions of the ancient world—here, Greek and Roman—should be seen as equivalent to modern monotheistic ones.

Granted that scholars of religion have long argued against such an approach to the subject matter of their studies,[5] it comes as a surprise that two important and highly praised volumes published in the last ten years begin from Cantwell Smith's "groundbreaking" positions, as it is argued, before proceeding to deconstruct the category "religion" specifically in relation to its applicability to the ancient world—with a focus, due to the extensive available sources, on Greek and Roman antiquity: Brent Nongbri's *Before Religion: A History of a Modern Concept* (2013) and Carlin A. Barton and Daniel Boyarin's *Imagine No Religion: How Modern Abstractions Hide Ancient Realities* (2016).[6]

–1–

Nongbri mentions Smith in various parts of his monograph, although, to be fair, he does not wholeheartedly accept his positions. Nevertheless, he informs his readers that "my initial curiosity about the history of the concept of religion is in large part due to my first reading of *The Meaning and End of Religion* more than a decade ago" (Nongbri 2013: 4). Similarly, Nongbri finds an ally in William T. Cavanaugh's work on religion, when he argues that "[Cavanaugh's] chapter titled 'The Invention of Religion' surveys some of the same evidence that I cover here in Chapters 5 and 6. This is not surprising, given that we seem to share a common starting point in the work of Wilfred Cantwell Smith …" (ibid.: 163, n. 14). Despite Nongbri's rejection of Smith's call to abandon the term "religion" altogether (ibid.: 228, n. 6), he eventually does suggest alternatives in an attempt to indicate (as he does throughout his volume) the term's inapplicability in antiquity. In a confusing manner, however, he closes his book with the following words:

> I do think the use of religion as an explicitly second-order or redescriptive concept has a place in the study of antiquity. … The different type of descriptive accounts that I have in mind would allow what we have been calling "ancient religions" … to be disaggregated and rearranged in ways that correspond better to ancient people's own organizational schemes. … We will end up not with slightly tweaked books on ancient Greek religion

or on Roman religion, but with books on Athenian appeals to ancestral tradition, Roman ethnicity, Mesopotamian scribal praxis, Christian and Muslim heresiological discourses, and other topics that will encapsulate and thoroughly rearrange those bits and pieces of what we once gathered together as "ancient religions." (Nongbri 2013: 158–9)

Wilfred Cantwell Smith's importance is equally evident in Barton and Boyarin's volume as well. Already in their introduction they acknowledge Smith, along with Talal Asad, as "the two most outstanding exponents of the latter view [i.e., that "religion" as a category is a post-Enlightenment construction] ... both of whom demonstrated how much of an imposition this invention was on the various cultures which Christian Europe met with in modernity" (Barton and Boyarin 2016: 9).[7] Similarly, Barton and Boyarin agree with E. A. Judge's assessment that "religion" should be discarded on the basis of being a post-fourth-century CE Christian construction when arguing that "we tend to agree *grosso modo* with this perspective" (ibid.: 219, n. 33; on Judge's assessment, see Chapter 1 of this volume).

To a great extent, the works of Nongbri and Barton and Boyarin have become a kind of normative references in relation to the (in-)applicability of the term "religion" to the Greek and Roman world. Instead of revisiting and doing anew an analysis of the Latin term *religio*—which has been dealt with extensively and in some respects rather successfully, not by accident considering that the Latin original is linguistically directly responsible for the emergence of the modern term "religion"[8]—I am here focusing on a Greek term that has been traditionally translated into English as "religion": namely, *thrēskeia*.[9] Contrary to the opinions expressed by scholars of religion regarding the problem of translatability and anachronism pertaining to conceptual schemes, tropes, and nuances, things are not as straightforward as they may seem.

A year after the publication of their jointly penned work, Daniel Boyarin offered an article that further builds on their book, entitled "The Concept of Cultural Translation in American Religious Studies" (2017). In summarizing their work in *Imagine No Religion*, Boyarin indicates that "we thus propose[d], at least for all important words, family-resemblance style mappings of usage to replace dictionaries."[10] Despite the popularity of family-resemblance approaches to the way religion could be defined—notably endorsed by Bruce Lincoln (2006: 5–7), among others—my skepticism in relation to Boyarin's argument lies at the need to replace dictionary explanations for all *important* words. Which are these words and why are they important? What makes *thrēskeia*, for example, an important term but ἄστυ (*astu*) an unimportant or insignificant one? Why continue utilizing terms such as democracy (δημοκρατία) or city-state (πόλις) despite their different connotations and associations within their cultural contexts?[11] Such call for a strict avoidance of anachronism only indicates, in my reading, *our* interests and *our* needs when dealing with terms that *we* deem important—for whatever reasons.

Nongbri takes the lexicographical corpus slightly more seriously, however, whereas Boyarin is more interested in the nuances of the term *thrēskeia*. By focusing more on the postclassical period and even more so on the early and later Christian era, Nongbri notes that

> the sense of "rite" or "worship" seems to persist from the earliest appearances of the term through the medieval period. The first century saw the transformation of *thrēskeia* into a more general term (the sum total of what goes on in the temples of a particular people), and at least by the fourth century, the word could refer to all the worship practices of a given ethnic group, such that people could be identified by "their *thrēskeia*." Throughout its history, then, the term seems to have been part of an ethnographic discourse. It is clear that a simple gloss of *thrēskeia* as "religion" will not do. (Nongbri 2013: 38)

Boyarin, on the other hand, dedicates more space on the classical and the earliest Christian period, drawing his examples from Plutarch and Herodotus (both also mentioned, albeit very briefly, by Nongbri [2013: 34–8]), but primarily by discussing Flavius Josephus (c. 37–c. 100 CE) in depth.[12] His summary is the following:

> I have found, indeed, that the contexts in which *thrēskeia* functions within the textual corpus just specified involve a range of usages that one might be inclined to see as opposites. *Thrēskeia* is used, on the one hand, by writers to indicate excessive, extravagant, and even harmfully distracting practices of others; but, on the other hand, can be used by participants to indicate their own cultic practices, thus presumably with a positive valence and not the negative charge associated with the first set of usages. It is as if a single word in Greek incorporates both our modern English

"religion" and "superstition," usually taken as opposites. (Barton and Boyarin 2016: 124)[13]

Both Nongbri and Boyarin deal with Herodotus's and Plutarch's testimonies to indicate the multifarious and divergent meanings of the term. Consider the example employed by Boyarin from Plutarch:

> A wife ought not to make friends of her own, but to enjoy her husband's friends in common with him. The gods are the first and most important friends. Therefore it is seemly for a wife to fear [*sebesthai*] and to know only the gods that her husband honors [*nomizei*], and to shut the outer door against all *periergoi trēskeiai* and *xenai deisidaimoniai*. (Plutarch, *Coniugalia praecepta* 140d; Barton and Boyarin 2016: 124)

In his assessment, proper *sebas* stands in opposition to improper *thrēskeia* and *deisidaimonia*, the latter two seen by Boyarin as virtually synonyms (ibid.: 124–6). Nowhere, however, does Plutarch indicate that *sebas* and *thrēskeia* and *deisidaimonia* are necessarily antonyms. Fearing the gods that a woman's husband honors could well constitute the husband's *thrēskeia* in this excerpt. By calling *thrēskeiai* all the other beliefs and/or practices that the woman's husband does not embrace, does not concurrently indicate that his beliefs and/or practices do not constitute his *thrēskeia*. As a matter of fact, Plutarch does not specify with a particular term what is constituted precisely by those beliefs maintained by the husband. But he does so, as both Nongbri and Boyarin denote, in his etymological explanation of the term in *Alexander* 2.5–6:

> But concerning these matters there is another story to this effect: all the women of these parts were addicted to the Orphic rites and the orgies of Dionysus from very ancient times (being called Klodones and Mimallones), and imitated in many ways the practices of the Edonian women and the Thracian women about Mount Haemus, from whom, as it would seem, the word "*thrēskeuein*" [θρησκεύειν] came to be applied to the celebration of immoderate and *periergoi* [overwrought, taking needless trouble, superfluous] ceremonies. (Barton and Boyarin 2016: 127)

For start, Orphic rites and Dionysian orgies constituted religious expressions nonetheless, albeit excessive and unnecessary ones as it is evidently expressed by Plutarch. For a priest of Apollo as the author from Boeotia (*An seni* 792f.), *deisidaimonia* in the context he mentions in the above passage does not mean nonreligious ceremonies; excessive and needless, yes. Yet, there is a paradox here at play: despite fashioning himself here as a "mainstream" religious person, Plutarch was actually initiated into the mysteries of Dionysus himself.[14] Furthermore, in another text, the priest of Apollo discusses the maenads who, possessed by the fury of Dionysus, used to tear animals into pieces and consume the raw meat within the context of a biennial festival night known as *Agrionia*. As Plutarch informs his readers, the maenads pretended to search for the god since he had presumably fled—only eventually mentioning, after their failure to encounter him, that Dionysus had ended up staying with the Muses. The end of the search was followed by a collective discussion between the participants to the *Agrionia*. In Plutarch's words:

> It is a good custom therefore of our women, who in their feasts called Agrionia seek after bacchus as if he were run away, but in a little time give over the search, and cry that he is fled to the Muses and lurks with them; and sometimes after, when supper is done, put riddles and hard questions to one another. For this mystery teaches us, that amidst our entertainment we should use learned and philosophical discourse, and such as hath a Muse in it; and that such discourse being applied to drunkenness, everything that is brutish and outrageous in it is concealed, being pleasantly restrained by the Muses. (*Quaestiones convivales* 716F–17A; trans. W. W. Goodwin, LOEB)

What is additionally perhaps of interest here is Plutarch's praise of the maenads for the intellectual endeavor following the end of their futile search for the god. His preference of discourse over practice in this excerpt could be taken as another instance of what constituted "proper religious activity" for Plutarch: theological discourse over and above mundane practices. In this respect, for Plutarch it is seemingly the contemplation about the divine that constitutes a worthy religious activity rather than *periergoi* and virtually pointless celebratory activities within the context of such orgies and rites.[15]

Given Plutarch's ambivalent approach to the Dionysian orgies and the ensuing uncertainly regarding the content of *thrēskeia*, it would perhaps be of interest to also turn our attention to another type of sources both from Plutarch's time and prior: that of inscriptions. It is problematic, in my view, that Nongbri and Boyarin do not take into serious consideration the inscriptional archive in respect to the way *thrēskeia* was used in different locations and chronological periods. The first is from Puteoli in Italy (dated 174 CE), and the second from the island of Paros (dated in the third century BCE). Since Plutarch is prominent in Nongbri's and Boyarin's studies in regard to the ambiguous meaning of the term, I begin with the contemporary inscription from Puteoli.

The text in question refers to the Tyrian inhabitants of the city of Puteoli, and their financial contributions to and maintenance of their traditional religious festivals, which are linked to their motherland, Tyros.[16] Of interest is the following excerpt:

> But now our number has dwindled to a few and, since we pay the expenses for the sacrifices and services [θρησκείας = *thrēskeias*] to our ancestral gods established here in temples. (*IG* XIV 830, lines 8–10; trans. Harland 2016)

Thrēskeia is here used as indicating the traditional beliefs and practices of the Tyrians corresponding to their official, accepted, and normative religious ideas and deities. Contrary to Plutarch's interpretation and utilization of the term as argued by Boyarin, the Tyrians' contemporary employment indicates an expression of the established and traditional religion rather than conflating it with superstition[17] or otherwise.

The second inscription from the island of Paros in the Aegean Sea discusses a prominent archon who had successfully completed his term of office. The following phrase encapsulates his doings:

> [— — —] comprehensively everything pertaining to the *thrēskeia* of the goddess from — — — — — — —. (*IG* XII, 5 141, line 5; my translation)[18]

Directly related to the official duties of the said archon, *thrēskeia* functions here as the established, anticipated, and proper manner of behavior and fulfillment of religious duties toward the goddess. Predating Plutarch's utilization by three centuries, the term is explicitly here related to formal and normative religious actions and obligations.

What these inscriptions unveil is a different utilization of the term *thrēskeia* than the one seemingly advocated in a one-sided manner by Plutarch and eagerly employed by Nongbri and (more vigorously) Boyarin as the prevalent one. When covering different historical periods and locales,[19] even succinctly, one readily observes that the Greek speaking people did not necessarily utilize the term as primarily a synonym of superstition (*deisidaimonia*) or foreign, immoderate, and overwrought (*periergoi*) ceremonies. Nor those examples point to an allegedly overwhelmingly negative connotation of the term. On the contrary, the term could well be perceived in the manner that nowadays people use "religion" for phenomena or movements they adhere to as well as they oppose to, in effect understanding the latter as religions that are "false," "weird," or even differentiating between their "real religion" and the others' "obscure or suspicious cults."[20]

–2–

This brings us to yet another puzzling argument made by Barton and Boyarin in their introduction of *Imagine No Religion*, where they attempt to justify as well as qualify their chosen title. As they put it, the title does *not* imply that they

> imagine that people did not make gods or build temples, praise and pray and sacrifice, that they did not ask metaphysical questions or try to understand the world into which they lived, conceive of invisible beings (gods, spirits, demons, ghosts), organize forms of worship and festival, invent cosmologies and mythologies, support beliefs, defend morals and ideals, or imagine other worlds. (Barton and Boyarin 2016: 4)

This is an unexpected and frankly rather confusing statement. It appears as if Barton and Boyarin insinuate that making gods, building temples, praising and praying and sacrificing to those gods, and so on, constitute *features* of "religion"—otherwise, why accentuate these particular aspects instead of, say, economics, politics, appeals to ancestral traditions (to recall Nongbri), or otherwise? This statement was immediately picked up by Russell McCutcheon, who in his review of the volume—which by the way he unsurprisingly praises and deems it a necessary read not only for specialists of the ancient world but for everyone interested in the academic study of religion—makes a baffling and quite defensive shift when realizing Barton and Boyarin's "slip up" in his view:

> So when we find a list … of such items as gods, temples, prayers, sacrifices, metaphysical questions, worship, and festivals, it's not that these are the

descriptive facts on the ground that we do or do not properly group together *as* religion (i.e., the bits and pieces); rather, it's theory and our imagination, all working to help us make sense of the world, all the way down. And not just at the level of the organizational category religion, for there are those who would argue, to pick but one example, that there's nothing sacrificial about sacrifice—not until someone armed with a theory of sacrifice shows up, becomes curious about what they see as, say, a part given for some whole, and who then does some selecting, ordering, and interpreting of their own. (McCutcheon 2018: 40; emphasis in original)

This is a fine example of a skeptic deconstructing another skeptic. In my reading, there are many problems in both excerpts that touch upon broader issues that have remained unresolved and virtually untouched by scholars working in the study of religions and being immersed into the enterprise of "historicizing religion."

The primary problem that emerges has little to do with whether the term is applicable to ancient cultures—as Barton and Boyarin argue in their book (as well as Nongbri in his)—but, rather, with what *we* decide to consider as constituent elements of "religion." In other words, the seemingly apparent issue is not if the term can adequately describe historically and/or spatially distant cultures, but what kind of a definition of "religion" one chooses and subsequently utilizes in examining such cultures before concluding that the category is not adequate as a descriptor. After all, there is no monopoly of one term over the other. Even if the ancients had terms that their meanings were diverse, such as *thrēskeia*, the elements that are mentioned here are deemed "religious" in the so-called modern sense—insofar as one has established, as the proper practice indicates, what the adjective amounts to for the purposes of their study.

This, however, seems like circular argumentation from my side, since deeming something "religious" in the modern sense still requires a proper definition for acknowledging it as such in the first place. In this respect Nongbri is far more precise than Barton and Boyarin. For example, already from the beginning of his work he explains what most people deem religion to be by utilizing a Protestant Christian approach to religion, although he does not seem to insinuate that such a definition is one that he espouses in general: "Because of the pervasive use of the word 'religion' in the cultures of the modern Western world (the 'we' here), we already intuitively know what 'religion' is before we even try to define it: religion is anything that sufficiently resembles modern Protestant Christianity" (Nongbri 2013: 18).[21] On the contrary, a statement of this kind is nowhere to be found in Barton and Boyarin's work. Their focus on the lack of agreement on a definition is mentioned only to push further their intended point regarding *religio* and *thrēskeia*. Thus, "a contextual study of the usages of *threskeia* in antiquity demonstrates a world of nuance that simply does not map onto the abstraction 'religion' as used in modern folk (and to a lesser extent, scholarly) language" (Barton and Boyarin 2016: 123). I am not the first to point out Barton and Boyarin's troubling approach to religion in general, and ancient religion in particular. For example, in his assessment of *Imagine No Religion*, Anders Klostergaard Petersen pointed out that desiring to demonstrate the lack of a concept in a particular culture, either ancient or modern, is predicated on the precondition of already having such a concept at our disposal in order to acknowledge the lack of it elsewhere. Similarly, in his review of their book, Todd Berzon faults Barton and Boyarin for their eagerness to deny the ancients of their "world of nuance" in regard to their linguistic contexts, while being perfectly content with the similar plurality of nuances of our modern terms—such as "religion"—and indicates Barton and Boyarin's avoidance of defining the category before going on to negate its applicability in the ancient Greek and Roman worlds.[22]

Turning to McCutcheon's assessment, however, another set of problems emerge as well. McCutcheon does not desire to focus on the issue of definition based on elements that we, the observers, decide to group together in an effort to create our conceptual category "religion"—and this is not the only place McCutcheon exhibits his reservations with the category in general. Despite his occasional pleas for stipulative definitions, his work has been overwhelmingly dedicated to the study of how the category is used by scholars, almost always indicating their failure to account for their choices altogether.[23] But McCutcheon is no specialist of Greek and Roman culture, has no knowledge of the linguistic structures of Greek (or Latin) or of the archaeological record, and has never published anything on Greek and Roman "religious" ideas and practices—as a matter of fact, he has never published anything on religious ideas and practices of any people, group, community, or culture. However, his interest in *Imagine No Religion* stems precisely from Barton and Boyarin's enterprise to historicize "religion"—in other words, he is not interested in delving into the data, but suffices to him that specialists in that field do so, without, however, being in a position to assess such attempts.

This by and of itself leaves the reader of his assessment with more questions than answers, given that statements such as "there's nothing sacrificial about sacrifice" or a list of "gods, temples, prayers, sacrifices, metaphysical questions, worship, and festivals [are] not … the descriptive facts on the ground that we do or do not properly group together *as* religion." McCutcheon's colleague at the University of Alabama, Michael Altman, has made similar statements when argued that "theory is how we decide what our object of study is … [that is, theory being the force that] guides the decision to pay attention to that person slitting the throat of a goat in one part of the world and not to my neighbor skinning a deer in Tuscaloosa, Alabama" (Altman 2017: 33). The answer seems simple but, apparently, not so much eventually: it is the perceived presence of something more than simply the person, the tool, and the animal that makes one event different compared to another. According to the person performing the act (and the audience, if any), that "presence" is a supernatural, superhuman, or transcendent agent that assigns some (symbolic) meaning to the person performing the action (and to the people observing it). It is not "we," the scholars, that deem such actions "different." They *are* different or, to recall Ann Taves's term, "special" (Taves 2009) *to the people performing them*. The issue, however, is not whether the slitting of a goat's throat, to return to Altman's example, really involves the perceived nonhuman agent(s), but whether it is believed to do so. If participants have such a perception, then the difference between a designated religious and a nonreligious act can be established—granted by also acknowledging that the categorization of such acts as "religious" are the scholars' categorization and not necessarily (if at all) indigenous: that is, the latter themselves calling them "religious." (However, in many modern cultures, it is the adherents themselves that do call such acts "religious.")

Let us consider an example from Homer's *Iliad*. The quarrel of Agamemnon with Achilles and the wrath of the latter lies at the very heart of Homer's magnum opus. Agamemnon had captivated Chryseis, the daughter of Chryses, Apollo's Trojan priest. Chryses asks for the god's help which results to nine days of plague, and, under pressure, Agamemnon agrees to return the priest's daughter but asks as compensation to be given Achilles's captive, the young Briseis. The famous hero is infuriated and refuses to further participate to the war, threatening to return to Greece. Eventually, Agamemnon admits his error and decides to return the girl to Achilles. And does so, as Homer narrates, after performing the following deed:

> Agamemnon drew a knife which he always wore in his sword's scabbard; setting aside as first-fruits hairs from a wild boar and raising his hands to Zeus, he prayed [Διὶ χεῖρας ἀνασχὼν εὔχετο]; and all the Argives stood silently by him in order, listening to the king. Making his prayer he looked toward broad heaven and said, "May now Zeus know first, most high and most perfect of the gods [Ζεὺς πρῶτα θεῶν ὕπατος καὶ ἄριστος], and Earth and Sun and the Furies who under the earth punish men who swear false oaths: I have not laid a hand upon the girl Briseis, neither to sleep with her nor for any other reason. She has remained, untouched, in my tent. If any of this is falsely sworn, may the gods give me all the many pains [ἐπίορκον ἐμοὶ θεοὶ ἄλγεα δοῖεν πολλὰ μάλ'] which they give to a person who commits sin against them when he swears." So he spoke, and slit the throat of the boar with the pitiless bronze. (*Iliad* 19.252–68; trans. Rice and Stambaugh 2009: 85)

The agreement Agamemnon proposes with his oath is sealed with a sacrifice—a *thysia* (θυσία)—which could be a bloody one or one that involved other non-animate goods.[24]

A number of questions thus arise that need to be addressed before making the leap from ancient sacrifice's reality to McCutcheon's "there's nothing sacrificial about sacrifice":

1. Does the action described by Homer constitute a mundane, merely political or social, or "traditional" practice without any reference to held beliefs in respect to nonhuman agents, such as Zeus?
2. Is belief in both the existence of Zeus and his ability to punish or reward humans an acceptable conclusion? If yes, what does that mean? If not, why?
3. If Agamemnon solely utilizes an existing system but holds no belief in regard to the consequences of his oath, can we account for the surrounding Greek observants who witness this ritual? Do they believe that Agamemnon will be punished if he is lying? If so, where is such belief grounded?[25]

Until such questions are answered, the difference between Agamemnon's act and accompanying oath and Altman's "neighbor skinning a deer in Tuscaloosa, Alabama" cannot be placed under the same rubric.

–3–

In the opening of this chapter, I argued that Wilfred Cantwell Smith had a specific agenda in mind: to demonstrate the insufficiency of the term "religion" when compared to the more appropriate, in his view, personalistic approach that takes "faith" at its core. The aim of Nongbri, Barton and Boyarin, or McCutcheon is in many respects radically different—despite their admiration and promotion of Cantwell Smith's work and their seemingly identical agenda. Their objections to the utilization of the term "religion" in premodern societies stems from their observation that the term is historically (Christian) theologically charged and that many scholars who employ it implicitly or explicitly accept or promote—once the critique is pushed further—an Eliadean *sui generis* outlook.[26] Despite the validity of such criticisms by and large, primarily in drawing attention to the pitfalls of an unexamined or unaware utilization of "religion," the content a term has acquired due to specific historical and political circumstances and within a specific spatial and temporal context does not automatically signify its ineffectiveness as a conceptual tool. This has been argued on several occasions by scholars of religion who are equally careful and aware of the said pitfalls. For example, Annette Yoshiko Reed has pointed out that "even if our current notion of 'religion(s),' for instance, originated as a modern Western taxonomic principle reinscribing Protestant ideals, its cultural effects are hardly limited to these origins, and its meanings today are no less shaped by its creative repurposing by a variety of nonChristian agents as well" (Reed 2015: 311). Similarly, and in response to Boyarin's latest work on Judaism (Boyarin 2019), Adele Reinhartz reminds us that "nothing prevents us from rejecting these inflections without relinquishing the term. ... Rejecting problematic usages does not require us to reject the term itself. We can use it and redefine it in ways that make sense to us, and future generations of scholars will be free to do the same" (Reinhartz 2019).

However, for all actors involved, the issue of definition remains open-ended—and, while it does so, anyone can historicize, deconstruct, criticize, or negate the utilization of the term. As such, in his assessment of a debate between Robert Segal and Brent Nongbri that resulted from the former's review of *Before Religion*,[27] Bryan Rennie engaged with the problem of defining religion as the quintessential issue to be addressed before arguing that a concept (category, descriptor, etc.) is or is not applicable across time and space. It seems a truism, but Rennie's argumentation is vital given that a lack of definition somehow goes unmentioned—or, worse, embraced—before scholars of the historicizing "mission" promote their theories and positions in regard to the applicability of the alleged contested category "religion." Rennie offers a direct reply to both raised issues:

> Until a more adequate taxonomy can be successfully propagated it is simply insupportable to conclude that we should dispense with it or cease to attempt to define it. The invention of religion resembles the invention of culture ... and the invention of tradition ... —they are all terms which may be absent from, but are certainly applicable to, native traditions. They may be invented and they should be used with caution but they are useful categories that refer to real members, and any call to abandon the terms, or the attempt to define them, without an available superior replacement, is misguided. We cannot hope to correct the mistaken popular understanding of religion by simply avoiding the word. (Rennie 2020: 83)

A similar articulation is to be found in the recent criticism by Jesper Sørensen and Anders Klostergaard Petersen regarding the usage or not of the category "magic"[28]—a position that is equally applicable to "religion" here:

> While criticism of categories is a necessary part of critical scholarship, the price paid for terminological cleansing is, at times, quite high—both in terms of clarity (how we construe our subject-matter) and in terms of scientificc integration (how our results engage in broader scientific discussions). To begin with clarity, giving up on categories usually means (a) that we revert to a higher, and more inclusive, classificatory level (i.e. arguing that 'magic' is merely a type or an aspect of 'religion'); (b) that we invent new, technical categories that fragment the phenomena in question differently; or (c) that we refrain from making any (implicit) generalizing assertions by exclusively using local, insiders' categories, preferably untranslated or even untransliterated. (Sørensen and Klostergaard Petersen 2021: 3)

A sober study of religion cannot overlook the points made here by both Rennie and Sørensen and Klostergaard Petersen, and, subsequently, scholars of Greek and Roman religion also need to address these positions before arguing that the category is inapplicable, inadequate, or irrelevant to the world of the Greeks and the Romans. One could side with the opposite pole if, say, *religio* and *thrēskeia* were the only "contested" terms in studying the religious ideas, practices, or vocabulary of the Greeks and the Romans. As numerous studies have clearly demonstrated, however, this is not the case. Examples abound, but it is worth noting, even in brief, an additional one that specialists of religion who work in the field of Greek and Roman religion(s) might find useful.

In her informative and detailed study on the adjective *hosios* (ὅσιος), a pivotal term in things religious in ancient Greek culture, Saskia Peels (2016) has masterfully shown how the term was used within different and broad semantic contexts: from a descriptor of moral or ethical evaluation in regard to interpersonal relationships to one of issues of purity, justice, or piety. What is of particular interest here, however, is how the term, predominantly related to the notion of piety, was also used to express two radically different and opposite meanings, those of sacred and profane. Already from the groundbreaking works of Émile Durkheim (1858–1917) and Sigmund Freud (1856–1939), and further illustrated by Mircea Eliade above all, the notions of sacred and profane are considered to be straightforward antonyms in the study of religions. Following Boyarin's explication in relation to the terms *thrēskeia*-qua-religion and *thrēskeia*-qua-superstition, one should also dismiss the usage of *hosios*-qua-sacred given that the Greeks tended to also utilize the term as *hosios*-qua-profane. In other words, the intended point here is no other than to emphasize how ancient Greek as a language is perhaps more nuanced, more pluralistic, and eventually different from our modern vocabularies. From this premise, the practice of using one term to describe radically opposite things should not surprise us but, rather, it should inform us that *our* semantic contexts are not *their* semantic contexts. And, therefore, a new approach to this issue is required.

4

Comparative Nausea

Be not the firſt by whom the New are try'd
Nor yet the laſt to lay the Old afide.

Alexander Pope (1688-1744)[1]

"Religion des Grecs & des Romains ... c'est la même religion; la greque est la mere, & la romaine est la fille," wrote Louis de Jaucourt (1704-1779) recapitulating perhaps the most common folk understanding—then, also scholarly one—of Greek and Roman religion(s).[2] Although scholarship has undoubtedly greatly advanced ever since in indicating the various differences (and, of course, similarities) between the religious ideas and practices of the Greeks and the Romans, what is of interest in de Jaucourt's unfortunate diagnosis is no other than his early comparative outlook. Without being interested here in discussing the positive and negative aspects of the comparative method, or its (in)adequacy as a tool in approaching religion overall,[3] what I am primarily drawn to is the very fact that for de Jaucourt—as for humans in general—an analogy is what makes a study of anything possible.

De Jaucourt's flawed comparativism, however, is not merely a relic of the past. A similar practice, this time following the opposite path—that of solely differences—is often dominant in contemporary studies on Greek and Roman religion(s). This outlook maintains that in an effort to indicate the "uniqueness" or "specialness" of the religious ideas and practices of the Greeks and the Romans—not qualitatively but as a way to delineate the need for a special, separate study—one needs to differentiate them from the dominant religion that emerged from within the Greek and Roman cultural and religious milieu, namely Christianity.[4] Some known examples demonstrate the argument attempted here:

1. "Classical Greek religion was at bottom a question of doing not believing, of behaviour rather than faith" (Paul Routledge).
2. "Greek religion is not theologically fixed and stable, and it has no tradition of exclusion or finality: it is an open, not a closed system" (John Gould).
3. "The reader will be struck first of all by the fact that pagan [Roman] priests are quite unlike their modern Christian counterparts. The priestly officials discussed in this volume bear no significant resemblance to the comforting image of the wise Christian pastor, guiding his flock through the spiritual perils of the world: they did not play the part (at least officially) of moral leaders; they were not involved with a congregation that looked to them for advice and guidance" (Mary Beard and John North).
4. "A system in which the emphasis falls primarily on the performance of ritual acts—not on the worshippers' belief, or religious emotions and experiences, or on theology or ethics—such a system inescapably makes it a primary value, though not necessarily the only value, that the known ritual should be successfully repeated" (John North).[5]
5. "[Roman religion] was a religion without revelation, without revealed books, without dogma and without orthodoxy. … It was a religion which kept explicit expression of belief quite separate from religious practice. … It was a religion that involved no initiation and no teaching. … It was a religion with no moral code. The ethical code by which it was ruled was the same as that which ruled other 'non-religious' social relations. … It was a religion that aimed for the earthly wellbeing of the community, not for the salvation of an individual and his or her immortal soul in the afterlife" (Scheid 2003: 18–19).

In his overall superb *On Greek Religion* (2011), Robert Parker dedicates the first two chapters on two arguably unnecessary questions: Why believe without revelation? How is it possible to have a religion without a church? Truth be told, Parker attempts to justify the use of "Greek religion" despite the lack of revelation and the absence of an organized, institutionalized church in the modern monotheistic fashion. Nevertheless, the fact that such questions need to be addressed in the twenty-first century still emphasizes the dominance of the traditional path of placing Greek and Roman religion(s) against the (apparently unquestionable) yardstick of what a religion is from a Western monotheistic perspective. To recall Brent Nongbri's (2013: 18) diagnosis, "because of the pervasive use of the word 'religion' in the cultures of the modern Western world (the 'we' here), we already intuitively know what 'religion' is before we even try to define it: religion is anything that sufficiently resembles modern Protestant Christianity."[6]

Such an approach to the religion(s) of the Greeks and Romans, however, points toward an oft-unacknowledged problem underlying the study of this subfield. Instead of addressing the category "religion" as a cross-cultural phenomenon—which would naturally require a general definition of the phenomenon/category and the subsequent analysis that follows from such a definition—scholars working in the subfield tend to be particularists. In other words, they are interested in Greek and Roman "religion" alone instead of dealing with and discussing such phenomena that belong to the Greek and Roman cultures as one more example of the category "religion." Before proceeding, however, I need to make a qualification that I hold to be necessary for further expanding on the topic of this chapter. By using the qualifier "cross-cultural" or "universal" I do not maintain that religion refers to some actual metaphysical reality—that is, an ontological reality that lies beyond time and space. Rather, I hold that religion refers to human activities, ideas, and thoughts that relate to and emanate from held beliefs by persons in the existence of agents that are thought to have superhuman or supernatural qualities or abilities. That being the case, I do not argue that all religions are similar or, worse, identical; rather, as it has been traditionally maintained by scholars of religion, such phenomena are to a great extent similar enough to allow for their categorization as "religions" and therefore can become objects for further theoretical reflection. As I will discuss below, there exist some appealing definitions of religion as a category that go beyond the mere limits of "antiquity"—and certainly overcome the dipole Greek/Roman religion(s) versus Christianity—which can become fruitful tools in the hands of scholars working in the field that covers the religious ideas, beliefs, and practices of the Greeks and the Romans.

–1–

Defining religion has proven to be an ongoing and hitherto contentious issue among scholars. Nevertheless, the very act of classifying phenomena, practices, ideas, concepts, actions, symbols, and such, as "religious" remains the norm despite this lack of consensus. This brings about more problems than it resolves for it allows for the utilization of the term without accounting for what is meant by it. There are two major clusters of definitions that scholars have typically suggested, adopted, or argued about. The one is usually called substantive definitions (or intellectualist—also known as essentialist, although some scholars make a distinction between substantive and essentialist); the other, functional definitions. The former addresses the question "what *is* religion?" whereas the latter focuses on "what does religion *do*?" The substantialist group suggests that there are one or more fundamental features—what could be called the "necessary condition(s)"—that allow us to identify religion on every occasion and at every place it is encountered. There are numerous examples of such definitions, but one of the most indicative one remains E. B. Tylor's (1871: vol. 1, 424) "belief in spiritual beings." The functionalist group has been traditionally exemplified by Émile Durkheim's (1995: 44) influential definition: "Religion is a unified system of beliefs and practices relative to sacred things, that is to say, things set apart and forbidden— beliefs and practices which unite into one single moral community called a Church, all those who adhere to them." Moreover, scholars have developed variants, such as by combining substantive and functional types of definitions, promoting experiential ones, or expanding upon Ludwig Wittgenstein's "family resemblance" metaphor. The latter has gained much support among scholars who are reluctant to employ a merely substantialist or functionalist definition. Those convinced by Wittgenstein's theory argue that a polythetic and pliable definition—that is, one that contains various elements but without identifying one or more of those elements as essential and/or universal—is the proper way to define religion.[7]

Given the seemingly endless discussions and disagreements pertaining to the definition of religion as a cross-cultural phenomenon and category, scholars seem more prone to either skillfully avoid or directly negate both the possibility and the need for a definition altogether. However, when acting as such, scholars of religion appear to be virtually talking about everything and nothing at the same time. For example, in a book resulting from the annual meeting of the North American Association for the Study of Religion (NAASR), Matt Sheedy responded to one of the main papers devoted to the Cognitive Study of Religion (CSR) by arguing that one of the main theoretical concepts to which cognitivists of religion usually refer to when discussing what is traditionally called "god(s)"—namely "minimally counterintuitive agents"—"appears to fall into an essentialist trap of proclaiming what religions *are*, rather than what they *do* and are made to do" (Sheedy 2017: 123; emphasis in original). Assuredly, religions *do* stuff. Yet, as a means to identify what they do, one needs to identify *them* in advance. Otherwise, how does one decide which action is classified as religious and which is not? Apparently, a religious action is deemed as such by the people who are performing it; in other words, their actions are the result of certain beliefs that involve such (minimally counterintuitive) agents. It goes without saying that whether these agents truly exist is irrelevant; it suffices that they do exist in the understanding and worldview of the persons who perform the said action. After all, as Jeppe Sinding Jensen (2020: viii) puts it in his discussion of the nature of religion,

> religious beliefs and behaviours refer to imagined entities or agents with strange and mysterious properties. ... However, they are imagined entities and agents and it is as such that they can be studied: namely as objects of the human imagination, the ability to have and hold objects in the mind.

Cato the Elder (234–149 BCE), for example, records the following within the context of farming in Roman society:

> Father Mars, I beg and entreat you to be well disposed toward me and toward our house and household. I have ordered an offering of pigs, sheep, and bulls to be led around my field, land, and farm on account of this request, so that you may prevent, ward off, and remove sickness, both seen and unseen, and barrenness and devastation, and damage to crops and bad weather, and so that you may permit my legumes, grain, vineyards, and shrubbery to grow and turn out well. Preserve my shepherds and flocks unharmed and give good health and strength to me, my home, and our household. For this purpose, to purify my farm and land and field and to make an expiatory offering, as I said, be increased by these offerings of suckling pigs, sheep, and bulls that are to be offered. Father Mars, for this same reason, be increased by these offerings of suckling pigs, sheep, and bulls. (Cato, *De Agri Cultura* 141.2–3; trans. King 2003: 281)

Does Cato here refer to something religious? The question seems naive—if not outrightly imprudent. There is hardly (if at all) any scholar that would not classify this as a prayer to the Roman god Mars. However, following the reservations that Sheedy and others have in regard to the question of what religion is, while focusing instead only on what religions do or are supposed to do, one can acknowledge that Cato's text is referring to a religious act (prayer, sacrifice, and anticipated reciprocity) without explaining why the categorization "religious" is employed, while simultaneously not addressing the question whether "prayers" and "sacrifices" are the elements that led to this categorization in the first place. To iterate: religions do things, and the prayer and accompanying sacrifice in Cato's text have end goals—which can be characterized variously, from economic sustainability to biological survival, without excluding, however, the need by Cato (and/or his readers) to simply be "religious"—that is, believe that their lives are indeed influenced by gods. The prerequisites for such end goals on behalf of the person uttering the prayer and performing the sacrifice are that (1) an agent called Mars exists, (2) who may grant requests, and (3) can be persuaded by humans to do so (via sacrifices).

In the previous chapter, I referred to the oath and the sacrifice made by Agamemnon to Zeus in the presence of the Greek army during the Trojan War. By merely focusing on the function of religion, one may again discuss how religion is used in that context to, say, maintain the army's morale and win the war; or how Agamemnon skillfully persuades the Greeks that he did not touch the young Briseis (thus, avoiding a punishment that could eventually be of death that could result from Achilles's wrath); or how a king secures his power by utilizing and perhaps manipulating public beliefs that he does not himself share. (Again, these possibilities do not negate the probability that Agamemnon himself was being "religious.") Nevertheless, none of the above has established that what Agamemnon does is indeed a "religious" activity. Whatever the sought outcome(s) might be, its success or failure is predicated on certain ideas: (1) there is an agent called Zeus, (2) who resides in the sky, and (3) who has the power—along with other agents, such as the Furies, Earth, Sun, and "the gods" in general—to severely punish whomever makes a false oath.

Undoubtedly, these elements are not the only ones that are traditionally seen as part of Greek and/or Roman religion(s). For example, our textual and archaeological records include, among others: ideas about the afterlife;

household religious traditions; reference to minor agents, such as demons, nymphs, heroes, heroines, and more; divination, auspices, and soothsaying. And, to further expand the list, how would one deal with cases of deified emperors and kings? Should magical practices also be considered?[8]

As a consequence, it becomes evident that formulating a definition of religion is extremely complicated but patently imperative. Some scholars have argued that defining religion is not that much of a Sisyphean task if the definition itself will be a stipulative one, whereas others have insisted that only by defining religion substantively can scholars then proceed to the explanatory quest.[9] Below I cite three appealing, in my view, definitions that correspond to such a perspective and may function as examples to define our subject matter—religion—in a way that is applicable *mutatis mutandis* across time and space, allowing for the subsequent theorization of the phenomenon, including its place within the Greek and Roman cultural milieus:

1. Religion is "an institution consisting of culturally patterned interaction with culturally postulated superhuman beings" (Spiro 1966: 96).[10]
2. "Religion, then, consists of *beliefs, actions and institutions which assume the existence of supernatural entities with powers of action, or impersonal powers or processes possessed of moral purpose*" (Bruce 2011: 112, emphasis in original).
3. "Religion is a cultural system and a social institution that governs and promotes ideal interpretations of existence and ideal praxis with reference to transempirical powers or beings" (Geertz 1997: 39).

When applying such attempts of defining religion to the two excerpts—that from Homer and that from Cato—one may observe that what is effortlessly acknowledged as expressions of ancient Greek and Roman religiosity seems to align with some or all of the conditions stipulated in the three aforementioned definitions. Other scholars, of course, may adopt another or promote their own definition of religion and proceed with it in examining Greek and Roman religious ideas and practices. But rejecting, avoiding, or even scorning the need to define the very category that shapes the subfield of Greek and Roman "religion(s)" generates serious problems in deciding what is and what is not "religious" within any given cultural context—including, of course, that of the Greeks and the Romans.

– 2 –

As Thomas Tweed recently pointed out, "definitions matter, in part, because they offer hints about theories, about what the definer thinks religion is" (Tweed 2020: 5).[11] Tweed's often neglected principle—especially so by many scholars working today in the field of the study of religion—requires further attention by those devoted to the study of the religion(s) of the Greeks and the Romans, as theorizing about those religious phenomena is virtually informed by an explicit or implicit definition and vice versa. (I am not conflating here definitions that seek to establish religion as "a thing of itself" ontologically speaking—a theological and long abandoned enterprise by scholars of religion—with definitions that seek to further develop our discussions on both the elements of what we classify as "religion[s]" and the phenomenon's nature and function.) Theories of religion have been pivotal in the development of the field of the study of religion, despite the recent vigorous rejection of the need for both defining and formulating such general theories about the phenomenon.[12] Nevertheless, and alarmingly to a certain degree, only a few scholars still insist on the need for definitions and theories of religion as academic prerequisites for a profitable study of the category and the phenomena subsumed under its rubric.[13] Despite the long and ongoing heated debates within the field known as the study of religion, scholars working on the religion(s) of the Greeks and the Romans still remain interested solely in "Greek and Roman" religion(s) and rarely—if at all—address such problems in their discussions and analyses.

Theories of religion are generalizations about religion as a cross-cultural phenomenon. They do not restrict themselves to particular religions, although the theoretician may—and some have explicitly done so—focus on one or two traditions as their case studies in order to proceed with their intended generalization (*pace* Émile Durkheim and Sigmund Freud, who both formulated their theories of religion by primarily focusing on the Australian Aborigines). In this respect, defining religion and formulating and advancing theories of religion seem to be the two sides of the same coin. A theory of religion purports to be in a position to account for religion wherever and whenever it is encountered, across both time and space. Typically, such inquiries concentrate on questions that may be presented in the following manner: Why, how, and when did religion appear? What prompts people to create, invent, or conceptualize religion, and why do people remain religious? The premise in such questions is that there is a need for which religion arises and persists. Such a need may vary, and, like definitions, theories may be classified as substantive, functional, experiential, and so on. Some theories stipulate needs that are intellectual or cognitive, such as ideas, emotions, instincts, and such—for instance, the need to come into contact with or experience god(s) (*pace* Mircea Eliade and Rudolf Otto)—whereas others seek the need behind the veil of religion's claims and encountering it in broader societal preoccupations or individual but unknown desires. For example, religion may appear to have emerged and continues to exist due to, say, a divine revelation as its adherents might argue about, but it is virtually a human by-product that eventually seeks to bring humans in contact with their unconscious (*pace* C. G. Jung). Or, it is about economic inequalities and class struggles and the call for a social revolution that will fulfill worldly material needs of the oppressed, such as food, clothing, and shelter (*pace* Friedrich Engels).[14]

Furthermore, although theories typically tend to focus on the questions of origin and function, some expand their scope to include the questions of religion's structure (that is, the role of the various elements typically identified as parts of religion, such as rituals, myths, institutions, etc.) and specificity (whether there is anything special or unique about religion)—the latter two also informing the project of definition, since they virtually address the question of what counts as religion in the first place (see, e.g., Stausberg 2009; Stausberg and Engler 2016).

A general theory of religion is not something alien to the Greek and Roman cultures. Perhaps the most representative example from antiquity can be found in the so-called Sisyphus fragment, dated in the fifth century BCE.[15] The author of the fragment—either the dramaturgist Euripides or the tyrant Critias—claims that religion sprung as a means for overseeing people's actions, thus maintaining social order and lawful behavior. The author here purports to explain the historical rather than the recurrent origin of religion. That is, when and why religion first emerged in human history—placing it, eventually, in a chronologically undetermined, prehistorical moment—instead of when and why religion occurs every time it does so throughout history:

> There was a time when the life of humans was disordered, and beast-like and subject to brute strength, when there was no prize for the decent, nor again any punishment for wrongdoers. And then I think men established laws for purposes of punishment, so that justice would be the ruler ... and keep transgression as its slave. And if someone were to do wrong they would be punished. Then, since the laws prevented them from doing violent deeds openly, they continued to do them in secret. I think that then ... some sound and clever-minded man invented fear [of the gods] for mortals, so that evil people would have some fear, even if they were acting or saying or thinking [something] in secret. Thereupon he introduced the divine being, saying: "There is a divinity, endowed with eternal life, who with his mind hears and sees and understands and attends to these things, bearing a divine nature, who will [both] hear everything that is said amongst mortals, and be able to see everything [that] is done. If ever you plan some evil in silence, you will not escape the notice of the gods in regard to this. For they are able to keep ... in mind." ... Around mortals he set up such fears, through which this man, by his words, nobly established the divinity in an auspicious spot, and he extinguished lawlessness with laws. ... Thus, I think, someone first persuaded mortals to believe that there is a race of gods. (Sextus Empiricus, *Adversus Mathematicos* 9.54; trans. O'Sullivan 2012: 171–2)

Although the Sisyphus fragment has been primarily dealt with as a case of atheism in antiquity by most (if not all) classicists and historians of antiquity,[16] it nevertheless advances a full-fledged theory of religion addressing both the historical origin and the function of religion. Pointing toward a type of surveillance system, the author of the fragment argues that religion emerged and persisted as a means for maintaining lawfulness, order, and societal serenity, whereas its necessary condition is the belief that there exists a group of agents (gods) that are indeed watching and do punish wrongdoers even when the misconduct occurs in secret. (The latter ostensibly also functioning as a definition of religion in the style of E. B. Tylor's "belief in spiritual beings.")

The antiquity of such a general theory of religion has sadly gone unnoticed, no less due to classicists' insistence on dealing with the fragment as an example of atheism tout court. As a result, in two books that appeared in the last decade from scholars working in different disciplines and who dealt with the issue of origins—albeit concealed behind the apparent priority and centrality of the function of religion in their view—the Sisyphus theory is strikingly absent: Ara Norezayan's *Big Gods* (2013) and Dominic Johnson's *God Is Watching You* (2016). In many respects, both works overlap in relation to the issue of the origins of religion. Both argue that the idea of superhuman, supernatural, omnipotent, omnipresent, and omniscient agents that act as surveillance mechanisms has played a decisive role in our species' evolution. This argument, in effect, tacitly maintains that the origins of religion could be potentially traced in the idea of one or many "watchers" that cannot be tricked, who are able to observe and scrutinize people's actions, and who are capable to and undoubtedly will punish the culprits. I do not argue, of course, that Norezayan and Johnson should have done a more careful research (none of them are classicists or historians of antiquity); but given that the Greek and Roman thinkers are deemed the specialization of scholars working in the field of classics (and, more often than not, in that of ancient philosophy), the one-sided approach to the fragment (that is, as a case of atheism in antiquity) has in a sense concealed the theory from colleagues working in adjacent fields in the humanities and the social sciences.

The vast majority of theories of religion from the Greek and Roman world, however, are particularistic in their scope and outlook, with the exception perhaps of Herodotus (fifth century BCE), given that the historian from Halicarnassus is often considered to be the first comparativist and ethnologist (often paired with Julius Caesar [100–44 BCE] and Tacitus [56–120 CE] from the Roman world).[17] From Xenophanes of Colophon (late sixth–early fifth century BCE) to Prodicus of Ceos (465–395 BCE), and from Euhemerus of Messene (c. third century BCE) to Varro (116–27 BCE) and Cicero (106–43 BCE), philosophers and thinkers in Greek and Roman antiquity dealt with the origins and/or the function of *Greek and Roman* religion(s) by primarily focusing their discourses on the protagonists of those phenomena, that is, the gods and other superhuman agents, and secondarily (but not always) with other elements of their religions, such as rituals, institutions, terminologies, religious servants, and so on.[18] In other words, their aim was to explain or account for the beliefs and practices of the Greeks and the Romans rather than every people they were aware of. Hence, for Xenophanes, the Greek gods should be freed from the anthropomorphic restrictions imposed by Homer and Hesiod; for Prodicus, language and naming of goods dictated the names of the (Greek) gods; for Euhemerus, the Olympians were simply deified kings of the past; whereas for Varro and Cicero, it is only the Roman gods, theology, divination, and other Roman traditions and institutions that are theorized. Therefore, it is no surprise that the vast majority of scholars working on Greek and Roman religion(s) focus on those writings and subscribe to such a perspective, creating, however, a rather isolated corpus of studies that is restricted to Greek and Roman religion(s) without "religion" as a category being addressed or theorized. On the contrary, however, the comparative outlook seems to be a common locus, albeit restricted, as presented at the beginning of this chapter, when it comes to Christianity.

The obvious historical reason for such a targeted comparativism is no other than the emergence of Christianity within the historical and cultural milieu of the Greek and Roman cultures and the latter's eventual dissolvement despite its rather vigorous and long-term resistance. Although specialists today are nonetheless ready to counterattack and argue that "the growth of studies of late antiquity ... has shown how imbricated Christianity and Greco-Roman culture continue to be—and make the recent claim that classics has attempted to 'quarantine' Roman history from Christianity only partially true at best" (Coneybeare and Goldhill 2021a: 6), this is not the actual case as Coneybeare and Godlhill's "culprit"—that is, Douglas Boin—points out. That is, in their criticism, Coneybeare and Goldhill refer to Boin's insightful and provocative review of Mary Beard's celebrated *SPQR: A History of Ancient Rome* (2015). In it Boint lashes a fierce criticism grounded on a very specific (and historically sound, I would add) argument: "Greeks and Romans have long been valorized as the cultural heroes of antiquity, enlightened pluralists who held out as long as they could until the 'victory of Christianity', as Beard terms it" (Boin 2016).[19] Boin's argument has merit insofar as one is willing to return to the changes brought about by the shifting power of *Altertumswissenschaft*.

In the eighteenth century, classicists lamented the long-established by then majesty of Christianity while forcefully strived to reinstate the glory of the pagan past. As James Turner put it:

> Altertumswissenschaft opened not merely a wider but a post-Christian view of classical antiquity. ... [W]riters skeptical of Christianity began to smash the shackles binding classical antiquity to Christianity. ... Altertumswissenschaft licensed scholars to find difference in the pagan past. Classical antiquity no longer walked side by side with Christianity. Socrates

and Cicero regained their pagan integrity, even under the gaze of pious Lutheran professors. (Turner 2011: 168–9)

The educational revolution of *Altertumswissenschaft* had consequences in higher education—and not merely during the eighteenth and nineteenth centuries, or only in Germany and the UK, but beyond these spatial and temporal limits.[20] Turner has also indicated how the conflict between classical philology and Biblical philology shaped so diverse paths that led to opposing camps ("Biblical philologists studied—and usually believed in—a divine revelation, not human creations" [Turner 2011: 357]), which started from and served very different research agendas. Recent attempts to examine such oppositions bear witness to an ongoing conflict that has yet to be overcome but slowly attracts serious attention.[21]

–3–

It is common ground among scholars of religion that Friedrich Max Müller (1823–1900) is considered to be the founding figure of the modern study of religion, followed by E. B. Tylor—the latter is deemed the founding figure of modern anthropology as well. There are scores of publications dealing with Müller's breakthrough that led to the academic study of religion as a category and cross-cultural phenomenon considering his passionate focus on comparison as the proper method for studying religion.[22] Nevertheless, as Ivan Strenski has pointed out, Müller's work owed much to the critical study of the Bible that antedated his own work on the sacred texts of the Hindus. As Strenski observes, "The method of the Higher Criticism was combined with a cross-cultural *comparative* method, and extended in principle to *all* religious texts from *all* traditions" (Strenski 2015: 29; emphasis in original). That is, the early study of religion emerged from within Christian theological anxieties, and, to a certain degree, adopted the hypotheses, ideas, and questions "critical textual scholars and historians had been asking about the Bible for well over a generation" (ibid.: 30).

Given such a slow diversion from a theological-only to a scientific-oriented approach to religion and religious texts, it should not be surprising that there is hardly a distinction between theology and the study of religion—for the most part encountered primarily as "religious studies"—in the mind of many outsider scholars. One of the first specialist in the study of religion, for example, was the Scottish Semiticist and Arabist William Robertson Smith (1846–1894), an Old Testament scholar, professor of divinity, and minister of the Free Church of Scotland—but who is also considered to be one of the forerunners of the social scientific study of religion.[23] Robertson Smith's study of ancient religion was not the same as the one promoted by philologists and classicists of the time. The nineteenth century was instrumental in creating separate and distinct disciplines, as has been recently demonstrated by Simon Goldhill, a century which "produced a particular configuration of the long battle between classics and theology as approaches to antiquity, as systems of values, and as understandings of the world" (Goldhill 2020: 215). Such configuration was readily and effortlessly extended to the "prodigal child" of theology, that is, the study of religion—especially when considering that the two fields were indistinguishable for a long time, whereas in Britain (as well as in many continental countries) they are still encountered jointly, with the practice in North America (especially after the 1960s) largely being the separation of the two disciplines.[24]

What is usually going unnoticed, however, is the equally long battle between theology and the study of religion—especially in North America and after the paradigm-shifting US Supreme Court's 1963 *Abington Township v. Schempp* decision, which saw teaching *of* religion (i.e., theological-confessional) as a violation of the First Amendment, and only permitting teaching *about* religion, which would allow any student in such classes to participate without the precondition of being a believer or a potential novice.[25] The decision, which was instrumental in the establishment of standalone departments of the study of religion in the country, also brought to the fore the radically different methods, theories, as well as ideas pertaining to religion that were espoused and promoted by the two disciplines. This distinction, however, has not been a painless one—and on many occasions, still remains highly problematic. Many scholars working in the study of religion have repeatedly argued about the diametrically different nature of the two disciplines, while lamenting the ongoing crypto-theological agenda of many scholars of religion, those whom Jonathan Z. Smith once called "the transcendentalists" (Lehrich 2013: 73–6). In some respects, the study of religion remains a contested field, a point that has been repeatedly tackled—on some occasions moderately and in other instances aggressively—by some scholars, among whom one should note the constant calls for a proper scientific study of religion by Donald Wiebe and Luther H. Martin. The failure of nerve in the academic study of religion, to recall Wiebe's (in)famous work, refers to this constant battle between theology and the study of religion,[26] whereas Martin (occasionally with Wiebe as his co-author) has persistently pointed out the difference between a theological and a theoretical (that is, scientific) study of religion (Martin 2014: 12–21; cf. Martin and Wiebe 2016).

Such tensions therefore indicate that, despite the recorded conflict between theology and classics with respect to the religious life, ideas, practices, and customs of the ancient Greeks and Romans, a similar but indirect and yet unrecorded one is at play: that between classics and the study of religion. The former in many respects explains—but does not justify—the one-sided comparativism between "pagan/Greek and Roman religions" and "Christianity," which is typically encountered in works penned by classicists. Since the nineteenth century, the quintessential opposite camp that has had a say about the "pagans" were theologians, Biblicists and New Testament scholars, as well as specialists of Church History. Naturally, scholars working from within the field of classics had to promote their own field's concepts, methods, and theories pertaining to those religions, leading to a constant interplay between the classical and the Christian world but simultaneously neglecting or overlooking the need for addressing the very category of contention, namely "religion" itself. The latter, on the other hand, is far more contemporary and less appealing, so to speak, given that the study of religion has had more battles to fight with other adjacent disciplines, such as theology, anthropology, or sociology. Nevertheless, some scholars working in the study of religion deal with and examine the religion(s) of the Greeks and the Romans based on their field's methods and theories, leading to an additional interplay, less popular and far more contemporary. Their approach to the Greek and Roman world is based on a broader comparative outlook and a different theorization of the category "religion" itself. And, thus, the religion(s) of the Greeks and the Romans remain split between two fields that have had, and still do, various tensions to address— but may advance further if they acknowledge such tensions, trace their pitfalls, and allow for more interconnections and collaborations.[27]

5

The Departing Gods

You do not believe our writings; then we do not believe your writings. We make up false things about Christ; then you make false and empty boasts about your gods. For neither has any god dropped from heaven or commented with his own hand on your affairs, or by the same token disparaged our affairs and religious beliefs. These are written by human beings; those too are written by human beings and set forth in mortal speech. Whatever you have in mind to say of our authors, you must accept and judge that these things are said with equal weight of your own.

Arnobius of Sicca (255–c. 327 CE)[1]

Whereas Arnobius, one of the most read early Christian apologists, had a specific theological agenda when writing his *Against the Nations*—a defense of Christianity against pagan accusations—the epigram above offers much more than simply an argument in opposition to what the pagans held regarding the life and miracles of Jesus of Nazareth. Unbeknownst to Arnobius, however, his argumentation here neatly summarizes, all things considered, the very core principle on which the study of religion as a field bases its theoretical and methodological self-understanding and distinguishes itself from other disciplines—particularly so, against the scholarly and other principles, methods, and approaches propagated by theology. Hence, apart from the historical as well as disciplinary tensions between the fields of classics and theology (as discussed in Chapter 4), another, yet fiercer and seemingly perpetual scholarly conflict exists between the study of religion and its historical matrix, that is, theology. What Arnobius's words against the pagans indicate has become—ironically so, given that it comes from an early Christian apologist—mainstream among scholars of religion: religious language, beliefs, concepts, and ideas are nothing more than mere human language, beliefs, concepts, and ideas. This has been concisely summarized by Willi Braun when arguing for an "anthropocentric study of religion." In his words:

> The distinction between Theology, which presumes and address supernatural or divine realities, and Religious Studies, which does not, is predicated on this identification of the subject matter of a secular, or humanistic, or scientific approach to the study of Religion, one which is not required to bow to the dictates of Theology, confessional or otherwise, nor address Theology's subject matter, not be bound by Theology's methods. (Braun 2020: 17)

This is perhaps old news to scholars working in either discipline, although the crypto-theological work of scholars of religion continues to be exposed by critics from within the field.[2] Despite thus the apparent wishful—or, as it turns out to be, occasionally superficial—distinction between theology and the study of religion, it comes as no surprise that often scholars outside these two fields have the tendency to either conflate them or identify them as one and the same.[3] This is perhaps due to the fact that the study of religion emerged from "within" theology—that is, as a field that takes its cue from theological ideas and beliefs but approaches them in an altogether different fashion, although this has not been so straightforward as critics maintain.[4]

For example, as recently as 2019, the British Academy published a report on the past, present, and future of the joint field in the UK. (Contrary to North America, the two disciplines are largely encountered within the same department in UK universities.) Entitled "Theology and Religious Studies Provision in UK Higher Education" (BA 2019), the report sketches a rather dim future for the field, which led the British Association for the Study of Religion (BASR) to issue a long counter-report. Numbers of student enrollments and graduates aside—which are diminishing without doubt—it is interesting to observe the points argued about by the BASR report, which clearly reveal that, despite the joint presentation of the two disciplines in the UK, scholars of religion do not seem either comfortable or content within such a scheme—which is further indication of the past and present disciplinary tension between the study of religion and theology. Already from BASR's President Bettina Schmidt's foreword, it becomes manifest that BASR is not willing to allow for the conflation of their work with that done by theologians: "Most of our members learnt about the report about our discipline from the press, where the study of religions was buried, mixed up with theology and related disciplines" (BASR 2021: 3). However, it is in the introduction of the report where the difference between the two disciplines is clearly sketched:

> The BA Report is presented as addressing Theology *and* Religious Studies, though it makes no differentiation between the disciplines, essentially ignoring their substantial and significant differences. ... We demonstrate that in eliding Theology and RS, the BA *Report* has critically misrepresented RS. ... Yet a lack of clarity on HESA codes, a strategy to present a "united front" under the "TRS" [theology and religious studies] banner, and the ongoing institutional predominance of Theology has obscured this fact. By presenting Theology and RS in such a way, the BA Report endangered our discipline. (BASR 2021: 4; emphasis in original)

BASR's response highlights some serious issues that remain unresolved—at least from a disciplinary perspective—both within and outside the field. The primary problem, however, is the obfuscation that apparently exists between the actual nature and aims of the two disciplines, theology and the study of religion/religious studies. Given that the latter is a relatively new discipline, it seems that it has not yet clearly defined its identity and scope, allowing therefore outsiders (such as the British Academy, or even the broader public) to continue conflating them and eventually leveling them.[5]

It is in this spirit that Braun adds that there is an inherent irony in the study of religion as a discipline, which on the one hand feeds itself from the theological principles propagated by insiders and theologians, while on the other hand strives to distinguish itself from such discourses: "'Religion' itself as a framework, a category, and thus as a demarcation for a non-theological discipline (Religious Studies) is defined by its theological content" (Braun 2020: 17). There is little doubt that Braun's diagnosis is apropos—one that is extensively discussed in Donald Wiebe's works (e.g., Wiebe 1999). What is at stake in such an ongoing entanglement between the two fields is no other than the very object of their study—an issue that, unfortunately, has taken many self-identified "critical" scholars of religion to a rather problematic path. It is a route that constantly finds itself encircling the same question: is "religion" an entity "out there," or is it simply (with a reverent nod to the late Jonathan Z. Smith) merely a classification by third parties (us, them, etc.) that needs to be declassified and reorganized (with a purposeful nevertheless avoidance to further cite Smith on such a secondary claim)? This is clearly posited in what Braun argues shortly before concluding his chapter from which I have been drawing upon:

> The aim of Religious Studies at the theoretical level is a fundamental deconstruction of its object, Religion. ... As an idea, religion itself is the very embodiment of a failure or refusal to think seriously and rigorously about certain classes of human practice. (Braun 2020: 21)

Initially one could mistakenly argue that Braun's vigorous critique here appears to be at least problematic, given that, from its inception, the study of religion has constantly attempted and more than often succeeded in indeed thinking seriously about such topics: from the formation of social scientific theories of religion to debunking religious claims and ideas as illiberal, oppressive, and harmful, and from copiously attempting to define religion from a comparative perspective to indicating the nuisance regarding such attempts given the malleability of the concept in both its past and present. One would be doing a disservice to many authors if merely the citation of a couple of works here would reinforce the aforementioned observation. For everyone who has done a serious reading of both the founding figures of the field and of contemporary scholars, it is evident that Braun's and others' criticisms (e.g., the usual names of Russell McCutcheon, Craig Martin, Naomi Goldenberg, and Timothy Fitzgerald come to mind) indicate a repetitive struggle against the likes of Rudolf Otto, Mircea Eliade, John Hick, and their followers within the field. Truth be told, such crypto- or phanæro-theological stances do indeed exist—and every so often seem to be in the majority.[6] This was precisely the case with Margaret Miles's 1999 Presidential Address to the American Academy of Religion (AAR) when she argued that

> theological studies, thought of as exploring a religious tradition from within, must also bring critical questions to the tradition studied. And the study of religion, often described as taking an "objective" or disengaged perspective, cannot be studied or taught without understanding the power and beauty, in particular historical situations, of the tradition or the author we study. Nor can religious studies avoid theology—the committed worldviews, beliefs, and practices of believers—by focusing on religious phenomenologies. Both "theological studies" and the "study of religion" must integrate critical and passionately engaged scholarship. I use, then, the providentially ambiguous

term "religious studies" to integrate the falsely polarized terms, "theological studies" and the "study of religion." (Miles 2000: 472)

Based on such startling views, Braun's and others' criticisms seem exceedingly accurate. What scholars of religion thus need is to eventually acknowledge that their actual "foe" is not *religion* as an analytical category and its possible cross-cultural utility (or any category and its utility for that matter), but scholars who attach to such a category something more (sacredness, holiness, transcendence, and the like) than simply a scholarly tool: that is, a classificatory system that, based on the similarities and differences between certain social phenomena, one may proceed and categorize them as "religions." Granted, such similarities and differences within the study of the taxon "religion" include various elements: from ideas and practices to superhuman agents that are usually called "gods" (yet again, another taxon). The latter, as it turns out, is the quintessential subject matter of theological conceptualization and argumentation. But there is a deep chasm between discussing, interpreting, and explaining people's ideas about gods and assessing the truth of those gods. And "ancient theology"—as some Greek and Roman thinkers pointed out centuries ago—may do both, but it is the former that is of value to the scholar of religion. In this respect, in what follows I am arguing that, despite the constant and often justified criticisms, scholars of religion have neglected the fact that "theology" does not by default mean Christian (or Western and, more particularly, Protestant) theology—especially so outside post nineteenth-century Western tertiary education. Once disciplinary anxieties informing such a dipole have been subsided, then the term seizes being a baleful one and becomes predominantly, if not exclusively, a tool—even more so within the field of the study of Greek and Roman religion(s).[7]

–1–

In her succinct but vastly important report on four very influential multi-authored compendia in the academic study of religion—namely: Mark C. Taylor's *Critical Terms for Religious Studies* (1998), Willi Braun and Russell McCutcheon's *Guide to the Study of Religion* (2000), John R. Hinnells's *The Routledge Companion to the Study of Religion* (2005), and Robert A. Segal's

The Blackwell Companion to the Study of Religion (2006b)—Ingvild Sælid Gilhus points out something rather alarming:

> Taking into consideration the importance of superhuman beings in the plural in almost all religions, it is strange that they are so elusive in textbooks. The difficulty to find adequate literature in companions and field guides written in English easily lead to the question: what has become of superhuman beings?[8] (Gilhus 2016: 375)

The answer is disheartening as well as disconcerting. Scholars of religion have regularly avoided talking about the very object of their subject matter (the latter being that of "religion"): that is, gods, goddesses, and other superhuman entities. Gilhus wonders why such an absence is recorded and postulates that "it could be due to a misplaced identification between God/gods and Theology," and given the continuous and forceful attempt by scholars of religion to free themselves from theology's "shadow," not paying central attention to gods could be "an effect of trying to keep all that smack of theology out" (ibid.: 381). Although she also makes an effort to find additional reasons for neglecting the gods as not central or even important to the study of religion, I am confident that Gilhus's initial hunch appears to be to the point. And despite the counterargument that she rightly cites, that is, that gods and other superhuman agents are relevant to believers but not to the scholar of religion, she correctly adds that "superhuman agents are, when all is said and done, typical for what is usually labelled religion" (ibid.: 382). Once again, however, we are faced with the same familiar conundrum: the more we avoid defining religion, the more we find ourselves struggling with the same problems, which will further persist until we acknowledge that, without a definition, we are constantly finding ourselves debating about our subject matter to no avail.

Are gods, goddesses, and superhuman agents central to the study of religion? Gustavo Benavides (2016) replies affirmatively, and so has done Benson Saler (2008) and many others.[9] Hence the problem appears to be twofold: firstly, it is linked to the aforementioned unresolved issue of definition and, secondly, it is related to the question of whether scholars of religion are in danger of "theologizing" when talking about gods and other superhuman agents—and, subsequently, be regarded therefore as theologians.

Such fear, however, seems to be unfounded. (At least beyond the apparent insecurity many scholars of religion feel when they have to address the entities in which people appear to believe within the different religious traditions across time and space.) In the case of Greek and Roman religion(s), a quick search in the *Thesaurus Linguae Graecae* (TLG), the research program at the University of California, United States, which since 1972 has amassed and digitized most literary texts written in Greek from the time of Homer to the fall of the Byzantine Empire in 1453 CE, returns thousands of examples of god-talk. Merely the term θεός, translated into English (and in all other Western languages) as "god," appears 65,909 times, a number that greatly increases once one adds other grammatical variations of the term or the numerous compounds.[10] Likewise, in Latin, a quick search of the term *deus* in the Packard Humanities Institute (PHI) Latin Corpus returns 1,293 results, *deorum* 1,439 results, and multiple others when one tinkers with the term.[11] In other words, both the Greeks and the Romans spoke and wrote extensively about their gods, but scholars of religion that work on materials from the world of Greek and Roman antiquity seem reluctant to discuss those agents and their centrality in Greek and Roman religion(s).

In the closing remarks of perhaps the best multi-authored recent discussion on the Greek gods, Andrew Erskine opens with the following words: "This volume has sought to put the gods back into Greek religion, a realm from which modern scholarship with its emphasis on ritual and anthropology had rather paradoxically ousted them" (Erskine 2010: 505).[12] It is rather unfortunate to read that, as late as 2010, the gods needed to be "put back into" the study of Greek religion—with the case being not that different in the study of Roman religion. Since then, however, some new publications have made great effort—with more or less success—to reinsert the gods into the core of the study of Greek and Roman religion(s), although none authored or edited by scholars of religion.[13] On the contrary, scholars of religion are consciously restricting their studies within the limits of discourses *about* religion, emphasizing practices and rituals (i.e., religion's function), discussing extensively the politics of religion and religious institutions, or merely highlighting the inadequacy of the term "religion" when studying the ancient world. In other words, scholars of religion will do anything to avoid god-talk without, however, offering solid justification for such a choice other than considering an examination of the

Greek and Roman gods and other superhuman agents as belonging to the field of theology or philosophy, and thus being irrelevant to the study of (ancient) religion, or as yet another instance of Christianizing ideas, concepts, and practices of people who lived before or beyond the purview of Christianity (see Chapter 3, this volume). In this respect, the scholar and student of Greek and Roman religion(s) need to turn their attention to the sources, an endeavor that has been successfully and prolifically addressed historically by classicists in various publications.

However, before proceeding, one needs to answer the fundamental question that informs the whole project of restating the gods and goddesses within the study of the religious ideas of the Greeks and the Romans: what is a Greek and Roman god or goddess? I have chosen two informative and influential accounts, one from a classicist (Albert Henrichs) and one from a scholar of religion (Einar Thomassen), which demonstrate both the complexity and the different approaches employed when studying the gods, goddesses, and other similar superhuman agents of the ancient Greeks and Romans. Nevertheless, despite the apparent different paths chosen by these representatives of the two disciplines, it turns out that there exist more points of agreement than disagreement.

In his illuminating essay "What is a Greek God?" Albert Henrichs (2010) identified three primary elements that answer this admittedly thorny question: immortality, power, and anthropomorphism. According to Henrichs, immortality is the most important aspect of a Greek (and one may add, Roman) god or goddess. "Immortality is the ultimate benchmark of their divinity. ... [It is] the privilege of the gods" (Henrichs 2010: 29, 32). Power, the most difficult of the three qualities to define, "is the driving force behind Greek polytheism in so far as it defines the relationships between the gods and their modes of interaction with humans" (ibid.: 37). By far the most widely spread concept regarding the Greek (and Roman) gods and goddesses is their anthropomorphic nature, that is, their human-like physical attributes. It is through these features that people were able to identify their gods when epiphany occurred—that is, the actual physical appearance of a god or goddess to an individual or a group of people: "Without the anthropomorphic gods, the Greek epiphanic experience would be very different; indeed, it might not exist at all" (ibid.: 33). In other words, Henrichs's tripartite analysis takes these features to be not simply significant but essential in identifying the Greek (and Roman) gods and goddesses whenever and wherever they appear in our sources and records. They work in tandem and cannot be isolated from one another. And as Henrichs laments, "these generic properties that are shared by all Greek gods have been largely ignored by scholars of Greek religion" (ibid.: 37), sacrificed to the trend of discussing individual gods and goddesses[14] but missing the opportunity to create a framework within which the category of "gods and goddesses" may be addressed.

Although in some respects similar, Einar Thomassen's discussion brings into the framework some additional features, more representative of a study of religion approach to such agents, and to a greater extent linked to a functionalist perspective one would add. In his view, what makes a god or goddess is related to three general principles: agency, communication, and distinct ontology. By arguing that gods and goddesses are agents, Thomassen reminds the reader that those entities appeared to and contacted with individuals or groups of people, which led to a communication between the latter and the former based on the belief that gods and goddesses were personal beings. Finally, and here Thomassen just about repeats Henrichs, gods and goddesses were perceived as different from and superior to humans, which can be validated by their power and immortality (Thomassen 2016: 368–70). Like Henrichs, Thomassen does not see his tripartite overview as a solidified set; rather, he rightly points out that

> it is possible in principle for a being to be considered a "god" in one of these senses but not in any of the others, though the possibility always exists to make the inference that if a being is a god in one of these senses, he or she must appear as a god in one or both of the others as well. (Thomassen 2016: 370)

The latter is of course related to the numerous agents in both Greek and Roman religion(s) that were, say, superior ontologically but were not sought by the people, or they had agency but lacked the power of other, superior to them agents. The examples abound, and some such agents played central role in the daily life of the Greeks and Romans despite not attempting to contact or worship them—and even being afraid of them due to their temperament and general inclination to cause misfortune and disaster. For example: river deities,[15] nymphs,[16] spirits of places or of the household,[17] the spirits of the dead,[18] gods that caused illnesses,[19] and more. After all, the number of agents that populated the religious world of the Greeks and Romans is vast, with many gods and goddesses being almost forgotten or overlooked by the student and scholar of Greek and Roman religion(s). For example: Aristaeus, Pales, Fons, Caerus, Dinlas, Vedionis, Eurus, Angitia, Molae, Humenaios, Paean, Nortia, Robigus, Pricus, Zelus, Summanus, and numerous others.[20]

Thomassen's and Henrichs's classifications indicate thus that there is a certain list of overall features that correspond to Greek and Roman theology—with the term being used here as Greek and Roman "narrations about the gods" (Borgeaud 2004: 408)—and it consists of (1) anthropomorphism, (2) communication, (3) power, and (4) immortality. All four necessary conditions qualifying an agent as a god, goddess, or superhuman entity are constantly present in the textual and archaeological corpus.

–2–

An initial note on the usage of theology: In the introduction to their superb *Theologies of Ancient Greek Religion* (2016), Esther Eidinow, Julia Kindt, and Robin Osborne enumerate various ways that the term can and has been used in the study of Greek religion—in many respects, the same applies to Roman religion as well. Observing a gradual stratification of the concept of theology, they move from a merely etymological usage of talking about the gods, a more elaborate one that involves questions about gods, an even more sophisticated one that accepts and promotes the existence of gods who intervene and respond to humans and takes the form of a coherent belief, to the most complex form of theology that offers a dogmatic or dogmatic-like system about beliefs and gods (Eidinow, Kindt, and Osborne 2016: 3–5). Despite one's objections to such a classification,[21] it is Julia Kindt's observance that "it may not be entirely misleading to say that ancient Greek religion was to a significant extent a theology of the story" (Kindt 2016: 14) that eventually summarizes the aforementioned stratification in a manner that allows for the utilization of the term "theology" in a broader way. In my view, Kindt's seemingly simplistic but extremely accurate summarization includes three of the most significant and important elements encountered among both the ancient Greeks and the Romans: a constant interest in stories and storytelling (what one would call "myth and myth-telling"); a linkage of such stories to various religious topics and questions of their time; and the continuous infusion of those stories with gods, goddesses, and other similar superhuman agents.[22] Although the stratification of theology(-ies) found in the introduction of their volume is a helpful taxonomy, it also complicates what theology amounts to—and for that we have many to blame: from the critics of traditional religion within the Greek and Roman world to post first-century CE Christian theologians in their attempt to formulate a consistent and acceptable theological system. As Denis Feeney (1991) and Richard Hunter (2018) have demonstrated, such different views of theology even within the ancient world merely indicate that a discourse and debate on the gods was vivid, continuous, and present within Greek and Roman thought and imagination, often encompassing more than one of the forenamed different levels of theology concurrently.[23]

A final, brief note on the usage of theology: If scholars of antiquity are willing to use terms such as soteriology[24]—despite whatever qualifications are employed, as if such terms are not Christian-centric or anachronistic—it should follow that theology in its basic understanding as god-talk (as well as the ensuing, more sophisticated discourses on those gods and their nature and function) remains a perfectly employable concept for further penetrating the religious world of the ancient Greeks and Romans. And for the still hesitant reader, I adopt an even more elaborate definition of theology to work with, formulated by T. M. Robinson (2008: 485): "a notion (however precisely or imprecisely systematized) of God/gods/the gods and his/their putative relationship, causal and directive, to the world and its operations, and to ourselves within that world." In many respects, such a definition echoes Cicero's view when, arguing against Plato,[25] indirectly offers the subject matter of both Greek and Roman theology:

> The inconsistencies of Plato are a long story. In the *Timaeus* he says that it is impossible to name the father of this universe; and in the *Laws* he deprecates all inquiry into the nature of the deity. Again, he holds that god [*deum*] is entirely incorporeal (in Greek, *asomatos*); but divine incorporeity is inconceivable, for an incorporeal deity would necessarily be incapable of

sensation, and also of practical wisdom, and of pleasure, all of which are attributes essential to our conception of deity [*deorum notione*]. Yet both in the *Timaeus* and the *Laws* he says that the world, the sky, the stars, the earth and our souls are gods [*deum esse*], in addition to those in whom we have been taught to believe by ancestral tradition [*maiorum institutis accepimus*]; but it is obvious that these propositions are both inherently false and mutually destructive. (*De natura deorum* I.12.30; trans. H. Rackham, LOEB)

One may desire to call such an exposition merely a philosophical one—as if there exist an alternative form of thinking and discussing about concepts other than "philosophically"—but the subject matter is no other than the nature, function, and place of the gods, that is, a *theologia*, a god-talk.[26]

–3–

Cicero's association of divine corporeality and agency brings us back to how both Greek and Roman gods and goddesses were conceived and thought of by persons living in those cultures. Evidently, Cicero's position reinforces Henrichs's and Thomassen's insistence on anthropomorphism as one of the core elements—if not the most representative one—determining what makes a Greek or Roman agent a god. From anthropomorphism, after all, stems the importance of epiphanies and of communication between the divine and the human world.

The Greeks employed a number of descriptions to sketch the anthropomorphic nature of their gods. Scent, shape and color of eyes, voice, posture, hair, and clothing are among the elements that indicated the human-like nature of the gods. And these traits were visible to people who claimed to have had an encounter with a superhuman agent. Sources abound: from the archaic epics and hymns to inscriptions one constantly witnesses a repetitive motif that leaves little doubt regarding the Greek perception in relation to the nature of the gods.[27] In her PhD thesis on divine epiphany (later published as a monograph), Georgia Petridou (2006: 311–407; 2015) enlists 367 cases of epiphanies from a wide range of sources, a number which grows exponentially when adding, for example, theatrical plays—both tragedies and comedies. The latter as a scene of demonstrating the nature of the Greek gods and goddesses through epiphanies has been thoroughly studied by many specialists, always indicating the centrality of the idea of interference as a demonstration of the gods' and goddesses' power, superhuman nature, and anthropomorphic characteristics (indicatively, Parker 2005: 136–53; 2008; Scullion 2014; Lefkowitz 2016; and more recently Lipka 2022). In such works, *theology* as discourse about the gods and accompanied by reflections on those issues holds a central place in the arguments promoted by the respective authors. And this does not come as a surprise considering how permeative was the idea that the gods appeared to many people having specific motives as well as goals. Among other scholars, Petridou has offered a working definition of epiphany as "the manifestation of a deity to an individual or a group of people, in sleep or in waking reality, in a crisis or cult context" (Petridou 2015: 2; similarly, Henrichs 2019b [2012]: 427). Perhaps one of the most known examples of an epiphany of a god in a dream is encountered in Apuleius's *Metamorphoses* or *The Golden Ass* penned in the second century CE.

The novel opens with Lucius traveling on business to Hypata in Thessaly (a region in eastern Greece), well known as a center of magic and as a home of witches. While in Hypata, Lucius is a guest of Milo, a friend of a friend. Milo's wife, Pamphile, is a sorceress and as Lucius was urged toward magic, he seduces Photis, Pamphile's servant girl. With her help, after secretly watching Pamphile transform herself into an owl, Lucius wishes to try the magic ointment himself but because of a mistake he is transformed into an ass. The antidote in order to retransform is to consume common roses. From then onward, Lucius, as an ass, wanders into the Hellenistic world without being able to find the so much desired roses and gets himself into different and occasionally bizarre situations. In the eleventh and final book of the narrative, Lucius is at Cenchreae, a harbor near Corinth in Central Greece. Disappointed and hopeless he prays to the unknown heavenly goddess and asks for her help. After his prayer, he falls asleep and goddesses Isis appears in his dream and assures him that the next day he will be retransformed into a man, but he will then have to dedicate his life to her. The next day Lucius, following Isis's instructions, is retransformed into a human, and dedicates his life to the goddess through several initiations into her cult.

Lucius's dream of Isis is illuminating as an example of "seeing" the gods in antiquity, both in respect to their anthropomorphic but superhuman nature and their epiphanic ability. It is worth citing it in its entirety:

I will try to convey to you, my readers, her astounding appearance; if, that is, the poverty of human speech can grant me the ability to explain it, or if the goddess's own godhead supplies my lack with the generous resources of her rhetorical eloquence. First, her hair: luxuriant, long-flowing, gently curled, falling free and unbound, it cascaded softly down around her divine neck. There was a crown of many shapes and symbols, and it ringed her lofty head with flowers of all sorts: in its center, upon her forehead, there was a flat disk, in the manner of a mirror or, better yet, an emblem of the moon, and from it flashed a pure white light; at the right and at the left it was flanked by coils of cobras, rearing up; above it was adorned with ears of waving wheat. There was a tunic of many colors woven of fine linen, here glowing with a white luminescence, there with the saffron flower's lutescence, there like flame in the rose's rubescence. On top of that was a cloak, black as blackness itself and, what dazzled my eyes more than anything else, it coruscated with a dark nigrescence. It ran round about her, under her right arm and back to her left shoulder; a part of its borders she let fall after the fashion of a knot; it hung down in files of accordion folds, an elegant waterfall ending in tassels and fringes at the hem of her gown. Along its embroidered border and scattered upon its surface were scintillating stars; in their center was the midmonth moon, breathing flame and fire. A crown composed of all flowers, all fruits, clung in bonds unbreakable to the flowing hem of that glorious cloak, wherever it swept. Most manifold were the things that she carried. In her right hand, you see, she bore a rattle made of bronze, and through the middle of its narrow strip of metal, bent backwards like a belt, passed three small rods, and this sistrum would give a shrill sound whenever the arm shook it in a triple flourish. But from her left hung down a vessel of gold, and from its handle, the part that I could see, rose up a cobra, lifting its head up high, its hood wide-swollen. Sandals woven of palm leaves, the prize of victory, covered her ambrosial feet. (Apuleius, *Metamorphosis* 11.3–4; trans. Relihan 2007)

Apuleius's description effectively constitutes a theological visual representation of this particular goddess, which was of course informed by Egyptian mythology given Isis's origins, but was also informative in regard to this goddess' nature to Apuleius's readership. The importance of "seeing the gods" as part and parcel of broader theological discourses—both advanced (or "elite") and daily (or "folk") ones—cannot be overstated, despite the fact that, as Verity Platt has accurately pointed out, the question "'what does it mean to see the gods?' inevitably highlights the limitations of approaches to Greek religion that prioritize praxis over theological and cognitive dimensions" (Platt 2015: 501). Platt's diagnosis merely iterates the continuous anxiety that scholars of the ancient world seemingly have when it comes to utilizing the term "theology."

The constant avoidance of god-talk (i.e., theology) is no less apparent in the study of Roman religion. In a recent book dedicated to gods and goddesses of ancient Italy, John North poignantly observes that, despite initial interests in those agents, "the gods and goddesses sometimes seemed to have been left out of the reckoning" in modern scholarship (North 2020: 3). It is indeed alarming that both Andrew Erskine regarding studies on Greek religion and John North in relation to Roman religion come to the same conclusion, despite writing ten years apart from each other. Similarly to Platt's "praxis first" in regard to Greek religion, Roman religion has been overwhelmingly studied as praxis-oriented, thus diminishing the discussions on theological issues pertaining to the actual receivers of Roman religious practices, the gods and goddesses. Consequently, one does not get caught off guard when encountering statements such as "I shall keep 'theology' in inverted commas in order to emphasize the difference between the less foundational role of these considerations among the Roman imperial elite and our modern expectations of the central role of theology for any religion" (Várhelyi 2010: 153).

Although Várhelyi is partly correct—primarily in respect to the absence of theological systematic thinking in the form of dogmatic truth among the Romans—theology does not require inverted commas, unless one is naive enough to claim that modern, Western, and monotheistic religions and their emphasis to theology are identical to premodern religions and their theology. In his excellent in many aspects *Legible Religion* (2016), Duncan MacRae allows for the usage of the term "civic theology" when referring to a set of texts that functioned, within Roman society, as means of demarcating, on the one hand, what was "perceived as particularly *Roman* religious culture" (*pace*, civic) and, on the other hand, what was "concerned with the intellectual discussion of the gods and their worship" (MacRae 2016: 4). Varro's oft-quoted three types of theology (*theologiae*) from his *Antiquitates rerum humanarum et divinarum*, that is, mythical, physical (philosophical), and civic theology (see Augustine, *De civitate Dei* 6.5), accompanied by Varro's elaborate narrations in relation to the names, the functions, and the genealogy of the Roman gods and goddesses (ibid.: 4.10; 4.23; 7.2; 7.28), corroborates MacRae's argument of dealing with such texts as part of a Roman "civic theology."[28]

However, our sources go well beyond the "classical authors" regarding the centrality of the gods and goddesses in Roman religion, which also indicates how important theology-as-"god-talk" was for the Romans in general. Teresa Morgan has amassed a number of proverbs, *gnomai*, fables, and *exempla* that contain various ideas about the nature and power of the Roman (and, occasionally, Greek) gods and goddesses (Morgan 2007). In addition to Morgan's work, theology's importance in the study of Roman religion has been slowly reemphasized by scholars in an attempt to rectify the excessive cautiousness and frankly unjustified choices of previous research.

Jacob Latham belongs among those scholars who do not shy away from utilizing the term "theology" in the study of Roman religion without the asterisks and extreme caution of other specialists. In his detailed work on Roman processions, Latham focuses on the *pompa circensis*, the circus procession which took place many times throughout the year from the late republic to late antiquity (c. 131 BCE to the fourth century CE). According to contemporary scholarship, large numbers of spectators observed those processions, with the number being estimated up to 150,000 persons, given that this was also the capacity of the Circus Maximus, the largest arena in antiquity (Latham 2015: 298). The *pompa circensis* went through the most important sites of the Roman capital, "from the temple of Capitoline Jupiter (the seat of Roman sovereignty); down into the Roman Forum; to the *vicus Tuscus*, which passed through the Velabrum into the Forum Boarium; and finally toward the plebian temple of Ceres on its way to the Circus Maximus, where the wildly popular races entertained the gods and their fellow Romans" (Latham 2016: 2). What is remarkable, according to Latham, is not merely the number of spectators, but primarily the function of those processions. Staged as a means of visual representation, the *pompa circensis* portrayed the Roman gods, superhuman agents, and other heroes and lesser figures through anthropomorphic statues and abstract symbols, consequently comprising "an implicit and embodied theology, an act of thinking and doing—a *savoir-fair* not simply a *savoir-penser*" (Latham 2015: 289). Latham is cautious in blindly relying on his sources—and correctly so, given that much of what we know about the *pompa circensis* comes only from Dionysius of Halicarnassus (*Roman Antiquities* 7.72.1–18) and Ovid[29]—but his work primarily seeks to bridge the chasm between theological thinking and orthopraxy-only, which has been forcefully argued by many a scholar of Roman religion.

Convincing or not, Latham's argumentation is worthy first and foremost for his assertion that Roman religion-cum-orthropraxy only tells us one side of the story. The *pompa circensis* in a way summarized the manner in which the Romans conceptualized their gods and their nature, including their relationship with the people. Hence, the latter corresponds to an explicit theological thinking, delineating the limits between humans and gods as well as indicating the most powerful superhuman agents and their interrelationships both among them and with the Romans themselves:

> That is, the other-than-human appeared as familiar and approachable, distant and threatening, or terrifying and ridiculous. The various modes of presencing the gods were themselves ordered and organized in pantheons, at least in the texts that represented and interpreted the procession. ... That is, the *pompa circensis* was fundamentally a *pompa deorum*—a procession of gods made present or represented in various ways in a performed theology. (Latham 2015: 317 and Latham 2016: 1, respectively)

Latham's argumentation is in essence based on the idea that the Romans in fact understood humans and gods as distinct and completely different categories, that is, contrary to the traditional view held by scholars that allows for a far more malleable line between the two spheres.[30] By and of itself, such a view can indeed be contested, but Latham's argumentation remains interesting and is worthy of further consideration.

A similar view of the place of theology in the study of Roman religion, also related to the work of Dionysius of Halicarnassus, is promoted by Lindsay Driediger-Murphy. In examining the place of traditional myths in Dionysius's work, Driediger-Murphy argues that theology was an essential element in Dionysius's analysis, despite the fact that his views have been traditionally categorized as related to philosophy. In her assessment, Dionysius's

> use of "theology" represents a departure from the contemporary philosophical view that "theological" ideas could and should be kept separate from myth and from cult practice, which in turn implies that ideas about the gods and

their nature played a much more important part in the religion of Greeks and Romans than many scholars currently allow. (Driediger-Murphy 2014: 333)

The inverted commas notwithstanding—an indication of how saturated is the idea that using the term theology in pre-Christian contexts is academically improper—Driediger-Murphy goes against the traditional flow. In her evaluation of Dionysius's theology, she points out the ancient historian's assessment of a variety of myths regarding the nature of the gods, which indicates that various theologies were at work at Dionysius's time—making theology as a mode of thinking a vibrant and ongoing exercise within the ancient world. As a result, Dionysius did not accept the idea that the gods had sexual relationships with humans but agreed that they had an interest (albeit limited) in human affairs (Driediger-Murphy 2014: 335, 337–9). Perhaps the most vivid example of Dionysius's own theological perspective in relation to the gods' nature is seen in his discussion of Romulus, the founder of the city of Rome.

> [Romulus] rejected all the traditional myths concerning the gods that contain blasphemies or calumnies against them, looking upon these as wicked, useless and indecent, and unworthy, not only of the gods, but even of good men; and he accustomed people both to think and to speak the best of the gods and to attribute to them no conduct unworthy of their blessed nature. ... Let no one imagine, however, that I am not sensible that some of the Greek myths are useful to mankind, part of them explaining, as they do, the works of Nature by allegories, others being designed as a consolation for human misfortunes, some freeing the mind of its agitations and terrors and clearing away unsound opinions, and others invented for some other useful purpose. But, though I am as well acquainted as anyone with these matters, nevertheless my attitude toward the myths is one of caution, and I am more inclined to accept the theology of the Romans [καὶ τὴν Ῥωμαίων μᾶλλον ἀποδέχομαι θεολογίαν], when I consider that the advantages from the Greek myths are slight and cannot be of profit to many, but only to those who have examined the end for which they are designed and this philosophic attitude is shared by few. (*Roman Antiquities* 2.18.3 and 2.20.1–2; trans. E. Cary, LOEB)

Reminiscent of Xenophanes of Colophon (late sixth, early fifth century BCE) and his criticism of Homer and Hesiod for portraying the gods as having the same vices as humans do,[31] Dionysius's theological understanding is indeed important, since Roman religion in his view was to be examined not just through "cult and ritual forms, but also from a theological perspective," which is "worthy of further consideration" (Driediger-Murphy 2014: 345).

Both Driediger-Murphy's and Latham's studies on the centrality of theology and theological thinking in Roman religion, which stress the importance of orthodoxy and not merely orthopraxy, constitute fine examples of a new stream in historical scholarship that attempts to free itself from the restraints of the past. Concurrently, such works clearly denote that, through the historical record, theology as a tool remains useful, applicable, and unequivocally necessary in discussing both the centrality and importance of the gods in what we now call Roman religion.

6

Re(ap)proaching the Study of Greek and Roman Religions

If the building of a bridge does not enrich the awareness of those who work on it, then that bridge ought not to be built and the citizens can go on swimming across the river or going by boat.

Frantz Fanon (1925–1961)[1]

Thus argued the prominent psychiatrist Frantz Fanon in his last published book, *The Wretched of the Earth* (originally appearing in French in 1961, with the title *Les Damnés de la Terre*). Although in this noteworthy work Fanon addressed both the effects of colonization and the ways to decolonize both the individual and people more broadly, I find in his excerpt a serious, careful, as well as realistic diagnosis fully applicable to what I have been discussing in the previous chapters regarding the way scholars of religion and classicists and historians of antiquity need to collaborate for a fuller, more accurate, and more appealing study of Greek and Roman religion(s). If my discussion up to this point has only brought about puffing and vexation, then undoubtedly any attempt to bring the two disciplines closer seems to me doomed to fail and, with it, the future of the study of Greek and Roman religion(s) as a subfield. However, I do not argue that my approach to the study of the religion(s) of the Greeks and the Romans is the best, only viable, or guaranteed to be successful one. But the problem of lack of collaboration is undeniable and readily observable, and still remains an obstacle that scholars of those religious traditions need to address, overcome, and leave behind—the "how," as in many other scientific and academic endeavors, naturally remains negotiable.

However, we still need to decide what our end goals should be when it comes to the academic study of religion in general and Greek and Roman religion(s) in particular. I have repeatedly addressed the need for defining our object of study before going on and attempting to understand, interpret, and explain the religious ideas and practices of the Greeks and the Romans—although, as one may object, it is the other way around when one has sufficient comparative data at hand. Yet, my call for a definition—be it a stipulative, a heuristic, or even a restricted one based on the data at hand—constantly bounces off primarily due to whether definitions should be employed at all and what they mean with reference to broader truths, knowledge, and scientific enterprises (even if the latter might seem to be a mirage at first). Contemporary theorization of religion(s)—as well as of anything else within the humanities and liberal arts, as it seems—is overwhelmed by what has been broadly called "postmodern theorization."[2] Despite the (limited, in my estimation at least) benefits of postmodernist thought broadly speaking, scholars of religion and of ancient religions as well have found themselves trapped within the allure of deconstructionist thinking and the vagueness of whatever remains after such a deconstruction.[3] In the preface of his latest book *Metamodernism: The Future of Theory* (2021), Jason Ānanda Josephson Storm gives a bold and rather gloomy description of the current, postmodern status quo of the exercise of theorizing in the humanities in general—including, of course, the study of religion past and present.

> Turning the techniques of a discipline inward on itself regularly appears theoretically sophisticated and intellectually ambitious, and sometimes even praised as revolutionary. But limiting one's research to critical scholarship about scholarship tends to undercut the work of the disciplines and to reduce them to little more than ideological formations themselves—an act which is, essentially, destructive rather than creative. It seems that deconstruction generally takes less effort and is better rewarded than construction. … [I]t can be seductive to take the stance of an epistemological anarchist and to start exploding fundamental concepts and then reveling in the chaos as disciplines disintegrate. … After something has been destroyed, something new must be built, and for something new to be built, a movement is necessary. (Josephson Storm 2021: ix–x)

But how do "disciplines disintegrate" through a deconstructionist-only approach to the key concepts, approaches, methods, and ideas they traditionally hold? Josephson Storm adds:

Skeptical dogmas of all sorts proliferated. Doubt was praised over understanding. Truth was said to be a sham. Knowledge was nothing more than power. ... Translation was believed impossible. Scholars became skeptical about the capacity of the word to reflect the world. ... For a time, many scholars imagined themselves to be masters of suspicion. Even today everything seems problematic and almost every thinker morally questionable. Such cynicism can be paralyzing. ... Postmodern skepticism was supposed to be liberating, but it failed us. (ibid.: 1–2)

One may be surprised by Josephson Storm's diagnosis. Although his work is dedicated to the future of theory in general within the humanities and the social sciences (not excluding, naturally, the study of religion given that he himself works at and is a member of the Department of Religion at Williams College, MA), consider the following statement by Tenzan Eaghll in his review essay of one of the most interesting collective works in the study of religion published recently—namely *Religion, Theory, Critique: Classic and Contemporary Approaches and Methodologies*, which was edited by Richard King and appeared in 2017:

I think it is more valuable to stress difference, incommensurability, multitude, fragmentation, and indeterminacy over continuity. I also think that stressing anarchy over continuity has more pedagogical value because it has the added benefit of introducing students to the contentious disagreements that still occupy academics. (Eaghll 2019: 39)

Admittedly, pointing out the disagreements and debates within a given field indeed has pedagogical, scientific, and in general significant value for both students and scholars. However, "stressing anarchy over continuity" makes Josephson Storm's position valid, accurate, and simultaneously alarming, since anarchy within such a discourse is another term for "anything goes."

–1–

Within the field of the study of religion such a deconstructionist stance has been intensely advocated by a number of scholars. Perhaps the most representative example of such current discourses and debates within the field may be found in a recent special volume of the journal *Implicit Religion* (vol. 20, no. 4) published in 2017, which was based on and resulted from an online debate between a number of scholars; a debate that was spurred by a podcast interview of Teemu Taira (University of Helsinki) to "The Religious Studies Project" and the response to the podcast by Paul Hedges (Nanyang Technological University, Singapore).[4]

Taira openly sides with the deconstructionists, many of whom also replied to the podcast and to Paul Hedges's criticism of Taira's positions. As Taira informs the listener, "I've been a big fan of scholars who have written critically about the category of 'religion' " (Taira 2017: 378), by which he refers to scholars who have asked whether one should even use the term "religion" given that, in their view, its emergence as an analytical category, its history, and its usefulness remain problematic (ibid.). This prevalent nowadays theoretical stance among many scholars of religion (especially of the newer generation) led Hedges to reply to Taira's arguments, which, in turn, apparently stimulated other like-minded deconstructionists who participated in the debate. Regrettably, it is only Hedges who maintains a different position—an indication of an unfortunate choice of contributors to this special volume, in which Hedges is virtually presented as a pariah of the academic study of religion. Hence, when Hedges points out the obvious, that is, that Taira "is clear in stating that he makes no claim as to whether anything is or is not a religion, nor does he try and give any definition to the term. It remains for him an empty signifier which others fill" (Hedges 2017: 390), he also draws the reader's attention to what remains problematic in such a "critical" study of religion as a category: "It is on the refusal to try and define or even to engage in discourse about how the term may be used that I see the problem arising" (ibid.: 390–1). As I have on numerous occasions indicated throughout the preceding chapters, the problem of definition—or even, to follow Hedges, our engagement in discourse on how we should eventually use the term—remains critical, essential, and central for a serious academic study of religion.

As it quickly becomes evident, however, both Hedges's and my preoccupations with defining our subject matter before attempting to historicize, deconstruct, dismantle, or whatever else we might wish to do with it, are not shared by either the other authors in the special volume or by many other scholars of religion of the historicization bend—which, in order to avoid any unsureness, takes its cue by Michel Foucault's genealogical work, plain and simple (with the occasional nod to Friedrich Nietzsche). Thus, Neil George informs us that "[w]e need words, but that does not mean we need all words. When presenting research at a conference a couple years ago, a senior scholar asked me about the possibilities for a viable definition of religion. ... 'I had no need of that hypothesis'" (George 2017: 399–400). In a similar vein, Russell McCutcheon argues that

> here the problem becomes evident: for many of our colleagues, I would argue, are, to put it frankly, native informants for this particular social classifications system (thereby taking this discourse's use as necessary and inevitable, given the social world they understand themselves to inhabit), making it near impossible for them to entertain that there are only religions in the world because many of us say and act like there are. (McCutcheon 2017: 404)

Likewise, McCutcheon's now colleague at the University of Alabama[5] Richard Newton opts for the term "culture" when he asserts that "we're better with the social facts of culture than we are with religion. In trying to move past the privileging of 'religion' that Taira and others critique, scholars are trying to bring at least the same order of questioning. That's the point of tethering religion and culture" (Newton 2017: 410). Newton's preference of "culture" over "religion" is also shared by Malory Nye, a known advocate of the study of "religion" without "religion." As he maintains, "'religion' does not need to be 'put back,' reconstructed after historicization. And nor do we need to 'make sure we take it seriously'" (Nye 2017b: 419–20).

Such positions have by and large dominated the discourse on religion and the study of religion in the Anglophone world in the past two decades, although the residual effects of such debates are also visible within other cultural and geographical contexts (e.g., Führding 2015; Horii 2018). The question that emerges, however, is related to the utility of such discourses beyond the evident need to historicize our terminologies and be certain that we are well aware: (1) that "religion" as a term has a history replete, among others, with unfortunate, contemptible, or outrightly inhumane theories and practices (what Nye points out in his contribution when arguing that such a scholarly practice unfolds and unveils the term's "colonial, racialized, and cis-male hetero-normative resonances" [Nye 2017b: 418]); (2) that although people across time and space produced, maintained, and promoted what we today call "religious beliefs, practices, and systems," this does not simultaneously mean that there is any empirical evidence that their beliefs, practices, and systems have any ontological validity whatsoever—that is, the truth of their "religions" can only be theologized or philosophized, but it cannot be the endeavor of the scholar of religion. Beyond these two important, essential, discipline-specific, and admittedly of high pedagogical value points in the study of religion, such debates, in my estimation, offer next to nothing when not accompanied by cross-cultural data, linguistic knowledge and mastery, comparative outlook, and a rigid theorization of what religion is and how it functions. Or, to invoke Bruce Lincoln's recent criticism, "religion" as a category[6] is defensible

> but admittedly imperfect and precarious to the extent that we a) base our definition on an inadequate number of examples; b) confer disproportionate privilege to some examples, while ignoring others; and c) misconstrue some examples by assimilating them to the ones we know better and the models we base upon them. For all these reasons, our terms, categories, definitions and theories always remain provisional at best, desperately needing the challenges and refinements that come from considering new examples and rethinking the old ones. (Lincoln 2021: 71)

This is where the contemporary study of religion has largely found itself today,[7] which has also led such debates to penetrate the study of Greek and Roman religions by scholars of religion and classicists alike—as I have demonstrated in the previous chapters—to a point that today seems of no return. Nevertheless, there are some voices that perhaps offer some alternatives that may allow the study of Greek and Roman religions to proceed beyond the impasse imposed by primarily (and often exclusively) focusing on a genealogical examination of "religion" or merely paying attention to how the term is inadequate, problematic, modern, and therefore ideally disposable. Concurrently, the virtually unexamined approach to the category "religion" by scholars who for the most part work exclusively with data (i.e., texts, material objects, archaeological archives, etc.) and who persistently avoid discussing what is meant by the term "religion" or how it is employed comparatively, has brought about an equally wide opening between the two disciplines responsible for studying, understanding, and explaining the religious beliefs, practices, and realities of the Greeks and the Romans: classics and the study of religion. That being the case, scholars from both sides repeatedly find themselves with a conundrum that more often than not goes either unnoticed or is skillfully avoided due to disciplinary "traditions," time and labor restrictions, or merely as "nonapplicable."[8] In the case of classicists: how to go about given the excessive theoretical discussions by scholars of religion on the term "religion" as a category and a taxon? Should one simply work from within the discipline and let "outsiders" do the theoretical work without, however, taking into consideration such findings? In the case of scholars of religion working on Greek and Roman religions: how should one master the immense volume of data on which classicists and ancient historians work? Also, and given that typically PhD degrees in the study of religion today only require an elementary (most usually) or intermediary (at best) knowledge of source languages, how can one talk about Greek and Roman "religion" and the category's applicability within a linguistic context of which one knows little?[9] The chosen solution in both cases is unfortunately to typically dismiss these questions as "inapplicable" or "irrelevant" to the type of work one wishes to do. However, as Cicero (106–43 BCE) pointed out more than two millennia ago when talking about how an orator might persuade and thus win an argument and the case of interest in general, there are two kinds of means of persuasion available (a point readily applicable to the student, both the classicist and the scholar of religion, of Greek and Roman religions):

> Now, for the purpose of proving, the orator has two kinds of material at his disposal. One consists of the things that are not thought out by the orator, but, inherent in the circumstances of the case, are treated methodically by him, such as documents, testimonies, agreements, evidence extracted by torture, laws, decrees of the Senate, judicial precedents, magistrates' rulings, legal opinions, and whatever else is not discovered by the orator, but is presented to him by the case and the parties involved. The other kind is that which entirely depends on the reasoning and argumentation of the orator. *So in dealing with the first type, one must think about how to treat the arguments; with the second, about discovering them as well.* (*De oratore* 2.116–17; trans. May 2016: 17, my emphasis)

–2–

Some scholars from both disciplines have been alerted to such a problem and have offered some solutions to bring closer the two fields (as well as other subfields, seemingly irrelevant to the subject) in order to promote an interdisciplinary and more vigorous study of Greek and Roman religion(s). Perhaps the most representative work of this kind is *Understanding Greek Religion* (2016), penned by classicist Jennifer Larson and expanding on the theories and ideas promoted by scholars (of religion and other disciplines) who work in the subfield of the cognitive study of religion (CSR). Larson's work capitalizes on a number of theories that have been put into test by specialists in the CSR: from theory of mind (ToM) and the principle of minimum counterintuitive concepts (MCI) to hyperactive agency detection device (HADD).[10] But what is the CSR?[11]

The cognitive study of religion is a fairly recently developed field of inquiry. Its basic principle is that religion is a by-product of the processes of ordinary human cognition and can be therefore studied according to those very processes—as would any other aspect of ordinary human thinking. As Luther H. Martin has put it, "cognitive scientists seek to explain the kinds of perceptual and conceptual representations—including 'religious' representations—which the mental processing of sensory input allows, the memory, transmission, and transformations of these mental representations, and the relationships, historical and potential, among them" (Martin 2004: 201). The cognitive science of religion does not attempt to explain away religion or to "promote" religion;[12] rather, it offers a series of tools to scholars dealing with religious phenomena and seek to understand and explain their origin and function. This new approach to religious phenomena that originated some forty years ago has produced an interesting cluster of riveting theories, stemming from various scientific disciplines such as anthropology, neuroscience, religious studies, and psychology among others. It is within such a scholarly ambiance that Larson attempts to present the study of an ancient and dead religion in a new key.

Larson opens with a question that typically creates a series of problems accompanied by numerous objections by traditional scholars, namely whether the Greeks believed in their gods—a question she replies to affirmatively.[13]

> In order to understand Greek religion, we need to begin with the mind. The Greeks were confident that their gods and goddesses existed and intervened in the world. For the most part, they gave credence to the content of their

myths. They believed that some people were powerful after their deaths, able to affect the world of the living. They thought that oracles revealed the will of the gods. (Larson 2016: 4–5)

Larson's argument was questioned by University of St. Andrews classicist Thomas Harrison in a recent review panel published in the *Journal of Cognitive Historiography* in 2017. Paying attention to the wording of Larson's aforesaid position ("were confident"; "gave credence"; "believed"; "thought"), he asks:

But what do we mean by such phrases? Were *all* the Greeks confident in, or giving credence to, their gods or myths? (Larson does acknowledge the variability of beliefs in passing, for example in relation to the "marvelous chaos of afterlife beliefs"; cf. 2016: 252). And did they do so consistently, or *all* of the time? And how is Greek "belief" sustained? (Harrison 2017: 32; emphasis in original)

These are certainly valid questions—and despite his mild criticisms in his review, Harrison does not reject the possibilities that are offered by CSR to the study of ancient religions (ibid.: 34). However, one may wonder whether these questions are restricted to ancient Greek (and/or Roman) religion alone—where "belief" is a contested term according to specialists—or within Christianity as well (and any other religion, for that matter). If one accepts Jeppe Sinding Jensen's position that "religion consists of beliefs and behaviours held and performed by humans," with the latter corresponding to what he calls e-religion (e standing for "mind-external") and the former to i-religion (i corresponding to "mind-internal") (Jensen 2020: viii),[14] it is then worth examining whether belief is such a clear and uncontested concept within, say, Christianity—and, the question can be readily asked in reference to other religions—but such a malleable and problematic one within the study of Greek and/or Roman religion(s).

In 1996 Justin Barrett and Frank Keil published the findings of their research with adults in India and the United States regarding their religious beliefs in two different contexts (Barrett and Keil 1996). Their experiments that included narrative tasks and questionnaires showed that when those subjects were asked to reflect on their theological ideas about supernatural beings, they responded in a theologically correct manner. That is, those beings were described according to the teachings of the established theological creed to which the subjects adhered. Thus, Christians participating to their experiment described God as infinite, boundless, unflawed, nonmaterial, almighty, omnipresent, eternal, omnipotent. However, in the narrative comprehension task, where the subjects were required to give quick replies to the stories presented to them (that included ideas such as "God finished one task in order to engage with another") then the same individuals reflected on the narratives and assigned anthropomorphic characteristics to God. That is, it seemed natural that God would first finish one task and then engage with another. As Barrett and Keil put it,

> despite theological descriptions, people seem to incorporate anthropomorphic and naturalistic characterizations into their intuitive God concepts. ... If subjects were asked directly what they believed about God, responses would tend to fit into an abstract theology. Even if people use an anthropomorphic God concept in daily life, they would be hesitant to articulate this as their personal theology because it might appear juvenile. (Barrett and Keil 1996: 223)

The study showed that there are two levels of representation of God, one that coincides with the abstract and sophisticated concepts maintained by informed theology, and one held by believers (Barrett 2000: 30). Barrett later expanded this theory into what he called "theological correctness," that is, "the coexistence of multiple levels of representation of religious concepts or relations … because when beliefs about God or other religious concepts are reflected on, they tend to be reported as more similar to dominant theological dogma, than the gut-level, basic concepts used in more mundane behavior" (Barrett 1999: 326). Such dual representation is informed by cognitive constraints that function in both religious and nonreligious concepts and are consistent with human intuitive knowledge. Consequently, when people need to use a god concept for a quick generation of interpretation of what happens around them, then the more abstract and theologically informed concepts tend to vanish. However, when no rapid interpretation or generation of inferences is needed, then people will return to the theologically correct concepts (ibid.: 328–9).

For Barrett, beliefs—of whatever kind, religious or otherwise—fall under two categories: reflective and nonreflective ones. The former require conscious and deliberate contemplation or explicit instruction; the latter contain beliefs that are generated automatically without the need of reflection or careful thought (Barrett 2004: 2–16). Any belief that requires some kind of elaboration is a reflective one. As such, informed theological concepts that an official creed articulates belong to this category once individuals adopt them as their own beliefs. On the contrary, beliefs held without any contemplation are nonreflective ones. The encounter, for example, with an animal that one has never seen before will automatically generate beliefs about it, which are based on intuitive knowledge acquired from previous experience. The person will therefore automatically believe that this new animal is bound to the laws of gravity, it has sensory organs, it reproduces in whatever way, it cannot go through solid objects, and such. The human tendency to look for an intentional explanation for a given situation that does not correspond to the nonreflective beliefs leads to the adoption of counterintuitive agents that can provide explanations when no other existing intuitive knowledge may do so. Steward Guthrie has argued that in such cases humans assign human-like agency following a trial-and-error method. A movement behind a bush while walking in a forest will generate the nonreflective belief that an agent is causing the movement. If it turns out to be the wind, then the benefit is bigger than ignoring the movement and face a predator hidden in the bush (Guthrie 1993).

This human-like, anthropomorphic assignment of agency is what informs the basic nonreflective religious concepts that Barrett distinguishes from the reflective ones. When the assignment of agency on something violates one of the three aspects of human cognition (or, occasionally, all of them), that is, "intuitive ontology (what kinds of things are in the world), intuitive causality (how do those things work), and intuitive probability (how are those things likely to work)" (Slone 2004: 122) then the basic nonreflective anthropomorphic and human-like religious concepts emerge. In contrast, the reflective religious concepts are the result of certain teachings that come from established theological institutions that an individual may adopt and believe in after personal contemplation. The two levels of representation led Barrett and Keil to argue that "it may be that the 'theological God' is radically different from the 'intuitive God' normally described in everyday discourse" (Barrett and Keil 1996: 223), which poses a rather complex and interesting problem as this should be considered as the source of two distinct theological discourses. An example from modern Greece might be helpful.

–3–

In contemporary Greece, an annual fire-walking ritual takes place at the village of Agia Eleni, in the district of Macedonia. The ritual, which according to the participants is a Christian one, involves extensive prayers to the patrons of the ritual, Saints Constantine and Helen (Eleni). According to the self-identified Orthodox Christian participants, no harm occurs to the fire-walkers due to the protection provided by the two saints, who are both accepted and honored by the official Greek Orthodox Church in its liturgical calendar, with May 21 being their official celebration day. However, the Church does not accept the ritual, since, according to the Holy Synod of the Greek Orthodox Church, its origin is to be found in ancient pagan Dionysian practices. The cognitive and experimental anthropologist Dimitris Xygalatas has extensively studied this ritual, the *Anastenaria* as the ritual is known among the participants. Although Xygalatas rightly points out that the reasons behind the prohibition of the ritual by the official Church should be deemed political and economic rather than theological (Xygalatas 2011: 67–8), what is of interest is the direct opposition of the fire-walkers to the official Greek Orthodox Church. One would expect the ritual to fall into oblivion after its condemnation by the Church. On the contrary, participants consider themselves more Christian than others precisely due to this ritual and openly express their depreciation toward the official position held by the Greek Orthodox Church. As one of the participants told Xygalatas during an interview,

> we are as good Christians as anyone. In fact, maybe more than the others, because we do all the things the rest of Christians do, but we also have this extra one, the Anastenaria. The priests say we are pagans. But we only worship the icons, the same icons that they have in the churches. And if they call us pagans, then why did they take our icons into their church? (Xygalatas 2012: 45).

How may one deal with such "low" theological concepts with which official religion disagrees?[15] In the case of the *Anastenaria* both the Patriarchate of Constantinople (the "Mother" Church of Greek Orthodox Christians and supervising body of the Greek Orthodox Church) and theology professors condemned the ritual as deviating from the practices and creed of the Mother

Church (Xygalatas 2011: 59–60). Such attitude should in turn mean that the people who are participating in the ritual are in effect heretics or pagans according to the official theological position. However, these participants not only believe in the teachings of the official Church and follow its liturgical calendar, but throughout the ritual they use icons depicting saints of the official religion that one may encounter when visiting an Orthodox church anywhere in Greece. In addition, they use the various elements that are used in liturgy, such as candles and incense (Xygalatas 2012: 46).

This type of folk religiosity, such as the fire-walking ritual of the *Anastenaria*, is an example of low (or folk) theology.[16] Although Greek Orthodox Christians (claim that they) believe in the official theological doctrines of the Church and will comply with its teachings and instructions, they will nevertheless often follow their own folk religious traditions. In the case of the *Anastenaria*, adherents hold the belief that the non-burning of the participants' feet is the result of a miracle performed by the two celebrated saints. According to the official doctrine of the Orthodox Christian Church, with the emphasis being explicitly on the trinitarian God, the saints "work powerfully in and through the grace of their one and common Lord" (McGuckin 2008: 364). If for the official Church the ritual is of pagan origins and therefore heretic in its essence, then it would be impossible for the two saints to intervene against God's will in order to bless and protect the participants. This theological idea contradicts the one propagated by the participants of the ritual; that is, the saints in effect act on their own accord, it is "their" ritual. One may appreciate the importance of the saints to the lives of Greek Christians. Once mortals, the saints were blessed by God due to their piety, faith, or martyrdom, earning a special place in the heavens. It is this previous state, that is, the mortal one that is of importance here. As Xygalatas puts it, the saints "have a more direct relationship with their devotees and most ritual practices are directed towards them" (Xygalatas 2012: 42), and it is common for Christians in Greece to appeal through prayers to the saints rather to God directly for their troubles and wishes. According to Barrett's theory, one may claim that people in Greece appeal to saints in their everyday activities precisely because those agents are closer to the people's intuitive knowledge. The saints, once mortals and thus with a biography that provides ample information to the believers, are more readily conceptualized as divine—that is, being transformed into something more than human than the more abstract trinitarian God—when it comes to rituals, divination, miracles, and intervention to everyday life. However, the official Church's position is explicit regarding the place, rank, and divine nature of the saints. Focusing on the importance of the two saints in the *Anastenaria* (ibid.: 49–60, 64–95), the participants seem to consider the saints more important than the official Church's dogma and teachings, which in turn leads to a different theological approach and belief than the one articulated by formal theology.

The question that arises after this brief detour is how one may apply such theories to our sources that deal with and refer to religious beliefs and practices related to the Greeks and the Romans. Barrett and Keil's observation that for some participants "God finished one task in order to engage with another" is not a nonreflective belief restricted to their interviewees and their religious/theological context. Rather, it is one that is encountered on several occasions in our sources, from Homer himself to daily religious conceptions and ideas. Especially in Homer one reads how misguided the human characters of the epics were about their gods overall—or what John Heath has described as Homer's "perfectly fallible gods":

> Homeric mortals, on the other hand, seem to assume that the gods know *everything*, including the future, *all the time*. And in this they are often proven wrong. Neither Zeus nor any other major god knows all—their "omniscience" is severely circumscribed by contextual demands. They know things when it is convenient for the story; they don't when it's important that they don't. As Paris and Menelaus prepare to duel, for example, Priam admits that he can't bear to watch, fearing for his son, and adds in typical Homeric fashion: "But Zeus no doubt knows this, and the other immortal gods, to which certain death is decreed" (3.308–9). As it turns out, the immortal gods don't know. It is only when Paris is about to be killed that Aphrodite rushes in to save him. (Heath 2019: 161; emphasis in original)

Similarly, Henk Versnel has offered a number of examples indicating the gods' rather perplexing powers for the Greeks:

> The Zeus of Hesiod's *Erga* 1–10 can do everything, see everything and know everything. The Zeus of *Il.* 14 does not know everything: he is deceived by Aphrodite. Yet she in turn is outmatched by him in the Hymn to Aphrodite with counter-deception. ... At one place Hesiod can tell how Zeus was

deceived by Prometheus, at another he can say that Zeus can never be deceived. The Zeus of Solon's Hymn to the Muses ... foresees and controls everything, eventually always punishing every sin. The Zeus of Solon's fourth fragment can*not* do everything he wishes. ... The Zeus of Aeschylus' *Oresteia* is the all-powerful supreme principle of justice, the Zeus of the *Prometheus Vinctus* is a pitiless and arbitrary tyrant. (Versnel 2011: 431; emphasis in original; cf. Heath 2019: 163–4 as well as Chaniotis 2017 and Larson 2016: 95–6)

For Versnel the explanation is rather straightforward: "Religious expression, especially of the type that we have been discussing, is mostly *unreflective*, very much gnomic, and with no deep interest in logical consistency" (Versnel 2011: 430; my emphasis). Naturally, this perspective allowed for a variety of responses by different agents and bodies once folk religiosity and "higher" theological ideas were at odds.

Perhaps the most known schematic presentation of the different theological ideas at play within Greek and Roman religion(s) was given by the Roman historian Varro (116–27 BCE), when he distinguished three forms of theology, as Augustine of Hippo (354–430 CE) informs us in his monumental *De civitate Dei* (6.5):

> [Varro's] own explanation runs as follows: "What they call 'mythical' is what is especially in use among the poets; 'physical' theology is used by the philosophers; and 'political' by ordinary citizens. In the first of these theologies are found many fictions unworthy of the dignity and nature of immortal beings. For, in this kind of theology one divinity [Minerva] was born from another's head, a second [Bacchus] from a thigh, a third [Pegasus] from drops of blood; some gods [for example, Mercury] were thieves, others [for example, Jupiter] adulterers, and still others [for example, Apollo] slaves of men, and in general deeds are attributed to gods which are not merely human but abnormal." (Trans. Zema and Walsh 1962)

Such a division was not unknown in Greek culture either. Rather, Poseidonius of Rhodes (c. 135–c. 51 BCE) had also laid out such a distinction:

> Those who handed down to us reverence (σεβασμόν) concerning the gods set it out for us through three forms (εἰδῶν), first that of "nature" (τοῦ φυσικοῦ), second that of "myth" (μυθικοῦ), and third that which has taken its evidence from the *nomoi*. The one of "nature" is taught by the philosophers, that of

"myth" by the poets, and that of *nomoi* is put together by each city. (Aëtius, *De placitis* 1.6.9; trans. Mikalson 2010: 17, n. 57)

Both Varro and Poseidonius partly recapitulate Herodotus's (c. 484–c. 425 BCE) famous observation regarding how the Greeks—and eventually the Romans as well—came to know and maintain their ideas about the gods: "And [it is Homer and Hesiod] who taught the Greeks of the descent of the gods, and gave to all their several names, and honours, and arts, and declared their outward forms" (Herodotus, *Histories* 2.53.2–3; trans. A. D. Godley, LOEB). However, the theology of the poets was from early on criticized despite its great popularity among people, most notably by the presocratic philosopher Xenophanes of Colophon (c. 570–c. 478 BCE), who in a known aphorism proclaimed:

Both Homer and Hesiod have ascribed to the gods all deeds which among men are matters of reproach and blame: thieving, adultery, and deceiving one another.... But mortals suppose that the gods are born, have human clothing, and voice, and bodily form. (Sextus Empiricus, *Adversus mathematicos* 9.193; Clement of Alexandria, *Stromateis* 5.109; trans. Curd 2011)

It appears that from early on one encountered a differentiation between ideas that most people held (due to the poets) and the reactions and alternative concepts offered by the intelligentsia of the time: in many respects, what we could readily classify as a dipole of folklore and "higher" theology. The former was outright anthropomorphic and therefore closer to intuitive knowledge, whereas the latter was deemed advanced, more abstract, and with more violations of human intuitive knowledge.[17]

This was further evident when philosophers and political authorities addressed the topic of epiphanies in the ancient world. An oft-appearing divine couple in both Greek and Roman religious history were Castor and Polux (the Dioskouri for the Greeks). Their epiphanies were common, and believers were quick to attest the gods' presence, power, and influence.[18] This did not, however, mean that every report was automatically taken at face value. Rather, skepticism was formally expressed by exponents of philosophical schools or by official bodies. For example, both Cicero and the historian Valerius Maximus (first century CE) inform their readers of a contested epiphany report that was eventually accepted after further proof was presented:

And in more modern history likewise these sons of Tyndareus brought the news of the defeat of Perses. What happened was that Publius Vatinius, the grandfather of our young contemporary, was returning to Rome by night from Reate, of which he was governor, when he was informed by two young warriors on white horses that King Perses had that very day been taken prisoner. When Vatinius carried the news to the Senate, at first he was flung into gaol on the charge of spreading an unfounded report on a matter of national concern; but afterwards a dispatch arrived from Paulus, and the date was found to tally, so the Senate bestowed upon Vatinius both a grant of land and exemption from military service. (Cicero, *De natura deorum* 2.6; trans. H. Rackham, LOEB; cf. Maximus Valerius, *Facta et Dicta Memorabilia*, where the author claims that Vatinius "thought" that the two young men who appeared to him were the divine twins)

In his *De natura deorum*, Cicero has the Academic representative Gaius Cotta questioning the gods' epiphany due to Vatinius's background, but also expanding further and offering a more general critique to popular beliefs about such phenomena *in toto*:

Then do you really think that the beings whom you call the sons of Tyndareus, that is mortal men of mortal parentage, and whom Homer, who lived not long after their period, states to have been buried at Sparta, came riding on white hacks with no retainers, and met Vatinius, and selected a rough countryman like him to whom to bring the news of a great national victory, instead of Marcus Cato, who was the chief senator at the time? Well then, do you also believe that the mark in the rock resembling a hoof-print, to be seen at the present day on the shore of Lake Regillus, was made by Castor's horse? Would you not prefer to believe the perfectly credible doctrine that the souls of famous men, like the sons of Tyndareus you speak of, are divine and live for ever, rather than that men who had been once for ail burnt on a funeral pyre were able to ride on horseback and fight in a battle? Or if you maintain that this was possible, then you have got to explain how it was possible, and not merely bring forward old wives' tales. (3.5; trans. H. Rackham, LOEB)[19]

It becomes therefore evident, I reckon, that Harrison's questions to Larson's position can be addressed not only through our sources themselves but also through theories such as the ones formulated by CSR. Harrison asks: "Were *all* the Greeks [and Romans] confident in, or giving credence to, their gods or myths? ... And did they do so consistently, or *all* of the time? And how is Greek [and Roman] 'belief' sustained?" Versnel's "unreflective religious expression" appears to be the key in approaching Harrison's valid skepticism. It seems that it was precisely the widely common practice to express opinions and beliefs about the gods without elaborate reflection that eventually urged both Varro and Poseidonius to distinguish between "low or folklore or popular" and "high or abstract or 'important'" religious ideas within both Greek and Roman discourses—or Cicero to address in a philosophical treatise the common phenomenon of divine epiphany. "Low" theological ideas, as I have attempted to sketch in this chapter, can be immensely benefited by Barrett's CSR theory, which takes concepts and notions more compatible to intuitive knowledge to be the most commonly held ones among people when they unreflectively respond to questions pertaining to their beliefs. "High" theological ideas, on the contrary, exemplified primarily by philosophers (and theologians) as well as institutional bodies influenced by the former, are the result of reflection since their premises require more counterintuitive abstractions for which people typically need more elaborate contemplation in order to master, recall, and maintain.

Given that my exposition here owes much to Larson's seminal work on CSR and Greek religion, I will conclude with her own response to Harrison's aporia, which also encapsulates: (1) the stagnancy of discourses claiming that "belief" is inapplicable to the study of Greek and Roman religion(s), and (2) the tendency to see such religions as somehow special and/or unique (to also recall my own criticism in Chapter 1, this volume). Instead of merely offering an individual hypothesis on such issues—which are usually addressed based on convictions long-held among scholars working solely within the limits of their disciplines—Larson: (1) calls for a new approach to traditional ideas based on new theories and findings from the interdisciplinary field of CSR, and (2) reminds us that such approach can only be materialized via the comparative lens:

> CSR is predicated on the idea that religious beliefs and behaviours have pan-human components shaped by our common mental architecture. Therefore, rigorous comparative work is methodologically feasible and (in my view) desirable. The exclusion of "belief" from Greek religion in favour of cult acts alone never made sense to me either. Humans do not function as mindless automata. ... We can question how widely certain beliefs were shared, with

what levels of confidence and conviction they were held, how they were formed, to what degree they were intuitive or reflective, and so on. But beliefs there were. (Larson 2017: 54)

Such new theorizing can indeed claim to offer a promising new approach to data, ideas, and hypotheses that it is time to be revised from more than one discipline—allowing us therefore to claim that an interdisciplinary study of Greek and Roman religion(s) has finally arrived.[20]

Appendix I

Re: Hesiod

Is it for these and such reasons that Hesiod was considered wise among the Greeks and in no way unworthy of that reputation, because he did not compose and sing his poems through human art, but because he had met the Muses and become their own pupil? As a result of this, whatever occurred to him, all of it he uttered musically and wisely, with nothing lacking purpose.
                                                    Dio Chrysostom (c. 40–c. 110 CE)[1]

For any student of ancient Greek religion, Hesiod's *Theogony* and *Works and Days* are among the first works to read. This is not due to some fixation with chronology given that the Hesiodic poems were compiled in the earliest times of Greek culture. Rather, the two works by the poet from Boeotia are considered, along with Homer's great epics, the quintessential sources of what we know about the Greek gods and the Greeks' ideas about the divine realm. Already from the fifth century BCE, as I argued in Chapter 6, Herodotus pointed out that the Greeks owed to both Hesiod and Homer all that they knew and maintained about their gods, and his diagnosis echoed the criticism of Hesiod and Homer by the presocratic philosopher Xenophanes of Colophon, who inveighed against the two epic poets. In both ancient criticisms the message is rather straightforward: the religious world of the Greeks was first and foremost informed by the great epic poems of the most widely acceptable figures among the Greeks—not simply due to the entertaining nature of their works but primarily due to the authority the Greeks assigned to their poets.[2]

The standard assessment of Hesiod's work has been uncomplicated (and traditionally unanimous among scholars and students of ancient Greek religion). The *Theogony* and *Works and Days*, just like the *Iliad* and the *Odyssey*, functioned as a pathway to early Greek theological conceptualizations, which in turn led to the formation and further development of the religious world of the Greeks:

> The *Theogony* recounts the genesis of the gods and the other eternal forces that regulate the cosmos; it culminates in the establishment of Zeus's order, henceforth permanent and unchanging, an order that encompasses both the brightness of Olympus above and murky Tartarus below. The *Works and Days* explores the character of human life as it has evolved and as it is now lived on earth under Zeus's dominion. ... The *Theogony*, authorised by the Muses, treats mankind from an Olympian perspective, while the *Works and Days* offers a terrestrial view of human life. ... As constructing his *Theogony* and his *Works and Days* as complementary visions of the cosmos, Hesiod reveals his ambition to encompass the whole that embraces the harsh realities of human life as well as the lovely songs of the Muses that make it bearable. (Strauss Clay 2003: 8, 99, 182)

There is hardly any scholar of ancient Greek religion that would disagree with the above description.[3] After all, and particularly regarding the *Theogony*, it is indeed the case that the vast majority of what we today know about the Greek gods and goddesses comes from the Hesiodic poem. From a study of religion point of view, therefore, one would anticipate that by dealing with the poem as a religious text—that is, as one that provides information about religious ideas and beliefs in relation to superhuman entities and agents and their place in the cosmos of a given culture or people—we could further advance to a better understanding of the Greek worldview at the time of Hesiod and the subsequent impact those texts had in the further development of what we today call Greek religion and its theology. This does not mean, however, that it is our duty as scholars of ancient religions to promote, propagate, or endorse such a religious text and its respective truth claims. As Bruce Lincoln has persuasively put it,

> [religious texts] connect themselves—either explicitly or in some indirect fashion—to a sphere and a knowledge of transcendent or metaphysical nature, which they purportedly mediate to mortal beings through processes such as revelation, inspiration, and unbroken primordial tradition. ... Scholars, however, ought not to replicate the stance of the faithful or adopt a fetishism at second hand. [Scholars need to] inquire about the human agencies responsible for the texts' production, reproduction, dissemination, consumption, and interpretation. (Lincoln 2012: 5)

This is a guideline that skillfully and aptly summarizes what a truly "critical" study of religion should entail, leading to tangible, stimulating, and appealing theories that offer points to ponder upon in regard to the religious ideas of the Greeks and the Romans—what in another, albeit different context has been called an attempt to "redescribe Graeco-Roman antiquity" (van den Heever 2005; cf. 2015). Instead of pausing here, however, I would like to turn my attention to another type of "critical" study of religion, which attempts to turn the tables, as it were, but without unfortunately offering any ideas of the sort that Lincoln advocates for or conforming with what is more than evident: that religious texts do exist and, despite the motivations of their author(s) (known or anonymous), these texts do have an impact in people's lives to the point of solidifying a religious tradition.

Such a "critical" study of religion is not by any stretch of the imagination free of ideological or other political agendas. My chosen example, which will be linked to Hesiod's poems to drive the point home, comes from Naomi Goldenberg and her approach to religion as a phenomenon across time and space. In an article that appeared in the *Journal of the British Association for the Study of Religion* in 2019, based on the keynote lecture she presented at the conference "Borders and Boundaries: 'Religion' on the Periphery" held at Queen's University Belfast in September 2018, Goldenberg from the outset informs her audience that "the deconstruction of religion and attendant categories in the subfield that some are calling 'critical religion' is crucial, I think, not only for improving academic analysis but also more broadly for promoting progressive politics. The subject fascinates me to the point of obsession" (Goldenberg 2019: 2). Despite sharing Goldenberg's aspiration to promote progressive politics, I lack her obsession—always a problematic trait in any theoretical endeavor, I would add—and I am first and foremost interested in proper academic analysis. Therefore, I turn to her own examination of Hesiod's *Theogony*, an excerpt worth citing in its entirety:

> I was struck by the transformation of the vile God Uranos in Hesiod's *Theogony*. After being castrated by his son Chronos, Uranos apparently reconciles with Gaia, who, in response to his cruelty toward their children, had commissioned his mutilation. In diminished form, Uranos morphs into a kindly yet distant wise counsellor. ... These are poetic (and, in a sense, patriotic) accounts of the succession of ruling orders in which a previous

government is moved away from the locus of contemporary power without being completely excised. That which was once truly supreme is now merely idealized. ... It is no coincidence that, in their new, largely symbolic role, these deities become supports for the regime that displaced them. ... I am not saying that the displacement and subsequent gestures of veneration toward Uranos ... [is an example] of the creation of "religion." Even though these sidelined powers are labeled deities and, in the latter example are accorded specific rites, the category of religion (as other than a set of ceremonial practices connected with government) had not yet entered history.[4] Hesiod [is] ... writing about the progression of governments. (ibid.: 6–7)

Although an interesting perspective, there is little data that can support Goldenberg's hypothesis in our corpus. The only manner such a hypothesis would be an operative one, I think, would be if we assume that Hesiod wrote not in the archaic age (800–500 BCE), but later, when indeed one encounters in Greek history a "progression of governments."[5] Goldenberg wishes to disperse with the possibility of "religion" as a category in Hesiod, just like she does for "religion" across time and space:

I argue that religions function as vestigial states composed of mutating institutions and ideologies that exist in relation to the dominant governing order that contains and defines them. Vestigial states are permitted some authority over particular behavioral or territorial jurisdictions pertaining to specific populations. (ibid.: 4)

Granted, this is indeed one way religions can function, and history is replete with such examples. However, to impose such a hypothesis to dead religions and, more so, to texts that belong in historical periods where organized religions did not exist so as to act as Goldenberg describes is a "critical" approach to ancient religions that takes its cue from modern religions. And in such way, Goldenberg's statement "the category of religion (as other than a set of ceremonial practices connected with government) had not yet entered history" becomes problematic, to say the least.[6]

Instead of adopting such a hypothesis, one may be more convinced by Armin Geertz's approach to religion as a category and phenomenon throughout history. In an article published in 1997, Geertz maintained that religious ideas are communicated through a number of media that include traditions, iconography, symbolisms, and (naturally) written sources. Such ideas, however, are typically propagated "in a typology of communication in terms of three main categories": cosmology, theology, anthropology. As Geertz went on to briefly explain: (1) cosmology contains ideas about how the world came to be, how it looks, what are its features, and who populates it; (2) theology promotes the ideas about gods, spirits, heroes, and other superhuman agents; and (3) anthropology discusses ideas about human beings, ranging from how they were created to their future here and after death (Geertz 1997: 40).

Hesiod's *Theogony* and *Works and Days* cover all of Geertz's three categories in detail and candidly so. Despite the plausibility or not of Goldenberg's approach, her "obsession" with doing away with "religion"—let alone with constantly avoiding to define her object of study altogether—remains a good example of a "critical" study of religion that is neither critical nor about religion.[7]

Appendix II

On Belief

Accomplishment is granted to the prayers of men in gratitude for their piety.
Pindar (c. 518–c. 438 BCE)[1]

A lot of ink has been spilled regarding whether "belief" (like, "religion" or "theology") is an applicable term for the study of Greek and Roman religion(s)—a question I discuss in Chapter 6 of this volume. And although one might think that the question has been settled after decades of debates, we are seemingly quite far from reaching an agreement. This became evident in a recent review panel of Jörg Rüpke's celebrated book *Pantheon: A New History of Roman Religion* (2018a), published in the journal *Religion in the Roman Empire* (vol. 4, no. 1) in 2018, with the participation of Jan Bremmer, Corinne Bonnet, Judith Lieu, and Zsuzsanna Várhelyi, followed by Rüpke's response. *Pantheon* is perhaps the best contemporary history of Roman religion by one of the most prominent specialists in the field, who has dedicated many years in formulating and promoting his approach called "Lived Ancient Religion" (LAR; see Chapter 2, this volume), around which *Pantheon* is built. Nevertheless, Bremmer's and Lieu's criticisms on the issue of "belief" in Roman religion, followed by Rüpke's response to them, are extremely interesting given that the debate demonstrates how much disagreement there is on whether scholars of ancient religions should use the term altogether—and an explicit indication that the debate is still ongoing.

Bremmer's overall positive assessment of Rüpke's hefty volume does not fail to indicate an astounding absence from the book: "The lack of attention to the gods and the absence of any discussion of belief make me wonder whether the LAR approach is not too much focused on action" (Bremmer 2018: 109). Similarly, Lieu's criticism turns to the problem of overlooking the need for a systematic study of gods as well as to the "problem" of belief: "At the same time [the volume] conspicuously follows that particular trend in the study of ancient religion that has consciously avoided exploring the phenomenon of 'belief'" (Lieu 2018: 120). What becomes clear from both Bremmer's and Lieu's criticisms is that, despite the detailed and overall magnificent work that Rüpke has conducted in his *Pantheon*, he has avoided (deliberately or not) to account for two pressing issues in the study of Roman (and Greek, one should here add) religion: defining and analyzing the gods as the quintessential agents in what we call "Greek and Roman religion(s)" more broadly, and settling the question of whether the Romans (and the Greeks, as one may justifiably argue) believed in their gods—a question reminiscent of Paul Veyne's influential *Did the Greeks Believe in Their Myths?* (1988).

Rüpke's long response to all four members of the panel deals with many themes, including the issues raised by Bremmer and Lieu on "belief." Rüpke's "solution," however, although interesting, seems somehow vague. The reader is informed that the manner the problem of belief is addressed is by replacing the term "belief" with that of "knowledge." It is worth citing this portion of Rüpke's response in length, since it manifests more than what meets the eye:

> This does not amount to a neglect of questions about the intellectual contents and framework of religious action and experience. Belief is represented by only two instances of *Glaubensbekenntnis* ("crede") in the index of the German version because I opted instead for the more neutral "knowledge," which has nineteen sub-entries with dozens of passages. Difficulties abound, however. For many periods and places, even the most basic assumptions are not attested and when they are attested, the correlation with specific practices is thin. Neither today nor for antiquity do burial practices, to take one example, say much about the ontological assumptions about the status of the deceased. (Rüpke 2018b: 148)

The conundrum is more than apparent: Rüpke has the same reservations as most (if not all) scholars working from primarily a classics or philological perspective, in which the dictum "when not in the sources, then avoid" has on numerous occasions restricted the possibility for a deeper theoretical reflection on the religion(s) of the Greeks and the Romans.

A list of works that specifically tackle the persisting problem of the place of "belief" in the study of Greek and Roman religion(s) is offered below.[2] Among them, a key role is played by works on the significance, centrality, and recently further examined category of divination, which was widely practiced in both cultures. Indubitably, this is not an exhaustive list; it rather serves as a mere starting point for the interested reader who has not been satisfied by the traditional view of the religion of the Greeks and the Romans as traditions that did not pay great attention to beliefs (to put it mildly).

***

Further Reading

Belief and Greek and Roman Religion(s)

Bowden, Hugh. 2019. "Believing in Oracles." In Anders Klostergaard Petersen, Ingvild Sælid Gilhus, Luther H. Martin, Jeppe Sinding Jensen, and Jesper Sørensen (eds.), *Evolution, Cognition, and the History of Religion: A New Synthesis. Festschrift in Honour of Armin W. Geertz*, 435–46. Leiden: Brill.

Champion, Craige B. 2017. *The Peace of the Gods: Elite Religious Practices in the Middle Roman Republic*. Princeton, NJ: Princeton University Press.

Chaniotis, Angelos. 2012. "Constructing the Fear of Gods: Epigraphic Evidence from Sanctuaries of Greece and Asia Minor." In Angelos Chaniotis (ed.), *Unveiling Emotions: Sources and Methods for the Study of Emotions in the Greek World*, 205–34. Stuttgart: Franz Steiner Verlag.

Collar, Anna. 2013. *Religious Networks in the Roman Empire: The Spread of New Ideas*. Cambridge: Cambridge University Press.

Dillon, Matthew. 2017. *Omens and Oracles: Divination in Ancient Greece*. London: Routledge.

Driediger-Murphy, Lindsay G. 2018. "'Do Not Examine but Believe': A Classicist's Perspective on Teresa Morgan's *Roman Faith and Christian Faith*." *Religious Studies* 54: 568–75.

Driediger-Murphy, Lindsay G. 2019. *Roman Republican Augury: Freedom and Control*. New York: Oxford University Press.

Driediger-Murphy, Lindsay G., and Esther Eidinow, eds. 2019. *Ancient Divination and Experience*. New York: Oxford University Press.

Eidinow, Eidinow. 2019. "The (Ancient Greek) Subject Supposed to Believe." *Numen* 66 (1): 56–88.

Harrison, Thomas. 2015. "Belief vs. Practice." In Esther Eidinow and Julia Kindt (eds.), *The Oxford Handbook of Ancient Greek Religion*, 21–8. New York: Oxford University Press.

Heineman, Kristin M. 2018. *The Decadence of Delphi: The Oracle in the Second Century AD and Beyond*. London: Routledge.

Johnston, Sarah Iles. 2018. *The Story of Myth*. Cambridge, MA: Harvard University Press.

Kindt, Julia. 2012. *Rethinking Greek Religion*. Cambridge: Cambridge University Press.

Kindt, Julia. 2016. *Revisiting Delphi: Religion and Storytelling in Ancient Greece*. Cambridge: Cambridge University Press.

King, Charles W. 2020. *The Ancient Roman Afterlife: Di Manes, Belief, and the Cult of the Dead*. Austin: University of Texas Press.

Mackey, Jacob L. 2017. "Das Erlöschen des Glaubens: The Fate of Belief in the Study of Roman Religion." *Phasis* 20: 83–150.

Morgan, Teresa. 2015. *Roman Faith and Christian Faith: Pistis and Fides in the Early Roman Empire and Early Churches*. Oxford: Oxford University Press.

Naiden, F. S. 2013. *Smoke Signals for the Gods: Ancient Greek Sacrifice from the Archaic Through Roman Periods*. New York: Oxford University Press.

Parker, Robert. 2011. *On Greek Religion*. Ithaca, NY: Cornell University Press.

Petrovic, Andrej, and Ivana Petrovic. 2016. *Inner Purity and Pollution in Greek Religion. Vol. 1: Early Greek Religion*. New York: Oxford University Press.

Pirenne-Delforge, Vinciane. 2020. *Le polythéisme Grec à l'épreuve d'Hérodote*. Paris: Les Belles Lettres, Collège de France.

Santangelo, Federico. 2013. *Divination, Prediction and the End of the Roman Republic*. Cambridge: Cambridge University Press.

Versnel, Henk S. 2011. *Coping with the Gods: Wayward Readings in Greek Theology*. Leiden: Brill.

Belief and the Study of Religion

Bivins, Jason C. 2016. "Belief." In Michael Stausberg and Steven Engler (eds.), *The Oxford Handbook of the Study of Religion*, 495–509. New York: Oxford University Press.

Blum, Jason N. 2018. "Belief: Problems and Pseudo-Problems." *Journal of the American Academy of Religion* 86 (3): 642–64.

Jensen, Jeppe Sinding. 2020. *What Is Religion?* 2nd ed. London: Routledge.

Martin, Craig. 2017. *A Critical Introduction to the Study of Religion*. 2nd ed. London: Routledge.

Palma, Anthony J., ed. 2019. *The Science of Religion: A Defence. Essays by Donald Wiebe*. Leiden: Brill.

Schilbrack, Kevin. 2014. *Philosophy and the Study of Religions*. Malden, MA: Wiley Blackwell.

Smith, Christian. 2017. *Religion: What Is It, How It Works, and Why It Matters*. Princeton: Princeton University Press.

Tweed, Thomas A. 2020. *Religion: A Very Short Introduction*. New York: Oxford University Press.

Appendix III

A Typology of Religions

Knowledge is of two kinds. We know a subject ourselves, or we know where we can find information upon it. When we enquire into any subject, the first thing we have to do is to know what books have treated of it. This leads us to look at catalogues, and at the backs of books in libraries.

James Boswell (1740–1795)[1]

In his latest book, *Unearthly Powers: Religious and Political Change in World History* (2019), Oxford University historian Alan Strathern attempts to investigate and explain how and why some, few religions have managed to be so dominant (e.g., Christianity, Islam, and Buddhism) on the global historical stage. In doing so, Strathern employs a typology of religions on the basis of which he unfolds his investigation. Given the scope of his work, Strathern is not interested that much in ancient Greece and Rome, although he draws on some examples from those cultures in order to further develop his broader comparative project. Nevertheless, his theoretical purview could be of great interest to specialists of Greek and Roman religion(s)—both scholars of religion and classicists and historians of antiquity—given that Strathern is drawing his data and theories from a number of scholarly fields (sociology, anthropology, history, study of religion, and more).

Contrary to what one might anticipate given the reluctance of most scholars to define religion as I have discussed in this book, Strathern is not shying away from formulating his own definition before proceeding with his comparative analysis. Religion, for him, is "that dimension of life which pertains to interactions with supernatural forces and metapersons" (Strathern 2019: 3, n. 5). The term "metapersons" is borrowed from the late Marshall Sahlins (1930–2021), who explained that he used the term, along with that of "metahumans," to describe "all those beings usually called 'spirits': including gods, ghosts, ancestors, demons, inua, and so on" (Sahlins 2017: 100)—an alternative to other prevalent terms among scholars of religion, such as "superhuman" or "supernatural" beings. Having delineated his definition of religion, Strathern advances by offering a typology of religions by identifying two prevailing types that he classifies as *immanentism* and *transcendentalism*. The former is based on the idea that "no society has lived without feeling these strange denizens [that is, the metapersons] moving amongst them," that is, such agents and forces are "potentially present—or 'immanent'—in the world and influencing it for the good or ill of human society" (ibid.: 4). The latter, on the contrary, is based on the idea that many religions, by and large, do not restrict themselves to the doings and influences of those metapersons in this world; rather, to a great extent, religions "push their conception of the sacred towards visions that are literally ineffable, transcending any capacity of the human mind to represent them" (ibid.: 5), with the aim of salvation. However, as he further qualifies his position, immanentism constitutes "a universal feature of religion, found in every society under the sun. Transcendentalism is not: it is rather the consequence of a series of intellectual revolutions that took place in particular parts of Eurasia in what has been called the 'Axial Age' of human history" (ibid.: 7).[2]

Addressing the validity of Strathern's typology would require a rather long exposition. What is of interest to the student of Greek and Roman religion(s), however, are the traits he identifies as being characteristic of each type—and even more so those of immanentism, to which Greek and Roman religions seem or have been argued to belong.

Immanentism

1. Attribution of agency in primarily an anthropomorphic form.
2. A cosmological conceptualization that focuses on "this" world.
3. A loose, superficial, or even unconcerned interest for what happens after death.
4. Religious thinking is almost exclusively interested in the here and now.[3]
5. Morality is relative, unsystematic, and restricted to small-scale groups.

6. Gods and other metahuman agents are not measured in terms of ethics but of power.
7. The success of religious activities (rituals, rites, etc.) determines their longevity.
8. Authoritative positions are essentially lacking.
9. Religious identity, thinking, and analysis are neither central nor instrumental to the success or continuation of a religion system.
10. Religious ideas, practices, and notions are characterized by plasticity rather than solidity (ibid.: 29–46).

Transcendentalism

1. The transcendent is qualitatively superior to the mundane.
2. Escapism and eventual salvation are identified as the end goal.
3. Ethics in the form of good/evil becomes central.
4. Ethical principles are informed by the transcendent.
5. Individualization replaces the communal.
6. Alternative visions of reality become dominant and more truthful.
7. Authority (in the form of scripture) and revelation take central stage.
8. Belief in the form of faith becomes the normative religious expression and verification.
9. Moral communities and an ideology of "specialness" place religious identity to the fore.
10. Small-scale groupings are extended on the basis of universalist creeds.
11. Metapersons are either demoted in favor of or elevated into a monotheistic hegemony.
12. Magic becomes problematic due to its non-soteriological nature.
13. Clergy and priesthood become powerful and influential institutions.
14. Religion becomes anti-political, and only later on is anew linked to the political arena.
15. When religion diminishes, it strikes back via reform to reestablish its priority (ibid.: 48–81).

Strathern's discussion offers an interesting turn when he argues that "transcendentalist traditions always form amalgams with immanentism" (ibid.: 84) for four reasons: (1) the transcendent requires the mundane world in order to be conceptualized, argued about, and disseminated; (2) our tendency to anthropomorphize[4] remains at place despite transcendentalism's thirst for overcoming the material and human world; (3) in defiance of transcendentalism's rejection of this world, transcendentalist religions eventually turn their full attention to this-worldly institutions and principles (family, cultural identities, etc.); and (4) in order to succeed and ultimately win, transcendentalists need to cope with, argue against, and mingle with immanentism's rigid ideas and long-established principles and traditions (ibid.: 84–7).

It is of value, in my view, to cite Strathern's words in relation to Greek religion, where he argues that within Greek culture one may encounter such an early amalgam, a position that surely offers food for thought:

> Indeed, let us consider the case of ancient Greece. What happens to a religious field that is not itself wholly restructured according to transcendentalism but yet sits within a society in which intellectuals have laid everything open to searching criticism, exhibiting some of the most impressive feats of second-order thinking and explicit debate? The result is an unmistakable distance that starts to open up between these elites and their religious inheritance—and it is surely worth pausing on the fact that it was often the *immanentist* qualities to the gods, their anthropomorphic features, or their amorality, for instance, that troubled various Greek thinkers. If gods fight battles, can they be wounded? Were cult statues instantiations of gods or representations of them? Did sacrifice as some sort of commercial exchange make any sense? Secular models of reality that simply left the gods out of the picture could be constructed; outright materialism asserted; idolatry mocked; tragic and comic poets could underline the perversity and unfathomableness of divine behaviour; and little bubbles of proto-transcendentalism could emerge, destined eventually to slip into the Christian tradition itself. (ibid.: 66)

Strathern's views anticipate a deeper examination, a dialogue between classicists, historians, theologians, scholars of religion, and other specialists, with the aim of reapproaching the Greek (as well as Roman) religious world by combining our data with theories and insights from a broader spectrum of disciplines.

Notes

Chapter 1

1. "Semper ego auditor tantum? numquamne reponam vexatus totiens rauci Theseide Cordi?" *Satires* 1.1–2 (trans. G. G. Ramsay, LOEB).
2. For an up-to-date discussion on the usage of the comparative method specifically in the study of religions, see Hughes (2017); Lincoln (2018); Freiberger (2019).
3. E.g., see the following publications which offer many cross-references to the broader debate about the future of classics (and of the humanities at large): Beard (2012); Fagan (2013); van Bommel (2016); Morley (2018); Stover (2018).
4. A quick search online will reveal a number of short and long publications dealing with this surprising, for many, move by Oxford, with many media voicing their disagreement with or outright anger for such a decision. E.g.: "Homer Phobia? Oxford Considers Making Iliad Optional." *The Times*, February 20, 2020: https://www.thetimes.co.uk/article/homer-phobia-oxford-considers-making-iliad-optional-shj7lr6zg (accessed: March 3, 2020); "Oxford Is in Danger of Making an Epic Mistake." *The Spectator*, February 20, 2020: https://www.spectator.co.uk/article/oxford-is-in-danger-of-making-an-epic-mistake (accessed: March 3, 2020); "Bis interimitur qui suis armis perit: It's Not All Greek to Oxford Classicists." *The Critic*, February 21, 2020: https://thecritic.co.uk/bis-interimitur-qui-suis-armis-perit/ (accessed: March 5, 2020); "'Fatal Mistake': Oxford Classics Department Considers Removing Homer and Virgil from Syllabus." *Washington Examiner*, February 19, 2020: https://www.washingtonexaminer.com/news/fatal-mistake-oxford-classics-department-considers-removing-homer-and-virgil-from-syllabus (accessed: March 5, 2020).
5. On Princeton's decision, see "Statement to Community—Undergraduate Concentration." *Princeton Classics*, June 1, 2021: https://classics.princeton.edu/department/news/statement-community-undergraduate-concentration (accessed: October 26, 2021). On reactions with a number of additional online resources cited therein, see "The Study of Classics Is Changing." *Inside Higher Ed*, June 15, 2021: https://www.insidehighered.com/views/2021/06/15/why-and-how-study-classics-changing-opinion (accessed: October 26, 2021). On the decision by Howard University to remove classics from its curriculum, see the passionate reply by Cornel West and Jeremy Tate "Howard University's

Removal of Classics Is a Spiritual Catastrophe." *Washington Post*, April 19, 2021: https://www.washingtonpost.com/opinions/2021/04/19/cornel-west-howard-classics/ (accessed: July 2, 2021). On a debate on how classics should be transformed (or, otherwise, perish, as the argument goes), see Johanna Hanink's vehement opinion in "A New Path of Classics." *Chronicle of Higher Education*, February 11, 2021: https://www.chronicle.com/article/if-classics-doesnt-change-let-it-burn (accessed: August 14, 2021); and the reply by James Kierstead "No, Classics Shouldn't 'Burn.'" *Chronicle of Higher Education*, February 23, 2021: https://www.chronicle.com/article/no-classics-shouldnt-burn?cid=gen_sign_in (accessed: August 14, 2021).

6 Quite surprising perhaps is the fact that theology is also seen as a field from which classics—when it comes to the study of Greek and Roman religions—has struggled to detach itself. This is briefly discussed in The Postclassicisms Collective (2020: 82–99). About the Collective, comprising nine classicists, which describes itself as a "network dedicated to redefining the study of classical antiquity," see http://www.postclassicisms.org (accessed: September 17, 2021).

7 For a discussion about the nature of the field one does not need to look deep into the nineteenth century. On the contrary, one may simply turn toward the very recent debate between Donald Wiebe (2020) and Satoko Fujiwara and Tim Jensen (2020) about the naming of the largest academic association devoted to the study of religions, the International Association for the History of Religions (IAHR).

8 Two very recent publications that stress the dichotomy between the study of religion and theology, thereby indicating the still prevalent disciplinary struggles, are Wiebe (2019) and Hughes (2020). Wiebe, along with Luther H. Martin, have repeatedly called for a nontheological scientific study of religion. It is worth examining the various essays and debates in Martin and Wiebe (2016), a publication that acts as a great summary of the inner struggles the study of religion has been facing in regard to its place in the modern university, its methods, and its theories.

9 Apart from the two works cited here, it is of interest to examine how scholars of the "caretaker" bend, as it were, have kept returning to McCutcheon's thesis, without nevertheless avoiding his reaction. E.g., see Slater (2007) as well as the exchange between Atalia Omer (2011) and McCutcheon (2012).

10 What I am arguing here is not by any means restricted to the study of Greek and Roman antiquity. In the *Companion to Religion in Late Antiquity*, which as so many other Companions—see more on this in Chapter 2—functions as the state of the art in its respective field, Thomas E. Hunt (2018) takes Smith, Nongbri, and other similarly-minded scholars as *the* (and only) proper theoreticians in his own analysis of the term "religion" along with his discussion of the classification "Late Antiquity." Thus, and not surprisingly, a group of "anticipated" names figure

prominently: Tomoko Masuzawa, Daniel Dubuisson, Timothy Fitzgerald, Michel de Certeau, Edward Said, Michel Foucault, Talal Asad, and David Chidester among others.

11 Although, as it will become evident, I shall not shy away from formulating various hypotheses and promoting my own views on what "Greek and Roman religion(s)" is or should be.

12 E.g., see Müller (1878: 190; emphasis in original): "In translating the hymns of the Vedas we always translate *deva* by *deus*, or by god, we should sometimes commit a mental anachronism of a thousand years." Similarly, as Arie L. Molendijk (2016: 96) has indicated,

> crucial to the whole programme of the *Sacred Books of the East* is the idea of translation. Therefore, it is no coincidence that Müller devoted a large part of the preface to the series as a whole to the character of the original texts and to the question how to translate these in a proper way. [In the initial volume of *SBE*, the *The Upanishads*, Müller] formulated three "cautions," the first concerning the character of the translated texts, the second with regard to the "difficulties making a proper use of translations," and the third about the possibilities and impossibilities of rendering "ancient thought into modern speech."

Cf. Martin (2019: 418, n. 16).

Chapter 2

1 *Rhetoric* 1354a.2 (trans. J. H. Fresse, LOEB).
2 Along with his colleagues, Thonemann has also studied the issue of gender bias in the *Journal of Roman Studies*, one of the flagship classics journals, covering the period 2005–2019. See Kelly et al. (2019).
3 https://global.oup.com/academic/content/series/o/oxford-handbooks-ohbk/?cc=gr&lang=en& (accessed: May 11, 2020); my emphasis.
4 https://www.cambridge.org/ar/academic/cambridge-companions (accessed: May 11, 2020); my emphasis.
5 There are different issues that arise from the extensive and excessive production of Companions and Handbooks, and scholars have occasionally pointed them out. E.g., in 2009, the then president of the American Philological Association (APA) Josiah Ober drew the attention of the association's members to the pitfalls of such trend. His preoccupation was targeted against three main aspects: the profit-driven view of such multi-authored volumes by major publishers in the field; the concern that scholars tend to dedicate their energy to such survey-based works, thus dedicating less time and energy into more groundbreaking projects; and the

"conventional" and "predefined" structure and topic/chapter-choice of such multi-authored works, leaving little space to scholars to expand into more productive areas. See Ober (2009). Ober's first preoccupation becomes especially apparent in Daniel Ogden's (2007) introductory chapter of his edited volume *A Companion to Greek Religion* (see later). In justifying the absence of an entry/survey on "Myth"—the importance of which for the study of ancient Greek religion is not debatable (see n. 9)—Ogden diverts the reader to another Companion, indicating thus that Ober's observation seems to be utterly accurate: "The subject of myth, whilst not addressed head-on here (see Ken Dowden's forthcoming *Companion to Classical Myth* in the same series [eventually published in 2011 and co-edited by the late Niall Livingstone]), nonetheless pervades the volume" (Ogden 2007: 2).

6 E.g., see Donald Wiebe's (2020: 11–36) as well as Robert Segal's (2021: xi–xvi) discussions on the issue.

7 Although not addressed here, an additional problem with publications of this kind seems to be that of language—i.e., they are primarily published in English, utilizing only (or largely) literature written in English, and therefore restricting the scope of scholarship available in a given field (including that of ancient religions in general, and Greek and Roman religions in particular). See Rubel (2019).

8 Another volume that I deliberately left out is the influential Johnston (2004), since it is more than merely a "Companion," including sections dedicated to the history of different cultures and geographical areas.

9 E.g., see Wiseman (2004); Dench (2005); Clark (2012); Edmunds (2014 and 2021). The choice of merely four volumes is not due to some hidden agenda but, rather, these are, to my knowledge, the only ones specifically dedicated to the study of Greek and Roman religion(s).

10 Bremmer studied classics and Spanish, received his PhD in 1979 with a dissertation on "The Early Greek Conception of the Soul" (subsequently published by Princeton University Press in 1983), and taught ancient history at the University of Utrecht for sixteen years (1974–1990) before moving to Groningen University as chair in religious studies in 1990. Despite her title (Professeur émérite d'histoire des religions à l'Université Marc-Bloch de Strasbourg), Dunand is an Egyptologist and archaeologist. In other words, both Bremmer and Dunand are historians of specific religions (and, thus, particularists in their approach to "religion") rather than scholars of the study of religion, while neither has published any work on the study of religion as a cross-cultural phenomenon from a theoretical and methodological point of view—at least none to my knowledge.

11 The added emphasis is not accidental. Dickie seems to be noting the lack of consensus regarding the definition of "religion" in general but proceeds with his suggestion of using the term despite this obvious hurdle.

12 I address the issue of "belief" in Chapter 6 and Appendix II.

13 For the reader interested in the field of material (or materiality of) religion, with a far more theoretical background, see Plate (2015) and Chidester (2018).
14 See the project's research outcomes as published on the European Commission's "CORDIS EU Research Results" platform at https://cordis.europa.eu/project/id/295555/results (accessed: September 11, 2020).
15 Rüpke has been a prolific author. Perhaps the best summarization of his conceptualization of how scholars should approach Roman (as well as other ancient) religion is to be found in Rüpke (2021)—which, despite its title, does not essentially address some of the most persisting issues. But it does offer a straightforward definition of religion, for which Rüpke is to be commended: "Hence, I define *religion in a specific moment and situation as the enlargement of the environment that is judged to be relevant by the introduction of one or several additional actors from beyond the unquestionably plausible social environment* of co-existing human beings in communication with one another (and hence observable by one another)" (2021: 43; emphasis in original).
16 Concerning the framework of Rüpke's project, see Albrecht et al. (2018).
17 It is inexplicable why Brent Nongbri's *Before Religion*, published two years before the Handbook, is not mentioned by any of the contributors. See Nongbri (2013). Cf. more recently, Barton and Boyarin (2016).
18 See Tylor (1871) and Durkheim (1995). On a discussion of Tylor's and Durkheim's influential as well as controversial definitions of religion and their importance, see Saler (2000: 71–3, 88–93) and Strenski (2015: 45–54, 129–41).
19 This latter point has been examined in a very appealing manner—and not restricted to the humanities—by Brecher and Trowler (2001). On the value of the comparative method but restricted in the study of Greek and Roman myth specifically, see the succinct but excellent Johnston (2017).
20 There is a plethora of works minutely discussing the ways disciplinary boundaries were formed in the modern university. Indicatively (and related primarily to the humanities and liberal arts): Bod (2013); Turner (2014); Podoksik (2020); Conybeare and Goldhill (2021b).
21 Billings (2014: 232). On the problem of what is (or whether we are in the right to talk about) the concept of the "classical," see Porter (2005).
22 E.g., the excerpt taken from Billings begins with the following sentence: "Classicists today are much more the descendants of Wilamowitz than of Nietzsche—and could not be otherwise" (Billings 2014: 232). Wilamowitz and Nietzsche represent two distinct approaches to the ancient world, also exemplified in the notorious debates between the two leading thinkers. For an overview with further bibliographical suggestions and interesting analyses, see: Lloyd-Jones (1982); Porter (2000); Ungefehr-Kortus (2006); Norton (2008); Reitz (2020). Cf. Güthenke (2020: 162–93).

23 The need to continue and, as it were, build on Wilamowitz's work was eloquently presented by Robert Fowler (1986: 71): "That kind of *Totalitätsideal* seems worth imitating; indeed, I should argue that it is necessary. Our task of keeping the classical heritage alive presumes that we keep the classical world's unity intact, so that it can continue to exert influence on the modern world. It cannot do so if it is reduced to fragments by its interpreters." (Cf. Fowler [2009] for a more thorough analysis.) William M. Calder is perhaps the most renowned supporter of Wilamowitz's work, having dedicated most of his career in rejuvenating the value of Wilamowitz's work for modern scholarship. E.g., see Calder (1998). Yet, Calder's work has not always been received positively—as is often the case in scholarship (cf. Chapter 1, this volume). As Hugh Lloyd-Jones (1986: 295) once put it, "we must be grateful to W. M. Calder III for the energy he has shown in collecting and publishing documents relative to W[ilamowitz], many of which are valuable. But we are less grateful for his own attempts to interpret their significance."
24 Bristol Classics Hub, University of Bristol, UK: https://www.bristol.ac.uk/classics/hub/what-is-classics/ (accessed: November 10, 2020).
25 Classical studies, Boston College, MA: https://www.bc.edu/bc-web/schools/mcas/departments/classics/what-is-classics.html (accessed: November 10, 2020).
26 Department of Classics, University of Kansas, USA: https://classics.ku.edu/what-classics (accessed: November 10, 2020).
27 Department of Classics, University of Buffalo, NY: https://arts-sciences.buffalo.edu/classics/about/what-is-classics.html (accessed: November 10, 2020).
28 From J. G. Droysen's (1808–1884) "Hellenistic Period" to Peter Brown's (b. 1935) "Late Antiquity," antiquity was never, and should not be, confined within particular historical limits as if a self-evident periodization is at play. E.g., see Martin (1987: 3–15); cf. Brown (1971).
29 E.g., see Ackerman (1978), especially letter VI.
30 On the myth and ritual theory and the Cambridge School, see Segal (1998).
31 On Murray's influence on classicists, see Stray (2007).
32 Cited in Wheeler-Barclay (2010: 215). On Wilamowitz versus the "Cambridge Ritualists," see Konaris (2016: 195–265).
33 See Momigliano (1982: 57–58). Cf. the short but very informative discussion of Wilamowitz's view of the gods in Bremmer (2010: 7–10). On Wilamowitz's "aristocratic" background and outlook, along with a set of excellent papers on his life and work, see Calder, Flashar, and Lindken (1985).
34 The Postclassicisms Collective (2020).
35 Hanink (2020).
36 Luttwak (2020).
37 Morales (2020).

38 Kessler (2020); emphasis in original.
39 See, e.g., Rutherford (2005: 16).
40 As one of the four anonymous reviewers of the proposal of the book at hand disapproved, "the problem may come from using 'companions and handbooks to ancient religions' as the source material instead of delving into the literature written for specialists." This is definitely a valuable criticism, but it is worth pointing out that Companions and Handbooks are far more influential across disciplines than more specialized literature. E.g., Paul Michael Kurtz, research fellow at Ghent University, Belgium, asked the following question on Twitter on September 3, 2020: "Do people actually read Oxford Handbooks and Cambridge Companions, or is my summerly labor entirely in vain?" The response included 377 replies, 74 retweets, and 1,855 likes (as of November 15, 2020). Not surprisingly, almost all replies were positive, with many respondents pointing out that such publications constitute their only contact with disciplines other than their own. E.g.: "Yes. Otherwise I would know nothing outside my own discipline and training"; "Such an important question. I think yes. Mostly grad students trying to get a glimpse at the questions asked and not asked"; "Speaking as an academic librarian, both the print and online are used heavily in libraries by students. Especially for survey courses. I consult them frequently for bibliography work"; "Yes, I use them to learn about other fields"; "All the time for teaching!"; "And just today my scholarship is helped on greatly by a Blackwell Companion in a field I know nothing about!"; "Yes, love them, for teaching & getting a handle on a new area"; "I find them very useful for teaching, but also as a starting point for new topics." I could go on, but I think that these representative answers drive my point home. See Kurtz (2020).

Chapter 3

1 "Nihil itaque absurdius, quam Auctoris judicium explodere, quia sequitur receptos sui temporis et populi mores." The quote is found in *Q. Curtius in integrum restitutus et vindicatus* (1703: 51).Translation drawn from Grafton (2007: 16).
2 For Jonathan Z. Smith's influential approach pertaining to the very category "religion," see primarily Smith J. Z. (1998); cf. Smith J. Z. (1982: xi). Concerning the abandonment of the term altogether, the commonly invoked work is Fitzgerald (2000), which was further elaborated in Fitzgerald (2007). On the modern, Western, Christian origins of the category "religion," see, among others, Asad (1993); Dubuisson (2003 and 2019); Masuzawa (2005).
3 For an interesting (but not throughout fruitful) discussion of Smith's book, see Talal Asad's assessment a year after Smith's passing, which he deems a

"masterpiece" and one that he regards to be an "indispensable reading for any student of comparative religion" (Asad 2001: 206).

4   For a discussion and criticism of Smith's positions from a social-scientific perspective and the academic study of religion, see Segal (2017). Segal's paper is found in a volume dedicated to Cantwell Smith's legacy, in which the tension between assessments of Smith's work from a theological versus study of religion/comparative religion stance is quite evident. E.g., see James L. Cox's informative words:

> Among the contributors to this book an inevitable unease can be found between those who represent theological disciplines, or are at least highly sympathetic to theology, and those who can be classified as scholars in comparative religion. The tension between theology and the science of religion found in this volume reflects Cantwell Smith's own awareness of the potential conflict between theological and empirical approaches. (Cox 2018: 602)

5   An interesting read on this topic is Elliott (2014).
6   Although the book is presented as co-authored, Barton and Boyarin indicate in the opening of the volume that it is virtually written independently: "This book is written in one scholarly voice but two authorial voices. Hence, we have chosen to write in the first-person singular throughout" (Barton and Boyarin 2016: ix). In practice, this means that the first part of the volume dedicated to the study of the Latin *religio* is penned by Barton, with the second part on the Greek *thrēskeia* by Boyarin.
7   The argument has become normative among religious studies scholars. E.g., see Kippenberg (2002) and Stroumsa (2010).
8   On *religio*, apart from the aforementioned works by Nongbri and Barton and Boyarin, one may consult Bremmer (1998) and Casadio (2010), which offer substantive bibliographical references for further reading. Equally well-informed are Scheid (2003) and Erker (2008). Cf. Despland and Vallée (1992); Feil (1986/2012).
9   *Thrēskeia* is the term still being used in modern Greek. E.g., the Greek Constitution, in Section 2, Article 3, which determines the relationship between State and Church, states:

> The prevailing religion [*thrēskeía*] in Greece is that of the Eastern Orthodox Church of Christ. The Orthodox Church of Greece, acknowledging our Lord Jesus Christ as its head, is inseparably united in doctrine with the Great Church of Christ in Constantinople and with every other Church of Christ of the same doctrine, observing unwaveringly, as they do, the holy apostolic and synodal canons and sacred traditions.

The English translation of the Greek Constitution can be found at http://www.hri.org/docs/syntagma/ (accessed: September 6, 2019).

10 Boyarin (2017: 18). The family-resemblance style mapping mentioned here refers to Ludwig Wittgenstein's (1889–1951) famous philosophical idea as formulated in his posthumously published *Philosophische Untersuchungen* (1953). The core of his theory maintains that a concept—for some, all concepts—is not restricted by a closed set of necessary and sufficient properties but it is rather open-ended in regard to its identifying features. Wittgenstein famously used the concept of "games" to explicate his idea.

11 A point made on good grounds in Morley (2004: 26).

12 It does not strike me that Boyarin, currently the Hermann P. and Sophia Taubman Professor of Talmudic Culture (emeritus) in the Department of Near Eastern Studies at Berkeley, dedicates the largest part of his discussion on Josephus, a first-century CE Jewish author. Expectedly so, he is far more confident working on Josephus given his specialization. Writing about and within a completely different cultural milieu than Herodotus, Plutarch, and other sources I will be discussing later, Josephus's assessment is rather problematic to me. I am not here interested in how the term was used outside its immediate linguistic and religious matrix, and thus I do not examine the Christian usage of the term either—on which Nongbri's work is very informative and rich in suggesting further readings to the interested reader.

13 This is not new. The same argument was made by Joseph C. A. van Herten (1934) almost ninety years ago, but without the polemical attitude that Boyarin employs here.

14 See Plutarch, *Consolatio ad Uxorem* 611D-E: "I know that you are better grounded in the doctrines delivered down to us from our ancestors, as also in the sacred mysteries of Bacchus, than to believe such stories; for the religious symbols are well known to us who are of the fraternity" (trans. W. W. Goodwin, LOEB).

15 For a good overview on Plutarch's views on religion, theology, and the so-called mystery cults, see Hirsch-Luipold (2021) (and especially p. 11, n. 3 for further references).

16 For a systematic examination of the inscription, see Lombardi (2013).

17 On superstition, see Martin (2004), which contains a plethora of examples on the similarly difficult conceptual content of the term in antiquity.

18 Pantelis Nigdelis has attempted a reconstruction of the inscription as follows: "[He fulfilled] comprehensively everything pertaining to the *thrēskeia* of the goddess [of himself])." In his view, the referred goddess is Hestia. See Nigdelis 1990: 171, n. 56 (my translation).

19 There are other inscriptions that corroborate what the two cases examined here demonstrate. E.g., see *IG* V, 2 268 (Mantinea, 10 BCE–10 CE); *IG* VII

3430 (Chaironeia, Roman period); *FD* III 4: 286 (Delphi, 52 CE); *IG* V,2 517 (Lykosoura, late second/early third century CE).

20 A good example to ponder upon is the Church of Scientology. As per the organization's website, "Scientology is *a religion* that offers a precise path leading to a complete and certain understanding of one's true spiritual nature and one's relationship to self, family, groups, Mankind, all life forms, the material universe, the spiritual universe and the Supreme Being." See https://www.scientology.org/what-is-scientology/#slide4, (accessed: May 25, 2019; my emphasis). However, in a survey conducted by CBS news and published in 2012, "70 percent of Americans say that Scientology is not a true religion; 13 percent believe it is; and 18 percent either don't know or don't care." One should pay attention to the articulation here. The vast majority does not deem Scientology a "true" religion—without further elaborating on what makes a religion a *true* one. Even those who do accept that Scientology is a religion, one could argue, perhaps do not necessarily deem it as "pristine," "unique," "fundamental," etc., as their own religion. See Groh (2012).

21 Needless to say that such a Protestant-centric definition of religion does not register well within other Christian denominations (i.e., Eastern Orthodox, Roman Catholic, etc.) or within non-Christian religions altogether—let alone outside the North American context with its very short and overall less complicated historical past.

22 See Klostergaard Petersen (2017a); Berzon (2018: 148–9).

23 Indicatively, see McCutcheon (2003 and 2015).

24 For another Homeric example of a detailed animal sacrifice, involving gods, see *Odyssey* 3.430–63. Works on Greek *thysia* (or *thusia*) abound. E.g., see Rives (2011) and Naiden (2013), which contain a plethora of bibliographical references. The issue of sacrifice (*sacrificium*) and its importance in Roman religion has received equal attention. Indicatively, see Scheid (2012) and Schultz (2016), whereas Beard, North, and Price (1998) contains numerous examples of sacrifices (see pp. 148–65). On theorizing about sacrifice, see the indispensable Hamerton-Kelly (1987); cf. Graf (2012) as well as Strenski (2003). It goes without saying that general theories of sacrifice go back at least to the nineteenth century, and more particularly in the works of E. B. Tylor (1832–1917), William Robertson Smith (1846–1894), J. G. Frazer (1854–1941), and Marcel Mauss (1872–1950), among others.

25 I leave these questions open here, but I will return to them in Chapter 5, albeit indirectly. However, on ancient Greek oaths and the rewards and punishments related to a truthful or fake oath, see Sommerstein and Torrance (2014).

26 Mircea Eliade (1907–1986) famously argued that a

religious phenomenon will only be recognised as such if it is grasped at its own level, that is to say, if it is studied *as* something religious. To try to grasp the essence of such a phenomenon by means of physiology, psychology, sociology, economics, linguistics, art or any other study is false; it misses the one unique and irreducible element in it—the element of the sacred. (Eliade 1963: xiii; emphasis in original)

E.g., see the criticism in McCutcheon (1997) and Ambasciano (2019), as well as Allen (2002) for a very substantial discussion of Eliade's overall work.
27 See Segal (2016) and Nongbri (2017).
28 On "magic" and the ancient world, see the discussions in Frankfurter (2019).

Chapter 4

1 Pope (1711: 21).
2 de Jaucourt (1765: 83).
3 There are numerous works addressing the comparative method in the study of religion. E.g.: Smith (1982 and 1990); Idinopulos, Wilson, and Hanges (2006); and Mancini (2007) for some general views. Also see Borgeaud (2009); van der Veer (2016); Candea (2019); Gagné, Goldhill, and Lloyd (2019). Cf. Chapter 1 (this volume), n. 2.
4 This, of course, is not the only case of such a differences-only comparativism. The example par excellence of such a practice is the centuries-old attempt of Christianity to separate and distance itself from its own "religious past," that is, Judaism. Scholars have pointed out that such a separation is nothing more than a mere artificial one aiming at no other than identity formation processes, and they have demonstrated that the argued chasm is not that evident after all. See Becker and Reed (2007) for a representative example.
5 The aforementioned and other similar examples are conveniently amassed in Morley (2000: 123–30), from where I am quoting. For more details of the original publications, the reader is invited to check Morley's work.
6 Cf. Chapter 3, this volume.
7 There are numerous works discussing the problem of defining religion. E.g., see Clarke and Byrne (1993); Idinopulos and Wilson (1998); Platvoet and Molendijk (1999); Saler (2000); Stausberg (2012); Stausberg and Gardiner (2016); Meylan (2019).
8 The literature on these topics is massive, but for the interested reader, see Gee (2020) and King (2020) (on afterlife); Bodel and Olyan (2008) (on household traditions); Larson (2001) (on nymphs); Jones (2010) (on heroes) and Lyons (1997) (on heroines); Driediger-Murphy (2019) and Driediger-Murphy and Eidinow (2019)

(on divination and auspices); Bulloch et al. (1993) and Cole (2013) (on deification of kings and emperors); Frankfurter (2019) and Watson (2019) (on magic).

9 E.g., see Bruce (2011) and Jensen (2020: 6–7).

10 This definition was also endorsed by the always skeptical Jonathan Z. Smith. See Braun and McCutcheon (2018: 52), although not without some reservations (e.g., see p. 31 in the same work).

11 Tweed has offered his own definition in the past, which he repeats and further analyzes in this latest book (Tweed 2020: 11–18).

12 E.g., see Martin (2017); Goldenberg (2018); McCutcheon (2018).

13 One should here mention Pals (2015) and Strenski (2015), both discussing the value of such endeavors, as well as Schewel (2017).

14 See, among others, Kunin (2006); Segal (2010); Pals (2015); Strenski (2015).

15 Another general theory of religion was formulated by Democritus of Abdera (c. 460–c. 370 BCE). Democritus assigned the origins of religion as belief in gods to the feelings of awe and fear experienced by humans in the face of terrifying natural phenomena (such as thunder, lightning, the movement of celestial objects, etc.) (Sextus Empiricus, *Adversus Mathematicos* 9.24). That being so, the function of religion for Democritus was about explaining the natural world.

16 The highly praised Whitmarsh (2015) is the latest example of such a take on the Sisyphus fragment.

17 Referring to Julius Caesar's *De bello Gallico* and Tacitus' *Germania*. On Herodotus, see Harrison (2002); Mikalson (2012); Roubekas (2019a). On ancient ethnography, see Skinner (2012); Almagor and Skinner (2013).

18 For examples of theories of (often, specifically Greek and Roman) religion from antiquity, see Thrower (1999: 93–8); Roubekas (2017: 15–50); Franek (2020: 9–29).

19 Boin is no stranger to the topic. He elaborates in detail on this issue in Boin (2015).

20 E.g., see Adler (2016 and 2020).

21 See the collection of papers in Coneybeare and Goldhill (2021b), as well as the chapter "God" in The Postclassicisms Collective (2020: 82–99).

22 Indicatively, see Stone (2002) and Molendijk (2016). Scholars have traced the roots of a nontheological study of religion primarily in the seventeenth century, as demonstrated by Stroumsa (2010). Cf. Strenski (2015: 9–18).

23 See, e.g., the discussions by Segal (2002) and (2008) on Robertson Smith's pioneering sociology of religion.

24 E.g., a quick scan online in British universities will find variations such as religious studies and theology, divinity (including religious studies as a subdiscipline), divinity and religious studies, whereas the study of religion in European universities by and large is still housed within faculties of theology,

catholic studies, etc. Despite the difference in the United States, one of the most important departments studying religion, found in Chicago, is still under the umbrella of The University of Chicago Divinity School (not less so, one may surmise, due to Eliade's foundational role in the study of religion in Chicago and in the United States more broadly, at least down to the 1990s).
25 See the discussion in Imhoff (2016).
26 On the "failure of nerve," see the original article and the numerous responds in Arnal, Braun, and McCutcheon (2014).
27 See, e.g., the various discussions in Roubekas (2019b).

Chapter 5

1 *Adversus Nationes* 1.57 (trans. Edwards [2015: 65]).
2 See, e.g., McCutcheon (2015) on the field's constant (implicit or explicit) relapse into valuing and employing theological thinking while arguing for a theologically free study of religion.
3 For explorations regarding the relationship between theology and the study of religion as disciplines, see Cady and Brown (2002); Warrier and Oliver (2008); Elliott (2014). On how departments present the study of religion—and its implicit or explicit relationship with theology—with 101 university webpages from 70 universities from 15 countries, see Melævr and Stausberg (2013).
4 On how the study of religion slowly established itself from within theology, see Turner (2011) (on the United States) and Hughes (2020) (on Canada) as representative examples. For a much broader, global perspective, see Alles (2008).
5 Granted, the authors of the BASR report do not shy away from the field's own failure in making such distinctions clear: "It may be that the failure is ours, for failing to differentiate RS's approaches from Theology, and for failing to make the case for the social-scientific non-confessional study of religion in public discourse" (BASR 2021: 23). Although such self-criticism is welcome, it would be interesting to learn why such a failure might have occurred. Given that the field of the study of religion has in the last decade been in the target regarding sustainability and its raison d'être in the academy (not only in the UK but also in North America, with a number of universities defunding, closing down, or threatening to do so Departments of Religious Studies and/or Departments of Theology and Religious Studies), it would be interesting to offer a diagnosis of the field's failure to convincingly argue about its necessity. And, in my view, the ongoing deconstruction of its very subject ("religion") has played a major role for such an apparent demise ever since the early 2000s.

6   Even so, this does not necessarily mean that the field of the study of religion should therefore only be populated by deconstructionists or similar-minded scholars. Indicatively, see the detailed criticisms in Ambasciano (2019) and in Ambasciano (2020) for a summary.
7   It is imperative to point out here that what follows is not a plea for a theologically informed study of religion in general, or of Greek and Roman religion(s) in particular. In this respect, my argument is fundamentally different from what is maintained by, e.g., Helmer (2012).
8   These are definitely not the only textbooks of this genre. A kindred circumstance is encountered in other similar publications, such as in Orsi (2012), whereas the situation is slightly better in non-English publications. E.g., Cancik, Gladikow, and Kohl (2001); Figl (2003). The only English work to my knowledge that contains an entry on "Gods"—and not merely from a Christian perspective like in the case of Taylor's *Critical Terms*—is found in Michael Stausberg and Steven Engler's *The Oxford Handbook of the Study of Religion*. See Benavides (2016). On "god/s" and comparativism in the academic study of religion, see Ahn (2012).
9   See, e.g., the definitions cited in Chapter 4, this volume.
10 Some hundreds of cases of the term's appearance in Greek literature were published in a reader in modern Greek consisting of 338 pages. See Kaktos Philological Group (2009).
11 It goes without saying that numbers increase exponentially once one adds inscriptions in their database.
12 Cf. Henrichs (2019a [1987]: 256): "Da werden die Götter historisch zergliedert und funktionsmäßig aufgeschlüsselt und verschwinden oft hinter der Fülle ihrer Komponenten."
13 E.g.: Fantham (2009); Lipka (2009); Graziosi (2013); Bonnet and Pironti (2017); Gagné and de Jáuregui (2019); Bispham and Miano (2020); cf. Long (1987). An interesting approach to how the Greeks saw their gods from an interdisciplinary perspective is offered by Eich (2011). On the names of the gods, see Parker (2017) as well as Bonnett (2021), although the latter also discusses deities beyond the religious world of the Greeks and the Romans. On divine attributes of the gods, see more recently Bonnett and Pironti (2021). Surprisingly, 2021 saw the English translation of Erika Simon's *Die Götter der Griechen*, originally published in 1969 (!). On whether her work remains relative today, I leave it to the readers. See Simon (2021).
14 Two examples are Miano (2018) and Hejduk (2020). Cf. the book series "Gods and Heroes of the Ancient World" published by Routledge: https://www.routledge.com/Gods-and-Heroes-of-the-Ancient-World/book-series/GHAW (accessed: January 4, 2021).

15 See Bremmer (2019).
16 E.g., Larson (2001).
17 See Dubourdieu (1989); Flower (2017).
18 See King (2020).
19 E.g., Borgeaud (1988).
20 I do not here imply that a study of the Greek and Roman gods and goddesses is incomplete if it does not include such agents. By default, and justifiably so, scholars have paid attention primarily to the agents that drew most attention and with whom most of the contemporary readers are acquainted with—this is also due to practical reasons given that the textual and archaeological records rarely offer any substantial information about those obscure, secondary, or archaic gods and goddesses. The short enumeration of such agents merely serves Thomassen's argument that allows for some flexibility when one takes into consideration gods and goddesses other than the popular or most known ones.
21 Rather than an objection per se, some years before the publication of this volume, Thomas Harrison also offered a number of different classifications of "theology" when discussing Greek religion: from the Presocratics's musings and the numerous miracle stories to ideas related to divination. See Harrison (2015: 172).
22 The importance of myth and myth-telling in Greek and Roman religion(s) cannot be overstated. The most current and appealing work on Greek myth is Johnston (2018). For the centrality of myth in Roman religion, one may consult the celebrated Wiseman (2004).
23 Most notably, the discourses on what has been now called Orphism, which covered both the basic understanding of theology as "talking about gods" and how they came to be, and a more sophisticated theological view, including after life and ethics. See, e.g., Edmonds (2013); Meisner (2018); Chrysanthou (2020).
24 See, e.g., the surprisingly circular argumentation in Adluri (2013).
25 It is well known that the term was first coined by Plato, and a lot of ink has been spilled concerning the place of theology in Plato and subsequent philosophical discourses and schools. Representatively, see Gladigow (1986); Naddaf (1995); Mayhew (2008); van Riel (2013).
26 John Scheid also employs the term in respect to Roman religion, despite his constant insistence on praxis rather than doxa; e.g., Scheid (2016 [2013]): "La théologie romaine paraît en fait comme une pensée et une pratique vivantes qui se caractérisent par une propension à la fragmentation des pouvoirs divins. Par ce biais, la pensée tentait de saisir tous les aspects de l'action divine, envisagés tantôt à l'état virtuel, comme des capacités traduisant la spécificité d'un mode d'action, tantôt dans ses différents effets" (Scheid [2009: 122–3]). On the theological terms used to describe the gods in Greek culture, see now Meister (2020).

27 E.g., we may recall the way Demeter's transformation is portrayed in the Homeric Hymns: "Thus speaking, the goddess changed her size and appearance, thrusting off old age. Beauty breathed about her and from her sweet robes a delicious fragrance spread; a light beamed far out from the goddess's immortal skin, and her golden hair flowed over her shoulders. The well-built house flooded with radiance like lightning" (*Homeric Hymn to Demeter* 275–80; trans. Foley [1994]).

28 On the importance of Varro in the study of Roman religion, see Rüpke (2014). On Varro's tripartite theology, see Rüpke (2005). I discuss this tripartite categorization in Chapter 6.

29 Also, though indirectly, from Virgil. See Nelis and Nelis-Clément (2011). On Dionysius's reliability considering his Greek background and his fondness for things Greek at times, see Wiater (2011).

30 For a discussion, see Gradel (2002) and Levene (2012).

31 See Sextus Empiricus, *Adversus Mathematicos* 9.193. I will be further discussing this excerpt in Chapter 6.

Chapter 6

1 Fanon (1968: 200–1).

2 For a splendid and lucid discussion on postmodernism and the study of religion(s) in general, see Heelas (2005).

3 E.g., see the critiques by Strenski (2004) and Segal (2006a). For a critique beyond the study of religion, see the amusing and contentious Sokal and Bricmont (1998). For a different yet informed approach, see Slingerland (2008).

4 The online debate can be found at http://www.religiousstudiesproject.com/podcast/categorising-religion-from-case-studies-to-methodology/ (accessed: June 5, 2021).

5 As Brian Pennington has put it, Russell McCutcheon's and his colleagues' work has created a new school, the "'Alabama School' of discourse analysis," of which he is rather critical (as I am too). See Pennington (2019, especially p. 334). McCutcheon himself has many times argued that he and his colleagues have brought about a new approach to the study of religion—to the point of "reinventing" it (more recently, McCutcheon [2021]).

6 On a discussion about "religion" as a "category" or/and "concept," see Amsler (2017).

7 There are still scholars who struggle to (re)establish the academic study of religion as a study of an actual field rather than one that ultimately deals with "no data." E.g., see more recently Hedges (2021).

8 E.g., this was openly admitted by Matt Sheedy, who, at the end of his contribution to a panel celebrating the late Jonathan Z. Smith, wrote:

> Although Smith's essays have become a staple of university classes in the study of religion ... his particular methods and theories are not easy to live up to. This is perhaps due in part to his prodigious breath of scholarly learning, where *very few have the time, training, or skill to read across such a wide range of data, or perhaps because it is so hard to separate the production of knowledge from our own human interests*, which leads us to look for similarity rather than explore how analyzing difference might open up new terrain. (Sheedy 2019: 44–5; my emphasis)

9 This is not the place to address the pressing issue of linguistic competency (not only of source languages but also of modern ones as is usually the case today—more so in the North American and less so in the British academic context). Moreover, such linguistic incompetence—regarding modern languages—is equally evident within classics in the same geographical contexts, as Alexander Rubel recently pointed out (Rubel [2019]). In many respects, I am equally guilty of the charge that Rubel puts forth about monolingualism in today's academic research and publishing in the humanities, given that in this book I am primarily referring and using works written in English. However, I am in agreement with his assessment which is worthy of perhaps a separate and broader study that could also involve statistics and metrics, with the aim of indicating that today's academic research in both the field of classics and the study of religion suffers from a broader outlook—that is only accomplished through linguistic competency—which most likely also affects the theoretical principles guiding those studies. If we are willing (and rightly so) to measure inequalities in the academic world (see the beginning of Chapter 2, this volume), we might as well be willing to measure academic problems that get at the heart of what it means to do academic research.

10 Larson is not the only scholar to integrate such concepts and tools into the study of Greek and Roman religions, but her work remains the most thorough and systematic one to date. For other recent examples, see Eidinow (2015) and Dilley (2019)—the latter found in a volume which, despite the appealing title, lamentably offers very little to the study of Greek and Roman religion(s) from a CSR perspective. For new attempts to bring the classics and CSR closer (not restricted, however, to the study of the religions of the period), see the online platform "Cognitive Classics" at https://cognitiveclassics.blogs.sas.ac.uk (accessed: October 10, 2021). The earliest explicit attempt to study these traditions from a CSR perspective (more hooked on biological and evolutionary theory) is Burkert (1998). Unfortunately, the writing of this book could not benefit from the promising Mackey (2022).

11 The literature on CSR is already extensive and growing. For a succinct overview (accompanied by criticisms and a rejoinder), see Claire White's (2017) chapter in a volume on theory in the study of religion, edited by Aaron W. Hughes. However, White has offered a far more detailed and informed introduction to the topic (White [2021]), highly recommended to the interested reader. Cf. Geertz (2004) and Pyysiäinen (2012).

12 E.g., see the criticisms in Arnal and McCutcheon (2013: 91–101) as well as Engler and Gardiner (2017).

13 For more on the inexplicably thorny issue of "belief" and a suggested up-to-date literature on the topic, see Appendix II. The main argument against the applicability of the term to premodern religions is based on the assumption that belief is a (Protestant) Christian trait, and therefore does not correspond to religions that do not resemble or simply antedate Christianity. Suffice it here to iterate Henk Versnel's words with which I am in full agreement:

> The statement that the ("religious") notion of "belief" is an exclusive privilege of the Christian creed and consequently can only be used with the full array of its Christian connotations is nothing less than an instance of modern Christian bias. ... [T]he question "did the Greeks believe in gods" is intrinsically absurd. ... Even if it could be demonstrated that Greek does not have a word that would match our *term* "belief/believe," this would never prove that the Greeks might not have a matching *concept*. (Versnel [2011: 554–5]; emphasis in original)

14 On the centrality and importance of beliefs in general (including religious beliefs) for our species and our evolution, see Bering (2011) and Fuentes (2019).

15 This classification ("high" and "low" theology) does not imply a qualitative distinction between the two categories, nor do I argue that the former should be considered more advanced or "real" than the latter. On the contrary, the classification here should be understood merely on the basis of complexity and sophistication. Larson uses another classification, equally valid in my view: implicit and explicit theology (the latter contained in traditional myths), but also accompanied by systematic theology, i.e., the "detailed, logically coherent description of divine matters that is shared, studied and grasped by relatively small groups of people within a culture" (Larson [2016: 67]).

16 Xygalatas has also discussed another example of folk religiosity versus official theological positions in Greece, namely the idea of the evil eye. See Xygalatas (2021).

17 On intuitive and counterintuitive knowledge, see Boyer (2001). A successful application of Boyer's theory in ancient Greek beliefs about nymphs and nature gods has been offered by Larson (2019).

18 On epiphany, see Chapter 5, this volume. On the various epiphanies of Castor and Polux in Greek and Roman history, see Geppert (1996); Platt (2018); Gartrell (2021).
19 Another example of "popular" versus "official" beliefs regarding the Dioscuri's epiphany is discussed by Claudia Santi (2017: 31–6) in connection with their appearance at Lake Regillus, about which Livy mentions nothing. For a counterargument, see Gartrell (2021: 77, 89–90).
20 Readers might object to such a final assessment, since scholars—as I argued in Chapter 1 of this volume—usually boast about being interdisciplinary. However, I am not alone in such an assessment. Most recently, and in relation to how historians have, by and large, a very limited interdisciplinary outlook, Nigel Raab argued the following:

> When historians advocate an interdisciplinary approach, more often than not they mean to say that we should turn to cultural anthropology or literary criticism rather than mathematics or political science or even philosophy. … Many historians are not trained in epistemology or theories of knowledge so a series of issues emerge when a relativist thesis appears in a historical argument. For example, knowledge and epistemology are treated as simple synonyms thus eliminating the subtleties of philosophical approaches. (Raab [2015: 8, 15])

On epistemology and the study of religion past and present, see Jensen (2011). Contrarily, it is worth mentioning here the groundbreaking study by Kyle Harper *The Fate of Rome: Climate, Disease, and the End of an Empire* (2017), which offers an exciting scientific explanation for the fall of the Roman Empire from the perspective of the natural sciences. Despite the promising and highly informed analysis, Harper's approach was quite critically discussed by Ohio State University historian of antiquity and of the medieval period Kristina Sessa (2019). In an extremely lengthy exposition, ranging over forty pages, Sessa makes a number of suggestions on how a future study of antiquity, which utilizes both data from the historical record and from the natural sciences, could be developed and further unveil to us the ancient world. And this is an example of how interdisciplinarity would allow us to study ancient ideas, realities, discourses, and other cultural and historical elements, among which religion should also feature prominently.

Appendix I

1 *Orationes* 77.1; trans. Hunter (2014: 8).
2 This was thoroughly discussed by Marcel Detienne already in 1967. See Detienne (1996).

3 Just as examples, see the chapters in Montanari, Rengakos, and Tsagalis (2009) as well as in Loney and Scully (2018). More recently, Romano (2020).
4 On the "anachronism" of "religion," see Chapter 3, this volume.
5 It would be an oversight of course not to mention the possible strong connection between the *Theogony* and the political system of kingship. However, this is not the same as arguing that through the poem Hesiod is writing about political shifts alone. On the contrary, as Richard Martin has argued, the *Theogony* "can be constructed as support—even propaganda—for the notion of kingship, the human institution being directly linked to the divine king Zeus." As Martin adds, this allowed Hesiod to put himself "on a level with the class of kings, since both they and the poet are Muse-gifted masters of the word" (Martin [2016: 44])—for the latter point, cf. Detienne (1996).
6 It is also problematic that Goldenberg's approach to the Hesiodic corpus overtly overlooks the long tradition of seeing Hesiod within the broader Indo-European cluster of origins mythology. For more on this, including a new and revived look, see Lincoln (2021: 239–64).
7 See Goldenberg (2018) as an example that hopefully corroborates my criticism.

Appendix II

1 *Olympian* 8.5 (trans. D. Arnson Svarlien; Perseus Project 1.0).
2 I have included only works written in the past ten years or so, restricting my choices in works written primarily in English. Given the excessive research being done recently, the interested reader will find numerous other works, both primary and secondary literature, on the topic of belief by resorting to the works mentioned here. The list is alphabetical rather than chronological.

Appendix III

1 Boswell (1953 [1791]: 627–8).
2 One may immediately recall Robert Bellah's work here (also on immanentism and transcendentalism). See Bellah (2011) and Bellah and Joas (2012). On the "Axial Age" and Greek and Roman religion(s)—particularly, the influence of Plato—see Klostergaard Petersen (2017b).
3 Both points #3 and #4 are not as straightforward as Strathern argues when it comes to Greek and Roman religious ideas. E.g., see the relevant chapters in Marlow, Pollmann, and Van Noorden (2021).
4 See Chapter 6, this volume.

References

Ackerman, Robert. 1978. "The Correspondence of Ulrich von Wilamowitz-Moellendorff with Sir James George Frazer." *Cambridge Classical Journal* 24: 31–40.

Adler, Eric. 2016. *Classics, the Culture Wars, and Beyond*. Ann Arbor: University of Michigan Press.

Adler, Eric. 2020. *The Battle of the Classics: How a Nineteenth-Century Debate Can Save the Humanities Today*. New York: Oxford University Press.

Adluri, Vishwa. 2013. "Philosophy, Salvation, and the Mortal Condition." In Vishwa Adluri (ed.), *Philosophy and Salvation in Greek Religion*, 1–27. Berlin: De Gruyter.

Ahn, Gregor. 2012. "Gottesvorstellungen als Thema vergleichender Religionswissenschaft." In Michael Stausberg (ed.), *Religionswissenschaft*, 169–81. Berlin: De Gruyter.

Albrecht, Janico, Christopher Degelmann, Valentino Gasparini, Richard Gordon, Maik Patzelt, Georgia Petridou, Rubina Raja, Anna-Katharina Riegera, Jörg Rüpke, Benjamin Sippel, Emiliano R. Urciuoli, and Lara Weiss. 2018. "Religion in the Making: The Lived Ancient Religion Approach." *Religion* 48 (4): 568–93.

Allen, Douglas. 2002. *Myth and Religion in Mircea Eliade*. New York: Routledge.

Alles, Gregory D., ed. 2008. *Religious Studies: A Global View*. London: Routledge.

Almagor, Eran, and Joseph Skinner, eds. 2013. *Ancient Ethnography: New Approaches*. London: Bloomsbury.

Altman, Michael J. 2017. "It's Hard Out There for a Theorist." In Aaron W. Hughes (ed.), *Theory in a Time of Excess: Beyond Reflection and Explanation in Religious Studies Scholarship*, 32–6. Sheffield: Equinox.

Ambasciano, Leonardo. 2019. *An Unnatural History of Religions: Academia, Post-Truth and the Quest for Scientific Knowledge*. London: Bloomsbury.

Ambasciano, Leonardo. 2020. "The Sisyphean Discipline: A Précis of *An Unnatural History of Religions*." *Religio: Revue Pro Religionistiku* 28 (1): 3–20.

Amsler, Monika. 2017. "How Could Religion Become a Category? Accounting for Classical and Fuzzy Logic in the Conceptualization of Religion." *Asdiwal: Revue genevoise d'anthropologie et d'histoire des religions* 12: 37–51.

Appiah, Kwame A. 2016. "There Is No Such Thing as Western Civilisation." *The Guardian*, November 9. https://www.theguardian.com/world/2016/nov/09/western-civilisation-appiah-reith-lecture (accessed: May 8, 2020).

Arnal, William E., and Russell T. McCutcheon. 2013. *The Sacred Is the Profane: The Political Nature of "Religion"*. New York: Oxford University Press.

Arnal, William E., Willi Braun, and Russell T. McCutcheon, eds. 2014. *Failure and Nerve in the Academic Study of Religion: Essays in Honor of Donald Wiebe*. London: Routledge.

Arnold, John H. 2000. *History: A Very Short Introduction*. Oxford: Oxford University Press.

Asad, Talal. 1993. *Genealogies of Religion: Discipline and Reasons of Power in Christianity and Islam*. Baltimore, MD: Johns Hopkins University Press.

Asad, Talal. 2001. "Reading a Modern Classic: W. C. Smith's *The Meaning and End of Religion*." *History of Religions* 40 (3): 205–22.

Badhe, Yaamir. 2020. "Classics Faculty Proposes Removal of Homer and Virgil from Mods Syllabus." *Oxford Student*, February 17. https://www.oxfordstudent.com/2020/02/17/94749/ (accessed: March 25, 2020).

Barrett, Justin L. 1999. "Theological Correctness: Cognitive Constraint and the Study of Religion." *Method and Theory in the Study of Religion* 11: 325–39.

Barrett, Justin L. 2000. "Exploring the Natural Foundations of Religion." *Trends in Cognitive Science* 4 (1): 29–34.

Barrett, Justin L. 2004. *Why Would Anyone Believe in God?* Lanham, MD: AltaMira Press.

Barrett, Justin L., and Frank C. Keil (1996). "Conceptualizing a Nonnatural Entity: Anthropomorphism in God Concepts." *Cognitive Psychology* 31: 219–47.

Barton, Carlin A., and Daniel Boyarin. 2016. *Imagine No Religion: How Modern Abstractions Hide Ancient Realities*. New York: Fordham University Press.

BASR. 2021. "BASR Response to the 2019 British Academy Report, *Theology and Religious Studies Provision in UK Higher Education*." https://basrblog.files.wordpress.com/2021/02/basr_response_final.pdf (accessed: February 22, 2021).

Beard, Mary. 2012. "Do the Classics Have a Future?" *New York Review of Books*, January 12. https://www.nybooks.com/articles/2012/01/12/do-classics-have-future/ (accessed: August 3, 2020).

Beard, Mary. 2015. *SPQR: A History of Ancient Rome*. London: Profile Books.

Beard, Mary, John North, and Simon Prince. 1998. *Religions of Rome. Vol. 2: A Sourcebook*. Cambridge: Cambridge University Press.

Becher, Tony, and Paul R. Trowler. 2001. *Academic Tribes and Territories: Intellectual Enquiry and the Culture of Disciplines*, 2nd ed. Buckingham: Society for Research into Higher Education and Open University Press.

Becker, Adam H., and Annette Yoshiko Reed, eds. 2007. *The Ways That Never Parted: Jews and Christians in Late Antiquity and the Early Middle Ages*. Minneapolis, MN: Fortress.

Bellah, Robert N. 2011. *Religion in Human Evolution: From the Paleolithic to the Axial Age*. Cambridge, MA: Belknap Press of Harvard University Press.

Bellah, Robert N., and Hans Joas, eds. 2012. *The Axial Age and Its Consequences*. Cambridge, MA: Belknap Press of Harvard University Press.

Benavides, Gustavo. 2016. "Gods." In Michael Stausberg and Steven Engler (eds.), *The Oxford Handbook of the Study of Religion*, 559–81. New York: Oxford University Press.

Bering, Jesse. 2011. *The Belief Instinct: The Psychology of Souls, Destiny, and the Meaning of Life*. New York: W. W. Norton.

Bernal, Martin. 1987. *Black Athena: The Afroasiatic Roots of Classical Civilization*. New Brunswick, NJ: Rutgers University Press.

Berzon, Todd. 2018. "Review of *Imagine No Religion*, by Carlin A. Barton and Daniel Boyarin." *Journal of Early Christian Studies* 26 (1): 147–9.

Billings, Joshua. 2014. *Genealogy of the Tragic: Greek Tragedy and German Philosophy*. Princeton, NJ: Princeton University Press.

Bispham, Edward, and Daniele Miano, eds. 2020. *Gods and Goddesses in Ancient Italy*. London: Routledge.

Bod, Rens. 2013. *A New History of the Humanities: The Search for Principles and Patterns from Antiquity to the Present*, translated by Lynn Richards. New York: Oxford University Press.

Bodel, John, and Saul M. Olyan, eds. 2008. *Household and Family Religion in Antiquity*. Malden, MA: Blackwell.

Boin, Douglas. 2015. *Coming Out Christian in the Roman World: How the Followers of Jesus Made a Place in Caesar's Palace*. New York: Bloomsbury.

Boin, Douglas. 2016. "Classicist's Christian Problem." *Chronicle of Higher Education* 62 (18). January 10. https://www.chronicle.com/article/classicists-christian-problem/?bc_nonce=4hy3id3omcltohp8graw5d&cid=reg_wall_signup (accessed: November 6, 2020).

Bond, Sarah E. 2019. "Reacting to the Racist Events At the SCS–AIA Annual Meeting in San Diego: A Roundup." *History from Below Blog*, January 18. https://sarahemilybond.com/2019/01/18/reacting-to-the-racist-events-at-the-scs-aia-annual-meeting-in-san-diego-a-roundup/ (accessed: March 3, 2020).

Bonnet, Corinne, ed. 2021. *Noms de dieux: Portraits de divinités antiques*. Toulouse: Anacharsis.

Bonnet, Corinne, and Gabriella Pironti, eds. 2017. *Les dieux d'Homère: Polythéisme et poésie en Grèce ancienne*. Liège: Presses Universitaires de Liège.

Bonnet, Corinne, and Gabriella Pironti, eds. 2021. *Les dieux d'Homère III: Attributs onomastiques*. Liège: Presses Universitaires de Liège.

Borgeaud, Philippe. 1988. *The Cult of Pan in Ancient Greece*, translated by Kathleen Atlass and James Redfield. Chicago: University of Chicago Press.

Borgeaud, Philippe. 2004. "Deities and Demons: Greece and Rome." In Sarah Iles Johnston (ed.), *Religions of the Ancient World: A Guide*, 408–13. Cambridge, MA: Belknap Press of Harvard University Press.

Borgeaud, Philippe. 2009. "Observe, Describe, Compare: A Small Meditation." *Historia Religionum* 1: 13–20.

Boswell, James. 1953 [1791]. *Life of Samuel Johnson*. London: Oxford University Press.

Boyarin, Daniel. 2017. "The Concept of Cultural Translation in American Religious Studies." *Critical Inquiry* 44: 17–39.

Boyarin, Daniel. 2019. *Judaism: The Genealogy of a Modern Notion*. New Brunswick, NJ: Rutgers University Press.

Boyer, Pascal. 2001. *Religion Explained: The Evolutionary Origins of Religious Thought*. New York: Basic Books.

Braun, Willi. 2020. *Jesus and Addiction to Origins: Towards an Anthropocentric Study of Religion*. Russell T. McCutcheon (ed.). Sheffield: Equinox.

Braun, Willi, and Russell T. McCutcheon, eds. 2018. *Reading J. Z. Smith: Interviews & Essay*. New York: Oxford University Press.

Braun, Willi, and Russell T. McCutcheon, eds. 2000. *Guide to the Study of Religion*. London: Cassell.

Bremmer, Jan N. 1998. "'Religion', 'Ritual' and the Opposition 'Sacred vs. Profane.'" In Fritz Graf (ed.), *Ansichten griechischer Rituale: Geburtstags–Symposium für Walter Burkert*, 9–32. Stuttgart: B. G. Teubner.

Bremmer, Jan N. 2010. "Introduction: The Greek Gods in the Twentieth Century." In Jan N. Bremmer and Andrew Erskine (eds.), *The Gods of Ancient Greece: Identities and Transformations*, 1–18. Edinburgh: Edinburgh University Press.

Bremmer, Jan N. 2018. "Jörg Rüpke's *Pantheon*." *Religion in the Roman Empire* 4 (1): 107–12.

Bremmer, Jan N. 2019. "Rivers and River Gods in Ancient Greek Religion and Culture." In Tanja S. Scheer (ed.), *Natur–Mythos–Religion im antiken Griechenland*, 89–112. Stuttgart: Franz Steiner Verlag.

Brown, Peter. 1971. *The World of Late Antiquity, AD 150–750*. London: Harcourt.

Bruce, Steve. 2011. "Defining Religion: A Practical Response." *International Review of Sociology* 21 (1): 107–20.

Bulloch, Anthony, Eric S. Gruen, A. A. Long, and Andrew Stewart, eds. 1993. *Images and Ideologies: Self-Definition in the Hellenistic World*. Berkeley: University of California Press.

Burkert, Walter. 1998. *Creation of the Sacred: Tracks of Biology in Early Religions.* Cambridge, MA: Harvard University Press.

Cady, Linell E., and Delwin Brown, eds. 2002. *Religious Studies, Theology, and the University: Conflicting Maps, Changing Terrains.* Albany: State University of New York Press.

Calder, William M. 1998. *Men in Their Books: Studies in the Modern History of Classical Scholarship.* John P. Harris and R. Scott Smith (eds.). Hildesheim: G. Olms Verlag.

Calder, William M., Hellmut Flashar, and Theodor Lindken, eds. 1985. *Wilamowitz nach 50 Jahren.* Darmstadt: Wissenschaftliche Buchgesellschaft.

Cancik, Hubert, Burkhard Gladikow, and Karl-Heinz Kohl. eds. 2001. *Handbuch religionswissenschaftlicher Grundbegriffe.* Vols. I–V. Stuttgart: Kohlhammer Verlag.

Candea, Matei. 2019. *Comparison in Anthropology: The Impossible Method.* Cambridge: Cambridge University Press.

Casadio, Giovanni. 2010. "*Religio* versus Religion." In Jitse Dijkstra, Justin Kroesen, and Yme Kuiper (eds.), *Myths, Martyrs, and Modernity: Studies in the History of Religions in Honour of Jan N. Bremmer*, 301–26. Leiden: Brill.

Chaniotis, Angelos. 2017. "The Life of Statues of Gods in the Greek World." *Kernos* 30: 91–112.

Chaudhuri, Nirad C. 1974. *Scholar Extraordinary: The Life of Professor the Rt. Hon. Friedrich Max Müller, P.C.* New York: Oxford University Press.

Chidester, David. 2018. *Religion: Material Dynamics.* Oakland: University of California Press.

Christensen, Joel P. 2018. "Classics and Theory: A Monday Rant." *Sententiae Antiquae*, August 6. https://sententiaeantiquae.com/2018/08/06/classics-and-theory-a-monday-rant/ (accessed: November 16, 2019).

Chrysanthou, Anthi. 2020. *Defining Orphism: The Beliefs, the Teletae and the Writings.* Berlin: De Gruyter.

Clark, Matthew. 2012. *Exploring Greek Myth.* Malden, MA: Wiley-Blackwell.

Clarke, Peter B., and Peter Byrne. 1993. *Religion Defined and Explained.* New York: St. Martin's Press.

Cole, Spencer. 2013. *Cicero and the Rise of Deification at Rome.* Cambridge: Cambridge University Press.

Conyebeare, Catherine, and Simon Goldhill. 2021a. "Philology's Shadow." In Catherine Conyebeare and Simon Goldhill (eds.), *Classical Philology and Theology: Entanglement, Disavowal, and the Godlike Scholar*, 1–11. Cambridge: Cambridge University Press.

Conybeare, Catherine, and Simon Goldhill, eds. 2021b. *Classical Philology and Theology: Entanglement, Disavowal, and the Godlike Scholar*. Cambridge: Cambridge University Press.

Cox, James L. 2018. "Review of *The Legacy of Wilfred Cantwell Smith*, edited by Ellen Bradshaw Aitken and Arvind Sharma." *Numen* 65 (5/6): 602–5.

Curd, Patricia, ed. 2011. *A Presocratics Reader: Selected Fragments and Testimonia*, 2nd ed. Indianapolis, IN: Hackett.

De Grazia, Margreta. 2010. "Anachronism." In Brian Cummings and James Simpson (eds.), *Oxford Twenty-First Century Approaches to Literature. Cultural Reformations: Medieval and Renaissance in Literary History*, 13–32. New York: Oxford University Press.

de Jaucourt, Louis. 1765. "Religion des Grecs et des Romains." *Encyclopédie ou Dictionnaire raisonné des sciences, des arts et des métiers* 14: 83–8.

Dench, Emma. 2005. *Romulus' Asylum: Roman Identities from the Age of Alexander to the Age of Hadrian*. New York: Oxford University Press.

Despland, Michel, and Gérard Vallée, eds. 1992. *Religion in History: The Word, the Idea, the Reality/La religion dans l'histoire: Le mot, l'idée, la réalité*. Waterloo, ON: Wilfrid Laurier University Press.

Detienne, Marcel. 1996 [1967]. *The Masters of Truth in Archaic Greece*, translated by Janet Lloyd. New York: Zone Books.

Detienne, Marcel. 2000. *Comparer l'incoparable*. Paris: Éditions du Seuil.

Dhindsa, Hardeep S. 2020. "What Studying Classics Taught Me about My Relationship with Western Civilisation." *CUCD Bulletin* 49. https://cucd.blogs.sas.ac.uk/files/2020/03/DHINDSA-What-Studying-Classics-Taught-me-about-my-Relationship-with-Western-Civilisation-2.pdf (accessed: June 9, 2020).

Dilley, Paul C. 2019. "Theory of Mind from Athens to Augustine: Divine Omniscience and the Fear of God." In Peter Meineck, William Michael Short, and Jennifer Deveraux (eds.), *The Routledge Handbook of Classics and Cognitive Theory*, 270–8. London: Routledge.

Douglas, Mary. 1984 [1966]. *Purity and Danger: An Analysis of the Concepts of Pollution and Taboo*. London: Routledge.

Driediger-Murphy, Lindsay G. 2014. "Theology as Historiographical Tool in Dionysius of Halicarnassus." *Phoenix* 68 (3/4): 330–49.

Driediger-Murphy, Lindsay G. 2019. *Roman Republican Augury: Freedom and Control*. New York: Oxford University Press.

Driediger-Murphy, Lindsay G., and Esther Eidinow, eds. 2019. *Ancient Divination and Experience*. New York: Oxford University Press.

Driscoll, Christopher M., and Monica R. Miller. 2019. *Method as Identity: Manufacturing Distance in the Academic Study of Religion*. Lanham, MD: Lexington Books.

Dubourdieu, Annie. 1989. *Les origines et le développement du culte des Pénates à Rome*. Rome: École française de Rome.

Dubuisson, Daniel. 2003. *The Western Construction of Religion: Myths, Knowledge and Ideology*, translated by William Sayers. Baltimore, MD: Johns Hopkins University Press.

Dubuisson, Daniel. 2019. *The Invention of Religions*, translated by Mary Cunningham. Sheffield: Equinox.

Durkheim, Émile. 1995. *The Elementary Forms of Religious Life*, translated by Karen E. Fields. New York: Free Press.

Eaghll, Tenzan. 2019. "Religion, Theory, Critique, and Epistemological Anarchy: A Review Essay." *Bulletin for the Study of Religion* 48 (1/2): 35–9.

Edmonds III, Radcliffe G. 2013. *Redefining Ancient Orphism: A Study in Greek Religion*. Cambridge: Cambridge University Press.

Edmunds, Lowell, ed. 2014. *Approaches to Greek Myth*, 2nd ed. Baltimore, MD: Johns Hopkins University Press.

Edmunds, Lowell. 2021. *Greek Myth*. Berlin: De Gruyter.

Edwards, Mark. 2015. *Religions of the Constantinian Empire*. New York: Oxford University Press.

Eich, Peter. 2011. *Gottesbild und Wahrnehmung: Studien zu Ambivalenzen früher griechischer Götterdarstellungen (ca. 800 v. Chr.–ca. 400 v. Chr.)*. Stuttgart: Franz Steiner Verlag.

Eidinow, Esther. 2015. "φανερὰν ποιήσει τὴν αὑτοῦ διάνοιαν τοῖς θεοῖς: Some Ancient Greek Theories of (Divine and Mortal) Mind." In Clifford Ando and Jörg Rüpke (eds.), *Public and Private in Ancient Mediterranean Law and Religion*, 53–73. Berlin: De Gruyter.

Eidinow, Esther, Julia Kindt, and Robin Osborne. 2016. "Introduction: What Might We Mean by the Theologies of Ancient Greek Religion?" In Esther Eidinow, Julia Kindt, and Robin Osborne (eds.), *Theologies of Ancient Greek Religion*, 1–11. Cambridge: Cambridge University Press.

Eliade, Mircea. 1963. *Patterns in Comparative Religion*, translated by Rosemary Sheed. Cleveland, OH: Meridian Books.

Elliott, Scott S., ed. 2014. *Reinventing Religious Studies: Key Writings in the History of a Discipline*. London: Routledge.

Engler, Steven, and Mark Q. Gardiner. 2017. "A Critical Response to Cognitivist Theories of Religion." In Richard King (ed.), *Religion, Theory, Critique: Classic* and *Contemporary Approaches and Methodologies*, 237–46. New York: Columbia University Press.

Erker, Darja Šterbenc. 2008. "Semantics of Latin Words *religio* and *ritus*." *Hōrin* 15: 13–31.

Erskine, Andrew. 2010. "Epilogue." In Jan N. Bremmer and Andrew Erskine (eds.), *The Gods of Ancient Greece: Identities and Transformations*, 505–10. Edinburgh: Edinburgh University Press.

Fagan, Garrett. 2013. "Classics and the 'Crisis' in the Humanities." *Society of Classical Studies Blog*, December 12. https://classicalstudies.org/scs-blog/garrett-fagan/classics-and-crisis-humanities (accessed: August 1, 2020).

Fanon, Frantz. 1968. *The Wretched of the Earth*, translated by Constance Farrington. New York: Grove Press.

Fantham, Elaine. 2009. *Latin Poets and Italian Gods*. Toronto: University of Toronto Press.

Feil, Ernst. 1986/2012. *Religio*. Vols. I–IV. Göttingen: Vandenhoeck & Ruprecht.

Feeney, Denis C. 1991. *The Gods in Epic: Poets and Critics of the Classical Tradition*. Oxford: Clarendon Press.

Figl, Johann, ed. 2003. *Handbuch Religionswissenschaft: Religionen und ihre zentralen Themen*. Göttingen: Vandenhoek & Ruprecht.

Fitzgerald, Timothy. 2000. *The Ideology of Religious Studies*. New York: Oxford University Press.

Fitzgerald, Timothy. 2007. *Discourse on Civility and Barbarity: A Critical History of Religion and Related Categories*. New York: Oxford University Press.

Flower, Harriet I. 2017. *The Dancing Lares and the Serpent in the Garden: Religion at the Roman Street Corner*. Princeton, NJ: Princeton University Press.

Foley, Helene P., ed. 1994. *The Homeric Hymn to Demeter*. Princeton, NJ: Princeton University Press.

Fowler, Robert L. 1986. "Review of *Wilamowitz nach 50 Jahren*, by William M. Calder, Hellmut Flashar, and Theodor Linken." *Classical Journal* 82 (1): 67–72.

Fowler, Robert L. 2009. "Blood for the Ghosts: Wilamowitz in Oxford." *Syllecta Classica* 20: 171–213.

Franek, Juraj. 2020. *Naturalism and Protectionism in the Study of Religions*. London: Bloomsbury.

Frankfurter, David, ed. 2019. *Guide to the Study of Ancient Magic*. Leiden: Brill.

Freiberger, Oliver. 2019. *Considering Comparison: A Method for Religious Studies*. Oxford: Oxford University Press.

Fuentes, Agustín. 2019. *Why We Believe: Evolution and the Human Way of Being*. New Haven, CT: Yale University Press.

Führding, Steffen. 2015. *Jenseits von Religion? Zur sozio-rhetorischen »Wende« in der Religionswissenschaft*. Bielefeld: Transcript Verlag.

Fujiwara, Satoko, and Tim Jensen. 2020. "What's in a (Change of) Name? Much—but Not *That* Much—and *Not* What Wiebe Claims." *Method and Theory in the Study of Religion* 32 (2): 159–84.

Gagné, Reanud, and Miguel Herrero de Jáuregui, eds. 2019. *Les dieux d'Homère II— Anthropomorphismes*. Liège: Presses universitaires de Liège.

Gagné, Renaud, Simon Goldhill, and Geoffrey E. R. Lloyd, eds. 2019. *Regimes of Comparatism: Frameworks of Comparison in History, Religion and Anthropology*. Leiden: Brill.

Gartrell, Amber. 2021. *The Cult of Castor and Pollux in Ancient Rome*. Cambridge: Cambridge University Press.

Gee, Emma. 2020. *Mapping the Afterlife: From Homer to Dante*. New York: Oxford University Press.

Geertz, Armin W. 1997. "Theory, Definition, and Typology: Reflections on Generalities and Underrepresentative Realism." *Temenos* 33: 29–47.

Geertz, Armin W. 2004. "Cognitive Approaches to the Study of Religion." In Peter Antes, Armin W. Geertz, and Randi R. Warne (eds.), *New Approaches to the Study of Religion. Vol. 2: Textual, Comparative, Sociological, and Cognitive Approaches*, 347–99. Berlin: De Gruyter.

George, Neil. 2017. "Is It Time to Become Theoretical Vegans? Notes on How to Practice Religious Studies without 'Religion.'" *Implicit Religion* 20 (4): 397–400.

Geppert, Stefan. 1996. *Castor und Pollux: Untersuchung zu den Darstellungen der Dioskuren in der römischen Kaiserzeit*. Münster: Lit.

Gilhus, Ingvild Sælid. 2016. "What Became of Superhuman Beings? Companions and Field Guides in the Study of Religion." In Peter Antes, Armin W. Geertz, and Mikael Rothstein (eds.), *Contemporary Views on Comparative Religion: Essays on Comparative Religion Presented to Tim Jensen on the Occasion of his 65th Birthday*, 375–87. Sheffield: Equinox.

Ginzburg, Carlo. 2013. "Our Words, and Theirs: A Reflection on the Historian's Craft, Today." *Cromohs: Cyber Review of Modern Historiography* 18: 97–114.

Gladigow, Burkhard. 1986. "Mythologie und Theologie: Aussagestufen im griechischen Mythos." In Heinrich von Stietencron and Jan Assmann (eds.), *Theologen und Theologien in verschiedenen Kulturkreisen*, 70–88. Düsseldorf: Patmos-Verlag.

Goldenberg, Naomi. 2018. "Forget About Defining 'It': Reflections on Thinking Differently in Religious Studies." In Brad Stoddard (ed.), *Method Today: Redescribing Approaches to the Study of Religion*, 79–95. Sheffield: Equinox.

Goldenberg, Naomi. 2019. "'Religion' and Its Limits: Reflections on Discursive Borders and Boundaries." *Journal of the British Association for the Study of Religions* 21: 1–15.

Goldhill, Simon. 2020. "Disentangling Antiquity: Classics and Theology in the Nineteenth Century." In Bernard Lightman and Bennett Zon (eds.), *Victorian Culture and the Origin of Disciplines*, 213–37. New York: Routledge.

Gradel, Ittai. 2002. *Emperor Worship and the Roman Religion*. Oxford: Clarendon Press.

Graf, Fritz. 2012. "One Generation after Burkert and Girard: Where Are the Great Theories?" In Christopher A. Faraone and F. S. Neiden (eds.), *Greek and Roman Animal Sacrifice: Ancient Victims, Modern Observers*, 32–51. Cambridge: Cambridge University Press.

Grafton, Anthony. 2007. *What Was History? The Art of History in Early Modern Europe*. Cambridge: Cambridge University Press.

Graziosi, Barbara. 2013. *The Gods of Olympus: A History*. London: Profile Books.

Groh, J. 2012. "Poll: Most Americans Don't Think Scientology Is a Religion." *Washington Post*. https://www.washingtonpost.com/national/on-faith/poll-most-americansdont-think-scientology-is-a-religion/2012/10/02/30381626-0cd4-11e2-ba6c-07bd866eb71a_story.html?utm_term=.e6a033deead1 (accessed: May 25, 2019).

Güthenke, Constanze. 2020. *Feeling and Classical Philology: Knowing Antiquity in German Scholarship, 1770–1920*. Cambridge: Cambridge University Press.

Guthrie, Stewart E. 1993. *Faces in the Clouds: A New Theory of Religion*. New York: Oxford University Press.

Hamerton-Kelly, Robert G., ed. 1987. *Violent Origins: Walter Burkert, René Girard and Jonathan Z. Smith on Ritual Killing and Cultural Formation*. Stanford, CA: Stanford University Press.

Hanink, Johanna. 2017. "It's Time to Embrace Critical Classical Reception." *Eidolon*, May 1. https://eidolon.pub/its-time-to-embrace-critical-classical-reception-d3491a40eec3 (accessed: August 2, 2020).

Hanink, Johanna. 2020. "Not All Classicists: Worrying Gaps in Well-Meaning Maps." *TLS*, July 24. https://www.the-tls.co.uk/articles/postclassicisms-postclassicisms-collective-book-review/ (accessed: September 17, 2020).

Harland, Philip. 2016. "Associations in the Graeco-Roman World: An Expanding Collection of Inscriptions, Papyri, and Other Sources in Translation." http://www.philipharland.com/greco-roman-associations/?p=1852 (accessed: May 25, 2019).

Harper, Kyle. 2017. *The Fate of Rome: Climate, Disease, and the End of an Empire*. Princeton, NJ: Princeton University Press.

Harrison, Thomas. 2002. *Divinity and History: The Religion of Herodotus*. Oxford: Clarendon.
Harrison, Thomas. 2015. "Review Article: Beyond the *Polis*? New Approaches to Greek Religion." *Journal of Hellenic Studies* 135: 165–80.
Harrison, Thomas. 2017. "Cognitive Science of Religion as a Challenge to Prevailing Models of Greek Religion?" *Journal of Cognitive Historiography* 4 (1): 30–5.
Hawes, Greta. 2017. "Review of *An Ancient Theory of Religion: Euhemerism from Antiquity to the Present*, by Nickolas P. Roubekas." *Bryn Mawr Classical Review* 2017.9.52.
Heath, John. 2019. *The Bible, Homer, and the Search for Meaning in Ancient Myths: Why We Would Be Better Off With Homer's Gods*. London: Routledge.
Hedges, Paul. 2017. "The Deconstruction of Religion: So What Next in the Debate?" *Implicit Religion* 20 (4): 385–96.
Hedges, Paul. 2021. *Understanding Religion: Theories and Methods for Studying Religiously Diverse Societies*. Oakland: University of California Press.
Heelas, Paul. 2005. "Postmodernism." In John R. Hinnells (ed.), *The Routledge Companion to the Study of Religion*, 259–74. London: Routledge.
Hejduk, Julia Dyson. 2020. *The God of Rome: Jupiter in Augustan Poetry*. New York: Oxford University Press.
Helmer, Christine. 2012. "Theology and the Study of Religion: A Relationship." In Robert A. Orsi (ed.), *The Cambridge Companion to Religious Studies*, 230–54. New York: Cambridge University Press.
Henrichs, Albert. 2010. "What Is a Greek God?" In Jan N. Bremmer and Andrew Erskine (eds.), *The Gods of Ancient Greece: Identities and Transformations*, 19–39. Edinburgh: Edinburgh University Press.
Henrichs, Albert. 2019a [1987]. "Die Götter Griechenlands. Ihr Bild im Wandel der Religionswissenschaft." In Albert Henrichs, *Greek Myth and Religion: Collected Papers II*, Harvey Yunis (ed.), 255–98. Berlin: De Gruyter.
Henrichs, Albert. 2019b [2012]. "Epiphany." In Albert Henrichs, *Greek Myth and Religion: Collected Papers II*, Harvey Yunis (ed.), 427–8. Berlin: De Gruyter.
Hinnells, John R., ed. 2005. *The Routledge Companion to the Study of Religion*. London: Routledge.
Hirsch-Luipold, Rainer. 2021. "Religions, Religion, and Theology in Plutarch." In Rainer Hirsch-Luipold and Lautaro Roig Lanzillotta (eds.), *Plutarch's Religious Landscapes*, 11–36. Leiden: Brill.
Horii, Mitsutoshi. 2018. *The Category of "Religion" in Contemporary Japan: Shūkyō and Temple Buddhism*. Cham: Palgrave Macmillan.
Hughes, Aaron W. 2017. *Comparison: A Critical Primer*. Sheffield: Equinox.

Hughes, Aaron W. 2020. *From Seminary to University: An Institutional History of the Study of Religion in Canada*. Toronto: University of Toronto Press.

Hunt, Thomas E. 2018. "Religion in Late Antiquity—Late Antiquity in Religion." In Josef Lössl and Nicholas J. Baker-Brian (eds.), *Companion to Religion in Late Antiquity*, 9–30. Malden, MA: Wiley-Blackwell.

Hunter, Richard. 2014. *Hesiodic Voices: Studies in the Ancient Reception of Hesiod's Works and Days*. Cambridge: Cambridge University Press.

Hunter, Richard. 2018. *The Measure of Homer: The Ancient Reception of the Iliad and the Odyssey*. Cambridge: Cambridge University Press.

Idinopulos, Thomas A., and Brian C. Wilson, eds. 1998. *What Is Religion? Origins, Definitions, and Explanations*. Leiden: Brill.

Idinopulos, Thomas A., Brian C. Wilson, and James Constantine Hanges, eds. 2006. *Comparing Religions: Possibilities and Perils?* Leiden: Brill.

Imhausen, Annette, and Tanja Pommerening. 2010. "Introduction: Translating Ancient Scientific Texts." In Annette Imhausen and Tanja Pommerening (eds.), *Writings of Early Scholars in the Ancient Near East, Egypt, Rome, and Greece: Translating Ancient Scientific Texts*, 1–10. Berlin: De Gruyter.

Imhoff, Sarah. 2016. "The Creation Story, or How We Learned to Stop Worrying and Love *Schempp*." *Journal of the American Academy of Religion* 84 (2): 466–97.

Jensen, Jeppe Sinding. 2011. "Epistemology." In Michael Stausberg and Steven Engler (eds.), *The Routledge Handbook of Research Methods in the Study of Religion*, 40–53. London: Routledge.

Jensen, Jeppe Sinding. 2020. *What Is Religion?* 2nd ed. London: Routledge.

Johnson, Dominic. 2016. *God Is Watching You: How the Fear of God Makes Us Human*. Oxford: Oxford University Press.

Johnston, Sarah Iles. 2004. *Religions of the Ancient World: A Guide*. Cambridge, MA: Belknap Press of Harvard University Press.

Johnston, Sarah Iles. 2017. "The Comparative Approach." In Vanda Zajko and Helena Hoyle (eds.), *A Handbook to the Reception of Classical Mythology*, 139–51. Hoboken, NJ: Wiley Blackwell.

Johnston, Sarah Iles. 2018. *The Story of Myth*. Cambridge, MA: Harvard University Press.

Jones, Christopher P. 2010. *New Heroes in Antiquity: From Achilles to Antinoos*. Cambridge, MA: Harvard University Press.

Josephson Storm, Jason Ānanda. 2021. *Metamodernism: The Future of Theory*. Chicago: University of Chicago Press.

Kaktos Philological Group, ed. 2009. *Θεός: Τι Είπαν οι Αρχαίοι Έλληνες*. Athens: Kaktos.

Kelly, Christopher, Peter Thonemann, Barbara Borg, Julia Hillier, Myles Lavan, Neville Morley, Alex Mullen, Silvia Orlandi, Emily Pillinger, Jonathan Prag, Henriette van der Blom, and Christopher Whitton. 2019. "Gender Bias and the *Journal of Roman Studies: JRS* EDITORIAL BOARD." *Journal of Roman Studies* 109: 441–8.

Kessler, Josef. 2020. "Letter to the Editor: Postclassicisms." *TLS*, October 2. https://www.the-tls.co.uk/articles/the-israel-defence-forces/ (accessed: October 11, 2020).

Kindt, Julia. 2016. "The Story of Theology and the Theology of the Story." In Esther Eidinow, Julia Kindt, and Robin Osborne (eds.), *Theologies of Ancient Greek Religion*, 12–34. Cambridge: Cambridge University Press.

King, Charles W. 2003. "The Organization of Roman Religious Beliefs." *Classical Antiquity* 22 (2): 275–312.

King, Charles W. 2020. *The Ancient Roman Afterlife: Di Manes, Belief, and the Cult of the Dead*. Austin: University of Texas Press.

Kippenberg, Hans G. 2002. *Discovering Religious History in the Modern Age*, translated by Barbara Harshav. Princeton, NJ: Princeton University Press.

Klostergaard Petersen, Anders. 2017a. "Words and Things: One or Two Things That I Know about Religion." *Studying Religion in Culture Blog*, February 15. https://religion.ua.edu/blog/2017/02/15/words-and-things-one-or-two-things-that-i-know-about-religion/ (accessed: March 15, 2019).

Klostergaard Petersen, Anders. 2017b. "Plato's Philosophy—Why Not Just Platonic Religion?" In Anders Klostergaard Petersen and George van Kooten (eds.), *Religio-Philosophical Discourses in the Mediterranean World: From Plato, Through Jesus, to Late Antiquity*, 9–36. Leiden: Brill.

Konaris, Michael D. 2016. *The Greek Gods in Modern Scholarship: Interpretations and Belief in Nineteenth and Early Twentieth Century Germany and Britain*. New York: Oxford University Press.

Kunin, Seth D. 2006. "Introduction." In Seth D. Kunin with Jonathan Miles-Watson (eds.), *Theories of Religion: A Reader*, 1–21. Edinburgh: Edinburgh University Press.

Kurtz, Paul Michael. (@paulmkurtz). 2020. "Do People Actually Read Oxford Handbooks and Cambridge Companions, or Is My Summerly Labor Entirely in Vain?" September 3. https://twitter.com/paulmkurtz (accessed: November 15, 2020).

Larson, Jennifer. 2001. *Greek Nymphs: Myth, Cult, Lore*. New York: Oxford University Press.

Larson, Jennifer. 2016. *Understanding Greek Religion: A Cognitive Approach*. Abington, MA: Routledge.

Larson, Jennifer. 2017. "A Response: Does a Cognitive Approach Challenge Prevailing Models of Greek Religion?" *Journal of Cognitive Historiography* 4 (1): 53–9.

Larson, Jennifer. 2019. "Nature Gods, Nymphs and the Cognitive Science of Religion." In Tanja S. Scheer (ed.), *Natur—Mythos—Religion im antiken Griechenland*, 71–85. Stuttgart: Franz Steiner Verlag.

Latham, Jacob A. 2015. "Performing Theology: Imagining the Gods in the *Pompa Circensis*." *History of Religions* 54 (3): 288–317.

Latham, Jacob A. 2016. *Performance, Memory, and Processions in Ancient Rome: The Pompa Circensis from the Late Republic to Late Antiquity*. New York: Cambridge University Press.

Lefkowitz, Mary. 2016. *Euripides and the Gods*. New York: Oxford University Press.

Lehrich, Christopher I., ed. 2013. *On Teaching Religion: Essays by Jonathan Z. Smith*. New York: Oxford University Press.

Levene, David S. 2012. "Defining the Divine in Rome." *Transactions of the American Philological Association* 142: 41–81.

Lewis, Thomas A. 2015. *Why Philosophy Matters for the Study of Religion—and Vice Versa*. New York: Oxford University Press.

Lieu, Judith M. 2018. "Jörg Rüpke's *Pantheon*: Some Personal Reflections." *Religion in the Roman Empire* 4 (1): 120–6.

Lincoln, Bruce. 2006. *Holy Terrors: Thinking about Religion after September 11*. Chicago: University of Chicago Press.

Lincoln, Bruce. 2012. *Gods and Demons, Priests and Scholars: Critical Explorations in the History of Religions*. Chicago: University of Chicago Press.

Lincoln, Bruce. 2018. *Apples and Oranges: Explorations In, On, and With Comparison*. Chicago: University of Chicago Press.

Lincoln, Bruce. 2021. *Religion, Culture, and Politics in Pre-Islamic Iran: Collected Essays*. Leiden: Brill.

Lipka, Michael. 2009. *Roman Gods: A Conceptual Approach*. Leiden: Leiden.

Lipka, Michael. 2022. *Epiphanies and Dreams in Greek Polytheism: Textual Genres and "Reality" from Homer to Heliodorus*. Berlin: De Gruyter.

Lloyd-James, Hugh. 1982. "Introduction." In Ulrich von Wilamowitz-Moellendorf, *History of Classical Scholarship*, translated by Alan Harris, v–xxxii. Baltimore, MD: Johns Hopkins University Press.

Lloyd-James, Hugh. 1986. "Review of *Wilamowitz nach 50 Jahren*, by William M. Calder III, Hellmut Flashar, and Theodore Lindken." *Classical Review* (n.s.) 36 (2): 295–300.

Lombardi, Paola. 2013. "*I Tirii en Potiolois Katoikountes* e la *Statio di Tiro* (IG XIV, 830)." *Mediterraneo Antico* 16 (2): 633–80.

Loney, Alexander C., and Stephen Scully, eds. 2018. *The Oxford Handbook of Hesiod*. New York: Oxford University Press.

Long, Charlotte R. 1987. *The Twelve Gods of Greece and Rome*. Leiden: E. J. Brill.

Luttwak, Edward. N. 2020. "Letter to the Editor: Classics and Postclassicism." *TLS*, September 11. https://www.the-tls.co.uk/articles/classics-and-postclassicism/ (accessed: September 17, 2020).

Lyons, Deborah. 1997. *Gender and Immortality: Heroines in Ancient Greek Myth and Cult*. Princeton, NJ: Princeton University Press.

Mackey, Jacob L. 2022. *Belief and Cult: Rethinking Roman Religion*. Princeton, NJ: Princeton University Press.

Mancini, Silvia. 2007. "Comparativism in the History of Religions: Some Models and Key Issues." *Religion* 37 (4): 282–93.

MacRae, Duncan. 2016. *Legible Religion: Books, Gods, and Rituals in Roman Culture*. Cambridge, MA: Harvard University Press.

Marlow, Hilary, Karla Pollmann, and Helen Van Noorden, eds. 2021. *Eschatology in Antiquity: Forms and Functions*. London: Routledge.

Martin, Dale B. 2004. *Inventing Superstition: From the Hippocratics to the Christians*. Cambridge, MA: Harvard University Press.

Martin, Craig A. 2017. *A Critical Introduction to the Study of Religion*, 2nd ed. London: Routledge.

Martin, Luther H. 1987. *Hellenistic Religions: An Introduction*. New York: Oxford University Press.

Martin, Luther H. 2004. "The Cognitive Science of Religion." *Method and Theory in the Study of Religion* 16: 201–4.

Martin, Luther H. 2014. *Deep History, Secular Theory: Historical and Scientific Studies of Religion*. Berlin: De Gruyter.

Martin, Luther H. 2019. "The Jabberwocky Dilemma: Take Religion for Example." In Nickolas P. Roubekas (ed.), *Theorizing "Religion" in Antiquity*, 414–38. Sheffield: Equinox.

Martin, Luther H., and Donald Wiebe, eds. 2016. *Conversations and Controversies in the Scientific Study of Religion: Collaborative and Co-authored Essays by Luther H. Martin and Donald Wiebe*. Leiden: Brill.

Martin, Richard. 2016. *Classical Mythology: The Basics*. London: Routledge.

Masuzawa, Tomoko. 2005. *The Invention of World Religions: Or, How European Universalism Was Preserved in the Language of Pluralism*. Chicago: University of Chicago Press.

May, James M., ed. 2016. *Marcus Tullius Cicero, How to Win an Argument: An Ancient Guide to the Art of Persuasion*. Princeton, NJ: Princeton University Press.

Mayhew, Robert. 2008. *Plato: Laws 10*. Oxford: Clarendon Press.

McCoskey, Denise E. 2018. "Black Athena, White Power: Are We Paying the Price for Classics' Response to Bernal?" *Eidolon*, November 15. https://eidolon.pub/black-athena-white-power-6bd1899a46f2 (accessed: August 2, 2020).

McCutcheon, Russell T. 1997. *Manufacturing Religion: The Discourse on Sui Generis and the Politics of Nostalgia*. New York: Oxford University Press.

McCutcheon, Russell T. 2001. *Critics Not Caretakers: Redescribing the Public Study of Religion*. Albany: State University of New York Press.

McCutcheon, Russell T. 2003. *The Discipline of Religion: Structure, Meaning, Rhetoric*. London: Routledge.

McCutcheon, Russell T. 2012. "A Direct Question Deserves a Direct Answer: A Response to Atalia Omer's 'Can a Critic Be a Caretaker too?'" *Journal of the American Academy of Religion* 80 (4): 1077–82.

McCutcheon, Russell T. 2015. *A Modest Proposal on Method: Essaying the Study of Religion*. Leiden: Brill.

McCutcheon, Russell T. 2016. "The Devil's in the Details." *Studying Religion in Culture Blog*, September 16. https://religion.ua.edu/blog/2016/09/16/the-devils-in-the-details/ (accessed: January 9, 2020).

McCutcheon, Russell T. 2017. "What Happens After the Deconstruction." *Implicit Religion* 20 (4): 401–6.

McCutcheon, Russell T. 2018. *Fabricating Religion: Fanfare for the Common E.g.* Berlin: De Gruyter.

McCutcheon, Russell T. 2021. *On Making a Shift in the Study of Religion and Other Essays*. Berlin: De Gruyter.

McGuckin, John A. 2008. *The Orthodox Church. An Introduction to Its History, Doctrine, and Spiritual Culture*. Malden, MA: Blackwell.

Meisner, Dwayne A. 2018. *Orphic Tradition and the Birth of the Gods*. New York: Oxford University Press.

Meister, Felix J. 2020. *Greek Praise Poetry and the Rhetoric of Divinity*. New York: Oxford University Press.

Melvær, Knut, and Michael Stausberg. 2013. "What Is the Study of Religion/s? Self-Presentations of the Discipline on University Web Pages." *Religious Studies Project*, December 6. http://www.religiousstudiesproject.com/2013/12/06/what-is-the-study-of- religionsself-presentations-of-the-discipline-on-university-web-pages/ (accessed: March 10, 2021).

Meylan, Nicolas. 2019. *Qu'est-ce qua la religion? Onze auteurs, onze définitions*. Genève: Labor et Fides.

Miano, Daniele. 2018. *Fortuna: Deity and Concept in Archaic and Republican Italy*. New York: Oxford University Press.

Mikalson, Jon D. 2010. *Greek Popular Religion in Greek Philosophy*. New York: Oxford University Press.

Mikalson, Jon D. 2012. *Herodotus and Religion in the Persian Wars*. Chapel Hill: North Carolina University Press.

Miles, Margaret R. 2000. "Becoming Answerable for What We See." *Journal of the American Academy of Religion* 68 (3): 471–85.

Molendijk, Arie L. 2016. *Friedrich Max Müller and the Sacred Books of the East*. Oxford: Oxford University Press.

Momigliano, Arnaldo. 1982. "Religious History Without Frontiers: J. Wellhausen, U. Wilamowitz, and E. Schwartz." *History and Theory* 21 (4): 49–64.

Montanari, Franco, Antonios Rengakos, and Christos Tsagalis, eds. 2009. *Brill's Companion to Hesiod*. Leiden: Brill.

Morales, Helen. 2020. "Letter to the Editor: Postclassicisms." *TLS*, September 18. https://www.the-tls.co.uk/articles/britain-first/ (accessed: September 22, 2020).

Morgan, Teresa. 2007. *Popular Morality in the Early Roman Empire*. Cambridge: Cambridge University Press.

Morley, Neville. 2000. *Ancient History: Key Themes and Approaches*. London: Routledge.

Morley, Neville. 2004. *Theories, Models and Concepts in Ancient History*. London: Routledge.

Morley, Neville. 2018. *Classics: Why It Matters*. Cambridge: Polity.

Müller, Friedrich Max. 1878. *Lectures on the Origin and Growth of Religion*. London: Longmans, Green.

Naddaf, Gerard. 1995. "Plato's Theologia Revisited." *The Society for Ancient Greek Philosophy Newsletter* 198. Online: https://orb.binghamton.edu/sagp/198 (accessed: June 23, 2020).

Neiden, F. S. 2013. *Smoke Signals for the Gods: Ancient Greek Sacrifice from the Archaic through Roman Periods*. New York: Oxford University Press.

Nelis, Damien, and Jocelyne Nelis-Clément. 2011. "Vergil, *Georgics* 1.1–42 and the *pompa circensis*." *Dictynna: Revue de poétique latine* 8: 1–15.

Newton, Richard. 2017. "Whither the Study of Religion and Culture?" *Implicit Religion* 20 (4): 407–11.

Nigdelis, Pantelis M. 1990. "Πολίτευμα και Κοινωνία των Πόλεων των Κυκλάδων κατά την Ελληνιστική και Αυτοκρατορική Εποχή." PhD thesis, Aristotle University of Thessaloniki, Greece.

Nongbri, Brent. 2013. *Before Religion: A History of a Modern Concept*. New Haven, CT: Yale University Press.

Nongbri, Brent. 2017. "The 'Proper' Way to Study Religion? A Rejoinder to Robert Segal." *Religion & Theology* 24 (1/2): 203–6.

Norezayan, Ara. 2013. *Big Gods: How Religion Transformed Cooperation and Conflict*. Princeton, NJ: Princeton University Press.

North, John. 2020. "Introduction." In Edward Bispham and Daniele Miano (eds.), *Gods and Goddesses in Ancient Italy*, 1–8. London: Routledge.

Norton, Robert E. 2008. "Wilamowitz at War." *International Journal of the Classical Tradition* 15 (1): 74–97.

Nye, Malory. 2008. *Religion: The Basics*, 2nd ed. London: Routledge.

Nye, Malory. 2017a. "I Don't Study Religion: So What Am I Doing in the Study of Religion?" *Religion Bites Blog*, April 21. https://medium.com/religion-bites/i-dont-study-religion-so-what-am-i-doing-in-the-study-of-religion-be2653682feb (accessed: November 22, 2019).

Nye, Malory. 2017b. "On Deconstructing the Deconstruction of the Deconstruction of the Category of Religion." *Implicit Religion* 20 (4): 413–21.

O'Sullivan, Patrick. 2012. "Sophistic Ethics, Old Atheism, and 'Critias' on Religion." *Classical World* 105 (2): 167–85.

Ober, Josiah. 2009. "Too Much Companionship?" *American Philological Association Newsletter* 32 (2): 1–3.

Ogden, Daniel. 2007. "Introduction." In Daniel Ogden (ed.), *A Companion to Greek Religion*, 1–17. Malden, MA: Blackwell.

Omer, Atalia. 2011. "Can a Critic Be a Caretaker too? Religion, Conflict, and Conflict Transformation." *Journal of the American Academy of Religion* 79 (2): 459–96.

Orsi, Robert A., ed. 2012. *The Cambridge Companion to Religious Studies*. New York: Cambridge University Press.

Pals, Daniel L. 2015. *Nine Theories of Religion*, 3rd ed. New York: Oxford University Press.

Parker, Robert. 2005. *Polytheism and Society at Athens*. New York: Oxford University Press.

Parker, Robert. 2008. "'Aeschylus' Gods: Drama, Cult, Theology." In Jacques Jouanna and Franco Montanari (eds.), *Eschyle à l'aube du théâtre occidental: Neuf exposés suivis de discussions*, 127–54. Vandoeuvres-Genève: Fondation Hardt.

Parker, Robert. 2011. *On Greek Religion*. Ithaca, NY: Cornell University Press.

Parker, Robert. 2017. *Greek Gods Abroad: Names, Natures, and Transformations*. Oakland: University of California Press.

Peels, Saskia. 2016. *Hosios: A Semantic Study of Greek Piety*. Leiden: Brill.
Pennington, Brian K. 2019. "Review of *Heathen, Hindoo, Hindu: American Representations of India, 1721–1893*, by Michael J. Altman." *International Journal of Hindu Studies* 23: 333–4.
Petridou, Georgia. 2006. "On Divine Epiphanies: Contextualising and Conceptualising Epiphanic Narratives in Greek Literature and Culture." PhD thesis, University of Exeter, UK.
Petridou, Georgia. 2015. *Divine Epiphany in Greek Literature and Culture*. New York: Oxford University Press.
Phillips, III, C. Robert. 2000 [1991]. "Misconceptualizing Classical Mythology." In Richard Buxton (ed.), *Oxford Readings in Greek Religion*, 344–58. New York: Oxford University Press.
Plate, S. Brent, ed. 2015. *Key Terms in Material Religion*. London: Bloomsbury.
Platt, Verity J. 2015. "Epiphany." In Esther Eidinow and Julia Kindt (eds.), *The Oxford Handbook of Ancient Greek Religion*, 491–504. New York: Oxford University Press.
Platt, Verity J. 2018. "Double Vision: Epiphanies of the Dioscuri in Classical Antiquity." *Archiv für Religionsgeschichte* 20 (1): 229–56.
Platvoet, Jan G., and Arie L. Molendijk, eds. 1999. *The Pragmatics of Defining Religion: Contexts, Concepts and Contests*. Leiden: Brill.
Podoksik, Efraim, ed. 2020. *Doing Humanities in Nineteenth-Century Germany*. Leiden: Brill.
Pope, Alexander. 1711. *An Essay on Criticism*. London: W. Lewis.
Popper, Karl R. 1998. *The World of Parmenides: Essays on the Presocratic Enlightenment*, A. F. Petersen (ed.). London: Routledge.
Porter, James I. 2000. *Nietzsche and the Philology of the Future*. Stanford, CA: Stanford University Press.
Porter, James I. 2005. "What Is 'Classical' about Classical Antiquity? Eight Propositions." *Arion* 13 (1): 27–61.
Pyysiäinen, Ilkka. 2012. "Cognitive Science of Religion: State-of-the-Art." *Journal for the Cognitive Science of Religion* 1 (1): 5–28.
Raab, Nigel A. 2015. *The Crisis from Within: Historians, Theory, and the Humanities*. Leiden: Brill.
Reed, Annette Yoshiko. 2015. "Christian Origins and Religious Studies." *Studies in Religion/Sciences Religeuses* 44 (3): 307–19.
Reinhartz, Adele. 2019. "Was the Word in the Beginning? On the Relationship between Language and Concepts." https://marginalia.lareviewofbooks.org/wordbeginningrelationship-language-concepts/ (accessed: June 20, 2019).

Reitz, Christiane. 2020. "Classical Philology: German *Altertumswissenschaften*, '*Professorenhaarspalterei*' and Organising the Classics in the 19th Century." In Efraim Podoksik (ed.), *Doing Humanities in Nineteenth-Century Germany*, 134–54. Leiden: Brill.

Relihan, Joel C. 2007. *Apuleius: The Golden Ass Or, A Book of Changes*. Indianapolis, IN: Hackett.

Rennie, Bryan S. 2020. "Robert Segal: Philosopher of Religion, Or: *Ye'll huvtae furgi'e oor Robert. He disnae ken his ane strength*." In Nickolas P. Roubekas and Thomas Ryba (eds.), *Explaining, Interpreting, and Theorizing Religion and Myth: Contributions in Honor of Robert A. Segal*, 70–85. Leiden: Brill.

Rice, David G., and John E. Stambaugh. 2009. *Sources for the Study of Greek Religion*. Atlanta, GA: SBL Press.

Rives, James B. 2011. "The Theology of Animal Sacrifice in the Ancient Greek World: Origins and Developments." In Jennifer Wright Knust and Zsuzsanna Várhelyi (eds.), *Ancient Mediterranean Sacrifice*, 187–202. New York: Oxford University Press.

Robinson, T. M. 2008. "Presocratic Theology." In Patricia Curd and Daniel W. Graham (eds.), *The Oxford Handbook of Presocratic Philosophy*, 485–98. New York: Oxford University Press.

Romano, Carman. 2020. "Works, Days, and Divine Influence in Hesiod's Story World." *Kernos* 33: 9–31.

Rood, Tim, Carol Atack, and Tom Phillips. 2020. *Anachronism and Antiquity*. London: Bloomsbury.

Roubekas, Nickolas P. 2017. *An Ancient Theory of Religion: Euhemerism from Antiquity to the Present*. New York: Routledge.

Roubekas, Nickolas P. 2019a. "Theorizing About (Which?) Origins: Herodotus on the Gods." In Nickolas P. Roubekas (ed.), *Theorizing "Religion" in Antiquity*, 129–49. Sheffield: Equinox.

Roubekas, Nickolas P., ed. 2019b. *Theorizing "Religion" in Antiquity*. Sheffield: Equinox.

Roubekas, Nickolas P. 2019c. "Review of *Method as Identity: Manufacturing Distance in the Academic Study of Religion*, by Christopher M. Driscoll and Monica R. Miller." *Researcher: European Journal of Humanities & Social Sciences* 4 (2): 132–3.

Rowe, Adam. 2020. "Diversity in Publishing Hasn't Improved in the Past 4 Years." *Forbes*, January 31. https://www.forbes.com/sites/adamrowe1/2020/01/31/diversity-in-publishing-hasnt-improved-in-the-past-4-years/#63912885c413 (accessed: February 26, 2020).

Rubel, Alexander. 2019. "Quo Vadis *Altertumswissenschaft*? The Command of Foreign Languages and the Future of Classical Studies." *Classical World* 112 (3): 193–223.

Rüpke, Jörg. 2005. "Varro's *Tria Genera Theologiae*: Religious Thinking in the Late Republic." *Ordia Prima* 4: 107–29.

Rüpke, Jörg. 2014. "Varro's *Antiquitates* and History of Religion in the Late Roman Republic." *History of Religions* 53 (3): 246–68.

Rüpke, Jörg. 2018a. *Pantheon: A New History of Roman Religion*, translated by David M. B. Richardson. Princeton, NJ: Princeton University Press.

Rüpke, Jörg. 2018b. "Reflecting on Dealing with Religious Change." *Religion in the Roman Empire* 4 (1): 132–54.

Rüpke, Jörg. 2021. *Religion and Its History: A Critical Inquiry*. London: Routledge.

Rutherford, Richard. 2005. *Classical Literature: A Concise History*. Malden, MA: Blackwell.

Sahlins, Marshall. 2017. "The Original Political Society." *HAU: Journal of Ethnographic Theory* 7 (2): 91–128.

Saler, Benson. 2000. *Conceptualizing Religion: Immanent Anthropologists, Transcendent Natives, and Unbounded Categories*. New York: Berghahn Books.

Saler, Benson. 2008. "Conceptualizing Religion: Some Recent Reflections." *Religion* 38 (3): 219–25.

Santi, Claudia. 2017. *Castor a Roma: Un Dio Peregrinus nel Foro*. Lugano: Agorà.

Scheid, John. 2002. "Religion, Institutions and Society in Ancient Rome: Inaugural Lecture Delivered on Thursday 7 February 2002." Paris: Collège de France, 2013. https://books.openedition.org/cdf/3010?lang=en (accessed: August 23, 2019).

Scheid, John. 2003. *An Introduction to Roman Religion*, translated by Janet Lloyd. Edinburgh: Edinburgh University Press.

Scheid, John. 2009. "Théologie romaine et représentation de l'action au début de l'Empire." In Ueli Dill and Christine Walde (eds.), *Antike Mythen: Medien, Transformationen und Konstruktionen*, 122–31. Berlin: De Gruyter.

Scheid, John. 2012. "Roman Animal Sacrifice and the System of Being." In Christopher A. Faraone and F. S. Neiden (eds.), *Greek and Roman Animal Sacrifice: Ancient Victims, Modern Observers*, 84–95. Cambridge: Cambridge University Press.

Scheid, John. 2016 [2013]. *The Gods, the State, and the Individual: Reflections on Civic Religion in Rome*, translated by Clifford Ando. Philadelphia: University of Pennsylvania Press.

Schewel, Ben. 2017. *Seven Ways of Looking at Religion: The Major Narratives*. New Haven, CT: Yale University Press.

Schilbrack, Kevin. 2014. *Philosophy and the Study of Religion: A Manifesto*. Malden, MA: Wiley Blackwell.

Schultz, Celia E. 2016. "Roman Sacrifice, Inside and Out." *Journal of Roman Studies* 106: 58–76.

Scullion, Scott. 2014. "Religion and the Gods in Greek Comedy." In Michael Fontaine and Adele C. Scafuro (eds.), *The Oxford Handbook of Greek and Roman Comedy*, 340–55. New York: Oxford University Press.

Segal, Robert A., ed. 1998. *The Myth and Ritual Theory: An Anthology*. Malden, MA: Blackwell.

Segal, Robert A. 2002. "Robertson Smith's Influence on Durkheim's Theory of Myth and Ritual." In Thomas A. Indinopulos and Brian C. Wilson (eds.), *Reappraising Durkheim for the Study and Teaching of Religion Today*, 59–72. Leiden: Brill.

Segal, Robert A. 2006a. "All Generalizations are Bad: Postmodernism on Theories." *Journal of the American Academy of Religion* 74 (1): 157–71.

Segal, Robert A., ed. 2006b. *The Blackwell Companion to the Study of Religion*. Malden, MA: Wiley Blackwell.

Segal, Robert A. 2008. "William Robertson Smith: Sociologist or Theologian?" *Religion* 38 (1): 9–24.

Segal, Robert A. 2010. "Theories of Religion." In John R. Hinnells (ed.), *The Routledge Companion to the Study of Religion*, 2nd ed., 75–92. London: Routledge.

Segal, Robert A. 2016. "Review of *Before Religion: A History of a Modern Concept*, by Brent Nongbri." *Religion & Theology* 23 (3/4): 423–7.

Segal, Robert A. 2017. "'Diagnosis Rather Than Dialogue as the Best Way to Study Religion.'" In Ellen Bradshaw Aitken and Arvind Sharma (eds.), *The Legacy of Wilfred Cantwell Smith*, 173–82. Albany: State University of New York Press.

Segal, Robert A. 2021. "Introduction." In Robert A. Segal and Nickolas P. Roubekas (eds.), *The Wiley Blackwell to the Study of Religion*, 2nd ed., xi–xvi. Hoboken, NJ: Wiley Blackwell.

Sessa, Kristina. 2019. "The New Environmental Fall of Rome: A Methodological Consideration." *Journal of Late Antiquity* 12 (2): 211–55.

Sfameni Gasparro, Giulia. 2011. *Introduzione alla storia delle religioni*. Bari: Editori Laterza.

Sheedy, Matt. 2017. "Of Elephants and Riders: Cognition, Reason, and Will in the Study of Religion." In Aaron W. Hughes (ed.), *Theory in a Time of Excess: Beyond Reflection and Explanation in Religious Studies Scholarship*, 121–8. Sheffield, UK: Equinox.

Sheedy, Matt. 2019. "Making the Familiar Strange: On the Influence of J. Z. Smith." *Journal of the American Academy of Religion* 87 (1): 41–6.

Simon, Erika. 2021. *The Gods of the Greeks*, translated by Jakob Zeyl. Madison: University of Wisconsin Press.

Skinner, Joseph E. 2012. *The Invention of Greek Ethnography: From Homer to Herodotus*. New York: Oxford University Press.

Slater, Michael. 2007. "Can One Be a Critical Caretaker?" *Method and Theory in the Study of Religion* 19 (3/4): 332–42.

Slingerland, Edward. 2008. *What Science Offers the Humanities: Integrating Body and Culture*. New York: Cambridge University Press.

Slone, D. Jason. 2004. *Theological Incorrectness. Why Religious People Believe What They Shouldn't*. New York: Oxford University Press.

Smith, Wilfred Cantwell. 1959. "Comparative Religion: Whither—and Why?" In Mircea Eliade and Joseph M. Kitagawa (eds.), *The History of Religions*, 31–58. Chicago: University of Chicago Press.

Smith, Wilfred Cantwell. 1962. *The Meaning and End of Religion: A New Approach to the Religious Traditions of Mankind*. New York: Macmillan.

Smith, Jonathan Z. 1982. *Imagining Religion: From Babylon to Jonestown*. Chicago: University of Chicago Press.

Smith, Jonathan Z. 1990. *Drudgery Divine: On the Comparison of Early Christianities and the Religions of Late Antiquity*. Chicago: University of Chicago Press.

Smith, Jonathan Z. 1998. "Religion, Religions, Religious." In Mark C. Taylor (ed.), *Critical Terms for Religious Studies*, 269–84. Chicago: University of Chicago Press.

Sokal, Alan, and Jean Bricmont. 1998. *Fashionable Nonsense: Postmodern Intellectuals' Abuse of Science*. New York: Picador.

Sommerstein, Alan H., and Isabelle C. Torrance, eds. 2014. *Oaths and Swearing in Ancient Greece*. Berlin: De Gruyter.

Sørensen, Jesper F., and Anders Klostergaard Petersen. 2021. "Manipulating the Divine—an Introduction." In Jesper F. Sørensen and Anders Klostergaard Petersen (eds.), *Theoretical and Empirical Investigations of Divination and Magic: Manipulating the Divine*, 1–20. Leiden: Brill.

Spiro, Melford E. 1966. "Religion: Problems of Definition and Explanation." In Michael Banton (ed.), *Anthropological Approaches to the Study of Religion*, 85–126. London: Routledge.

Stausberg, Michael. 2009. "There Is Life in the Old Dog Yet: An Introduction to Contemporary Theories of Religion." In Michael Stausberg (ed.), *Contemporary Theories of Religion: A Critical Companion*, 1–21. London: Routledge.

Stausberg, Michael. 2012. "Religion: Begriff, Definitionen, Theorien." In Michael Stausberg (ed.), *Religionswissenschaft*, 33–47. Berlin: De Gruyter.

Stausberg, Michael, and Steven Engler. 2016. "Theories of Religion." In Michael Stausberg and Steven Engler (eds.), *The Oxford Handbook of the Study of Religion*, 52–72. New York: Oxford University Press.

Stausberg, Michael, and Mark Q. Gardiner. 2016. "Definition." In Michael Stausberg and Steven Engler (eds.), *The Oxford Handbook of the Study of Religion*, 9–32. New York: Oxford University Press.

Stone, Jon R., ed. 2002. *The Essential Max Müller: On Language, Mythology, and Religion*. New York: Palgrave Macmillan.

Stover, Justin. 2018. "There Is No Case for the Humanities." *Chronicle of Higher Education*, March 4. https://www.chronicle.com/article/there-is-no-case-for-the-humanities/ (accessed: May 12, 2020).

Strathern, Alan. 2019. *Unearthly Powers: Religious and Political Change in World History*. Cambridge: Cambridge University Press.

Strauss Clay, J. 2003. *Hesiod's Cosmos*. Cambridge: Cambridge University Press.

Stray, Christopher, ed. 2007. *Gilbert Murray Reassessed: Hellenism, Theatre, and International Politics*. New York: Oxford University Press.

Strenski, Ivan. 2003. *Theology and the First Theory of Sacrifice*. Leiden: Brill.

Strenski, Ivan. 2004. "Ideological Critique in the Study of Religion: Real Thinkers, Real Contexts and a Little Humility." In Peter Antes, Armin W. Geertz, and Randi R. Warne (eds.), *New Approaches to the Study of Religion. Vol. 1: Regional, Critical, and Historical Approaches*, 271–93. Berlin: De Gruyter.

Strenski, Ivan. 2015. *Understanding Theories of Religion: An Introduction*, 2nd ed. Malden, MA: Wiley Blackwell.

Stroumsa, Guy G. 2010. *A New Science: The Discovery of Religion in the Age of Reason*. Cambridge, MA: Harvard University Press.

Taira, Teemu. 2017. "The Religious Studies Project—Podcast Transcription: Categorizing 'Religion': From Case Studies to Methodology." *Implicit Religion* 20 (4): 377–84.

Taves, Ann. 2009. *Religious Experience Reconsidered: A Building-Block Approach to the Study of Religion and Other Special Things*. Princeton, NJ: Princeton University Press.

Taylor, Mark C., ed. 1998. *Critical Terms for Religious Studies*. Chicago: University of Chicago Press.

The British Academy. 2019. "Theology and Religious Studies Provision in UK Higher Education." https://www.thebritishacademy.ac.uk/documents/288/theology-religious-studies.pdf (accessed: February 22, 2021).

The Postclassicisms Collective. 2020. *Postclassicisms*. Chicago: University of Chicago Press.

Thomassen, Einar. 2016. "What Is a 'God' Actually? Some Comparative Reflections." In Peter Antes, Armin W. Geertz, and Mikael Rothstein (eds.), *Contemporary Views on Comparative Religion: Essays on Comparative Religion Presented to Tim Jensen on the Occasion of His 65th Birthday*, 365–74. Sheffield: Equinox.

Thonemann, Peter. 2019. "Gender, Subject Preference, and Editorial Bias in Classical Studies, 2001–2019." *CUCD Bulletin* 48. https://cucd.blogs.sas.ac.uk/files/2019/09/THONEMANN-Gender-subject-preference-editorial-bias.pdf (accessed: May 7, 2020).

Thrower, James. 1999. *Religion: The Classical Theories*. Edinburgh: Edinburgh University Press.

Turner, Camilla, and Fin Kavanagh. 2020. "Oxford Could Remove Homer and Virgil from Compulsory Classics Syllabus amid Diversity Drive." *The Telegraph*, February 19. https://www.telegraph.co.uk/news/2020/02/19/oxford-could-remove-homer-virgil-compulsory-classics-syllabus/ (accessed: March 22, 2020).

Turner, James. 2011. *Religion Enters the Academy: The Origins of the Scholarly Study of Religion in America*. Athens: University of Georgia Press.

Turner, James. 2014. *Philology: The Forgotten Origins of the Modern Humanities*. Princeton, NJ: Princeton University Press.

Tweed, Thomas A. 2020. *Religion: A Very Short Introduction*. New York: Oxford University Press.

Tylor, Edward B. 1871. *Primitive Culture: Researches into the Development of Mythology, Philosophy, Religion, Art, and Custom*, 2 vols. London: Murray.

Ungefehr-Kortus, Claudia. 2006. "Nietzsche-Wilamowitz-Kontroverse." In Hubert Cancik, Helmuth Schneider, and Manfred Landfester (eds.), *Der Neue Pauly*. http://dx.doi.org/10.1163/1574-9347_dnp_e1508910 (accessed: November 5, 2020).

van Bommel, Bas. 2016. "Classics between Prosperity and Crisis: Greek and Latin Education in 21st-Century Holland." *Addisco Blog*, May 3. https://www.addisco.nl/classics-between-prosperity-and-crisis-greek-and-latin-education-in-21st-century-holland/ (accessed: August 2, 2020).

van den Heever, Gerhard. 2005. "Redescribing Graeco-Roman Antiquity: On Religion and History of Religion." *Religion & Theology* 12 (3/4): 211–38.

van den Heever, Gerhard. 2015. "What Do You Read When You Read a Religious Text? Open Question and Theses towards an Anti-hermeneutic." *Religion & Theology* 22 (3/4): 187–218.

van der Veer, Peter. 2016. *The Value of Comparison*. Durham, NC: Duke University Press.

van Herten, Joseph C. A. 1934. *Θρησκεία, Εὐλάβεια, Ἱκέτης: Bijdrage tot de Kennis der Religieuze Terminologie in het Grieksch*. Amsterdam: H. J. Paris.

van Riel, Gerd. 2013. *Plato's Gods*. Farnham: Ashgate.

Várhelyi, Zsuzsanna. 2010. *The Religion of Senators in the Roman Empire: Power and the Beyond*. New York: Cambridge University Press.

Vernant, Jean-Pierre. 1991. "Greek Religion, Ancient Religions." In Jean-Pierre Vernant, *Mortals and Immortals: Collected Essays*, Froma I. Zeitlin (ed.), 269–89. Princeton, NJ: Princeton University Press.

Versnel, Henk S. 2011. *Coping with the Gods: Wayward Readings in Greek Theology*. Leiden: Brill.

Veyne, Paul. 1988. *Did the Greeks Believe in Their Myths? An Essay on the Constitutive Imagination*, translated by Pausa Wissing. Chicago: University of Chicago Press.

Warrier, Maya, and Simon Oliver, eds. 2008. *Theology and Religious Studies: An Exploration of Disciplinary Boundaries*. London: T&T Clark.

Watson, Lindsay C. 2019. *Magic in Ancient Greece and Rome*. London: Bloomsbury.

Wheeler-Barclay, Marjorie. 2010. *The Science of Religion in Britain, 1860–1915*. Charlottesville: University of Virginia Press.

White, Claire. 2017. "What the Cognitive Science of Religion Is (and Is Not)." In Aaron W. Hughes (ed.), *Theory in a Time of Excess: Beyond Reflection and Explanation in Religious Studies Scholarship*, 95–114. Sheffield: Equinox.

White, Claire. 2021. *An Introduction to the Cognitive Science of Religion: Connecting Evolution, Brain, Cognition, and Culture*. London: Routledge.

Whitmarsh, Tim. 2015. *Battling the Gods: Atheism in the Ancient World*. New York: Alfred A. Knopf.

Wiater, Nicolas. 2011. *The Ideology of Classicism: Language, History, and Identity in Dionysius of Halicarnassus*. Berlin: De Gruyter.

Wiebe, Donald. 1999. *The Politics of Religious Studies: The Continuing Conflict with Theology in the Academy*. New York: St. Martin's Press.

Wiebe, Donald. 2019. *The Learned Practice of Religion in the Modern University*. London: Bloomsbury.

Wiebe, Donald. 2020. "A Report on the Special Executive Committee Meeting of the International Association for the History of Religions in Delphi." *Method and Theory in the Study of Religion* 32 (2): 150–8.

Wiseman, Timothy P. 2004. *The Myths of Rome*. Exeter: University of Exeter Press.

Wittgenstein, Ludwig. 1953. *Philosophische Untersuchungen*. Frankfurt am Main: Suhrkamp.

Xygalatas, Dimitris. 2011. "Ethnography, Historiography, and the Making of History in the Tradition of the Anastenaria." *History & Anthropology* 22 (1): 57–74.

Xygalatas, Dimitris. 2012. *The Burning Saints: Cognition and Culture in the Fire-Walking Rituals of the Anastenaria*. Sheffield: Equinox.
Xygalatas, Dimitris. 2021. "Evil Eyes and Baking Pies: Aspects of Greek Divination." In Jesper F. Sørensen and Anders Klostergaard Petersen (eds.), *Theoretical and Empirical Investigations of Divination and Magic: Manipulating the Divine*, 105–23. Leiden: Brill.
Zema, Demetrius B., and Gerlad G. Walsh. 1962. *Saint Augustine, The City of God: Books I–VII*. Washington, DC: Catholic University of America Press.
Zuckerberg, Donna. 2018. "What's So Special about Classics?" *Eidolon*, January 29. https://eidolon.pub/whats-so-special-about-classics-b82ef435f52b (accessed: August 1, 2020).

Index

Agamemnon 48–50, 58
Altertumswissenschaft 34, 36, 64–5
anachronism 11–14, 37, 40–1, 79, 125 n.12, 142 n.4
Anastenaria 100–2
Anthropomorphism 63, 76, 78, 80–1, 84, 98–9, 104, 120, 122
Apollo 42–3, 48, 103
Apuleius 81–2
Atheism 62–3

Barrett, Justin 97–9, 101–2, 106
belief(s)
    irrational 12
    phenomenon of 24, 32, 42, 49, 58
    reflective and nonreflective 98–9, 102
    religious 16, 24, 28, 44–5, 54–5, 56–7, 59, 62–3, 69–70, 72, 77–8, 94, 97, 101–2, 105–7, 110, 114–16, 121, 126 n.12, 141 n.19, 142 n.2
Bernal, Martin 5
Boin, Douglas 64, 134
Boyarin, Daniel 7–8, 13, 39, 40–50, 52, 130 n.6, 131 n.12
Braun, Willi 70–3
Bremmer, Jan N. 22, 29, 114–15, 126 n.10
British Association for the Study of Religion (BASR) 70–1, 135 n.5

Castor and Polux (Dioskouri) 104–5
Cato the Elder 57–9
Christianity 8, 10, 53, 67, 97
    -centric view of religion 11, 32, 37, 39–40, 46–7, 50, 54–5, 64–5, 76, 79
    early 45, 69
    era 13, 41
    Orthodox 100–1, 130 n.9, 132 n.21
    Protestant 46–7, 50, 55, 73, 132 n.21
Cicero 63–5, 79–80, 95, 104–6
Cognitive Study of Religion (CSR) 27, 56, 96–8, 100, 105–6, 139 n.10

comparative
    method 1, 28, 32, 35, 53, 64–5, 67, 94, 106, 119
    religion 6, 14, 37, 72, 130 n.4
deconstruction 11, 17, 46, 72, 90–2, 111, 135 n.5, 136 n.6
deisidaimonia (*see also* superstition) 12–13, 42, 45
Demeter 138
Detienne, Marcel 1
Dionysius of Halicarnassus 85–7, 138 n.29
Dionysus 42–3
disciplinary
    anxieties 7, 70, 73
    boundaries 2, 12, 17, 30, 36
Douglas, Mary 4, 22, 25, 28
Durkheim, Èmile 22, 32, 52, 56, 60

Eliade, Mircea 22, 50, 52, 61, 72, 134–5 n.24
epiphany 76, 80–1, 84, 104–6
Euhemerus of Messene 2–3, 5, 63

Foucault, Michel 9, 17, 92, 124–5 n.10
Frazer, James G. 22, 35, 132 n.24
Freud, Sigmund 22, 52, 60

Geertz, Armin W. 112–13
Goldenberg, Naomi 72, 111–13, 142 n.6

Harrison, Ellen 35
Harrison, Thomas 22–3, 30, 97, 105–6, 137 n.21
Henrichs, Albert 76–8, 80
Herodotus 3, 41–2, 63, 104, 109, 131 n.12
Hesiod 63, 86, 102, 104, 109–13, 142 n.5
historization 13
Homer 6, 13, 48–9, 59, 63, 75, 86, 102, 104–5, 109, 132 n.24, 138 n.27
humanities 5–6, 20, 33, 63, 90–1, 127 n.19

immortality 76–8
interdisciplinary
    collaboration 1, 26, 33, 141 n.20
    study of religion(s) 15, 21, 96, 107
Isis 81–2

Jupiter 84, 103

Klostergaard Petersen, Anders 14, 47, 51–2

Larson, Jennifer 96–7, 105–7, 140 n.15
Lincoln, Bruce 28, 31, 40, 94, 110–11
Lucius 81

Mars 57–8
Martin, Luther H. 28, 67, 96
McCutcheon, Russell T. 7, 9–10, 25, 28, 31, 45–50, 72, 124 n.9, 138 n.5
metaperson(s) 119–21
Müller, Friedrich Max 11, 17, 65, 125 n.12
myth 23–4, 61
    Egyptian 82
    Greek and Roman 21, 79, 85–6, 97, 103, 105, 115, 126

Nietzsche, Friedrich 9, 34–6, 93, 127 n.22
Nilsson, Martin P. xi
Nongbri, Brent 7, 13, 39–47, 50–1, 54
Nye, Malory 8–10, 93

Orphism 42, 137

paganism 54, 64–5, 67, 69, 100–1
Plutarch 41–4, 131 n.14
pompa circensis 84–5
Popper, Karl 4
Poseidonius of Rhodes 103–4, 106
postmodern 5, 13, 90–1

religion
    classification of 8–9, 11, 20, 71
    concept of 13–14, 23, 38–9, 47, 50–1, 72, 138 n.6
    definition of 9–11, 23–4, 28–9, 32, 46–7, 51, 55–6, 59–62, 74, 90, 92–4, 119–20, 127 n.15
    e-religion and i-religion 97
    essence of 32, 132–3 n.26
    explanation of 59, 103

function of 32, 56, 58, 60–3, 75, 94, 96, 112, 134 n.15
interpretation of 44, 59, 110
phenomenon of 9–10, 20–1, 30, 32, 35, 45, 51, 55–6, 59–60, 65, 73, 111–12, 126 n.10, 133 n.26
theory of 27, 56, 60–3, 134 n.15
Rennie, Bryan 51–2
ritual 24, 32, 49, 54, 61, 63, 75, 87, 100–2
Rüpke, Jörg 24–8, 114–15, 127 n.15

sacrifice 44–6, 48–9, 58, 77, 122, 132 n.24
Scheid, John 14–6, 54, 137 n.26
Segal, Robert 25, 28, 51, 130 n.4
Sisyphus (fragment) 61–2
Smith, Jonathan Z. 7–9, 14, 22, 25, 28, 37, 66, 71–2
Smith, Wilfred Cantwell 37–40, 50
superhuman
    agent(s) 48, 55, 59, 63, 73–4, 76, 78–80, 84–5, 110, 113, 120
    nature 81
    power(s) 27
supernatural
    agent(s) 48, 55, 63
    being(s) 97, 120
    entity(-ies) 59
    power(s) 12, 119
    reality(-ies) 70
superstition 12–13, 35, 42, 44–5, 52

theology
    folk 82, 101
    high 103–4, 106, 140 n.15
    low 106
    and religious studies 65–7, 70–1, 130 n.4, 135 n.5
    theologia 80, 83
    theological correctness 98
Thomassen, Einar 76–8, 80, 137 n.20
thrēskeia 13, 40–4, 46–7, 52, 130 n.9, 131 n.18
Tylor, E. B. 32, 62, 65
Tyros 44

Varro 63–4, 83, 103–4, 106
Vernant, Jean-Pierre 14–17
Versnel, Henk 102–3, 106

von Wilamowitz-Moellendorff, Ulrich
    34–6, 127 n.22

Wiebe, Donald 25, 28, 67, 71, 124 nn.7–8
Wittgenstein, Ludwig 56, 131 n.10

worldview(s) 57, 72, 110

Xenophanes of Colophon 63, 86, 104, 109

Zeus 49, 58, 102–3, 110, 142 n.5

www.ingramcontent.com/pod-product-compliance
Lightning Source LLC
Chambersburg PA
CBHW061836300426
44115CB00013B/2405